ALFA ROMEO GIULIA COUPES 1963-1976

Compiled by
R.M. Clarke

ISBN 0 946489 64 5

Distributed by
Brooklands Book Distribution Ltd.
'Holmerise', Seven Hills Road,
Cobham, Surrey, England
Printed in Hong Kong

BROOKLANDS BOOKS

BROOKLANDS BOOKS SERIES
AC Ace & Aceca 1953-1983
AC Cobra 1962-1969
Alfa Romeo Alfasud 1972-1984
Alfa Romeo Alfetta Coupes GT.GTV.GTV6 1974-1987
Alfa Romeo Giulia Berlinas 1962-1976
Alfa Romeo Giulia Coupés 1963-1976
Alfa Romeo Spider 1966-1987
Allard Gold Portfolio 1937-1958
Alvis Gold Portfolio 1919-1967
Aston Martin Gold Portfolio 1972-1985
Austin Seven 1922-1982
Austin A30 & A35 1951-1962
Austin Healey 3000 1959-1967
Austin Healey 100 & 3000 Collection No. 1
Austin Healey 'Frogeye' Sprite Collection No. 1
Austin Healey Sprite 1958-1971
Avanti 1962-1983
BMW Six Cylinder Coupés 1969-1975
BMW 1600 Collection No. 1
BMW 2002 1968-1976
Bristol Cars Gold Portfolio 1946-1985
Buick Automobiles 1947-1960
Buick Riviera 1963-1978
Cadillac Automobiles 1949-1959
Cadillac Automobiles 1960-1969
Cadillac Eldorado 1967-1978
Camaro 1966-1970
Chevrolet Camaro & Z-28 1973-1981
High Performance Camaros 1982-1988
Chevrolet Camaro Collection No. 1
Chevrolet 1955-1957
Chevrolet Impala & SS 1958-1971
Chevelle & SS 1964-1972
Chevy II Nova & SS 1962-1973
High Performance Corvettes 1983-1989
Chrysler 300 1955-1970
Citroen Traction Avant 1934-1957
Citroen DS & ID 1955-1975
Citroen 2CV 1948-1988
Cobras & Replicas 1962-1983
Cortina 1600E & GT 1967-1970
Corvair 1959-1968
Daimler Dart & V-8 250 1959-1969
Datsun 240Z 1970-1973
Datsun 280Z & ZX 1975-1983
De Tomaso Collection No. 1
Dodge Charger 1966-1974
Excalibur Collection No. 1
Ferrari Cars 1946-1956
Ferrari Dino 1965-1974
Ferrari Dino 308 1974-1979
Ferrari 308 & Mondial 1980-1984
Ferrari Collection No. 1
Fiat-Bertone X1/9 1973-1988
Fiat Pininfarina 124+2000 Spider 1968-1985
Ford Automobiles 1949-1959
Ford Fairlane 1955-1970
Ford Falcon 1964-1970
Ford RS Escort 1968-1980
High Performance Escorts MkI 1968-1974
High Performance Escorts MkII 1975-1980
High Performance Mustangs 1982-1988
Honda CRX 1983-1987
Hudson & Railton Cars 1936-1940
Jaguar Cars 1957-1961
Jaguar Cars 1961-1964
Jaguar XK120 XK140 XK150 Gold Portfolio 1948-1960
Jaguar MK2 1959-1969
Jaguar E-Type Gold Portfolio 1961-1971
Jaguar E-Type 1966-1971
Jaguar E-Type V12 1971-1975
Jaguar XJ6 1968-1972
Jaguar XJ6 Series II 1973-1979
Jaguar XJ6 & XJ12 Series III 1979-1985
Jaguar XJ12 1972-1980
Jaguar XJS Gold Portfolio 1975-1988
Jensen Cars 1946-1967
Jensen Cars 1967-1979
Jensen Interceptor Gold Portfolio 1966-1986
Jensen Healey 1972-1976
Lamborghini Cars 1964-1970
Lamborghini Cars 1970-1975
Lamborghini Countach Collection No. 1
Lamborghini Countach & Urraco 1974-1980
Lamborghini Countach & Jalpa 1980-1985
Lancia Stratos 1972-1985
Land Rover 1948-1973
Land Rover Series II & IIa 1958-1971
Land Rover Series III 1971-1985
Land Rover 90 & 110 1983-1989
Lotus Cortina 1963-1970
Lotur Elan Gold Portfolio 1962-1974
Lotus Elan Collection No. 2
Lotus Elite 1957-1964
Lotus Elite & Eclat 1974-1981
Lotus Turbo Esprit 1980-1986
Lotus Europa 1966-1975
Lotus Europa Collection No. 1
Lotus Seven 1957-1980
Lotus Seven Collection No. 1
Marcos Cars 1960-1988
Maserati 1965-1970
Maserati 1970-1975
Mazda RX-7 Collection No. 1
Mercedes 190 & 300SL 1954-1963
Mercedes 230/250/280SL 1963-1971
Mercedes 350/450SL & SLC 1971-1980
Mercedes Benz Cars 1949-1954
Mercedes Benz Cars 1954-1957
Mercedes Benz Cars 1957-1961
Mercedes Benz Competition Cars 1950-1957
Metropolitan 1954-1962

MG TC 1945-1949
MG TD 1949-1953
MG TF 1953-1955
MG Cars 1957-1959
MG Cars 1959-1962
MG Midget 1961-1980
MGA Collection No. 1
MGA Roadsters 1955-1962
MGB Roadsters 1962-1980
MGB GT 1965-1980
Mini Cooper 1961-1971
Mini Moke 1964-1989
Morgan Cars 1960-1970
The Morgan 3-Wheeler Gold Portfolio 1910-1952
Morgan Cars Gold Portfolio 1968-1989
Morris Minor Collection No. 1
Oldsmobile Automobiles 1955-1963
Old's Cutlass & 4-4-2 1964-1972
Oldsmobile Toronado 1966-1978
Opel GT 1968-1973
Packard Gold Portfolio 1946-1958
Pantera Gold Portfolio 1970-1989
Pantera & Mangusta 1969-1974
Plymouth Barracuda 1964-1974
Pontiac Fiero 1984-1988
Pontiac GTO 1964-1970
Pontiac Firebird 1967-1973
Pontiac Firebird and Trans-Am 1973-1981
High Performance Firebirds 1982-1988
Pontiac Tempest & GTO 1961-1965
Porsche Cars 1960-1964
Porsche Cars 1964-1968
Porsche Cars 1968-1972
Porsche Cars in the Sixties
Porsche Cars 1972-1975
Porsche 356 1952-1965
Porsche 911 1965-1969
Porsche 911 1970-1972
Porsche 911 1973-1977
Porsche 911 Carrera 1973-1977
Porsche 911 SC 1978-1983
Porsche 911 Turbo 1975-1984
Porsche 914 Gold Portfolio 1969-1976
Porsche 914 Collection No. 1
Porsche 924 Gold Portfolio 1975-1988
Porsche 928 1977-1989
Porsche 944 1981-1985
Reliant Scimitar 1964-1986
Riley 1½ & 2½ Litre Gold Portfolio 1945-1955
Rolls Royce Silver Cloud 1955-1965
Rolls Royce Silver Shadow 1965-1980
Range Rover Gold Portfolio 1970-1988
Rover 3 & 3.5 Litre 1958-1973
Rover P4 1949-1959
Rover P4 1955-1964
Rover 2000 + 2200 1963-1977
Rover 3500 1968-1977
Rover 3500 & Vitesse 1976-1986
Saab Sonett Collection No. 1
Saab Turbo 1976-1983
Studebaker Hawks & Larks 1956-1963
Sunbeam Tiger and Alpine Gold Portfolio 1959-1967
Thunderbird 1955-1957
Thunderbird 1958-1963
Thunderbird 1964-1976
Toyota MR2 1984-1988
Triumph 2000-2.5-2500 1963-1977
Triumph Spitfire 1962-1980
Triumph Spitfire Collection No. 1
Triumph Stag 1970-1980
Triumph Stag Collection No. 1
Triumph TR2 & TR3 1952-1960
Triumph TR4.TR5.TR250 1961-1968
Triumph TR6 1969-1976
Triumph TR6 Collection No. 1
Triumph TR7 & TR8 1975-1982
Triumph GT6 1966-1974
Triumph Vitesse & Herald 1959-1971
TVR Gold Portfolio 1959-1988
Volkswagen Cars 1936-1956
VW Beetle 1956-1977
VW Beetle Collection No. 1
VW Golf GTi 1976-1986
VW Karmann Ghia 1955-1982
VW Scirocco 1974-1981
VW Bus-Camper-Van 1954-1967
VW Bus-Camper-Van 1968-1979
VW Bus-Camper-Van 1979-1989
Volvo 1800 1960-1973
Volvo 120 Series 1956-1970

BROOKLANDS MUSCLE CARS SERIES
American Motors Muscle Cars 1966-1970
Buick Muscle Cars 1965-1970
Camaro Muscle Cars 1966-1972
Capri Muscle Cars 1969-1983
Chevrolet Muscle Cars 1966-1972
Dodge Muscle Cars 1967-1970
Mercury Muscle Cars 1966-1971
Mini Muscle Cars 1961-1979
Mopar Muscle Cars 1964-1967
Mopar Muscle Cars 1968-1971
Mustang Muscle Cars 1967-1971
Shelby Mustang Muscle Cars 1965-1970
Oldsmobile Muscle Cars 1964-1970
Plymouth Muscle Cars 1966-1971
Pontiac Muscle Cars 1966-1972

BROOKLANDS ROAD & TRACK SERIES
Road & Track on Alfa Romeo 1949-1963
Road & Track on Alfa Romeo 1964-1970
Road & Track on Alfa Romeo 1971-1976
Road & Track on Alfa Romeo 1977-1989
Road & Track on Aston Martin 1962-1984

Road & Track on Auburn Cord & Duesenberg 1952-1984
Road & Track on Audi 1952-1980
Road & Track on Audi 1980-1986
Road & Track on Austin Healey 1953-1970
Road & Track on BMW Cars 1966-1974
Road & Track on BMW Cars 1975-1978
Road & Track on BMW Cars 1979-1983
Road & Track on Cobra, Shelby &
  Ford GT40 1962-1983
Road & Track on Corvette 1953-1967
Road & Track on Corvette 1968-1982
Road & Track on Corvette 1982-1986
Road & Track on Datsun Z 1970-1983
Road & Track on Ferrari 1950-1968
Road & Track on Ferrari 1968-1974
Road & Track on Ferrari 1975-1981
Road & Track on Ferrari 1981-1984
Road & Track on Fiat Sports Cars 1968-1987
Road & Track on Jaguar 1950-1960
Road & Track on Jaguar 1961-1968
Road & Track on Jaguar 1968-1974
Road & Track on Jaguar 1974-1982
Road & Track on Jaguar 1983-1989
Road & Track on Lamborghini 1964-1985
Road & Track on Lotus 1972-1981
Road & Track on Maserati 1952-1974
Road & Track on Maserati 1975-1983
Road & Track on Mazda RX7 1978-1986
Road & Track on Mercedes 1952-1962
Road & Track on Mercedes 1963-1970
Road & Track on Mercedes 1971-1979
Road & Track on Mercedes 1980-1987
Road & Track on MG Sports Cars 1949-1961
Road & Track on MG Sports Cars 1962-1980
Road & Track on Mustang 1964-1977
Road & Track on Peugeot 1955-1986
Road & Track on Pontiac 1960-1983
Road & Track on Porsche 1951-1967
Road & Track on Porsche 1968-1971
Road & Track on Porsche 1972-1975
Road & Track on Porsche 1975-1978
Road & Track on Porsche 1979-1982
Road & Track on Porsche 1982-1985
Road & Track on Porsche 1985-1988
Road & Track on Rolls Royce & Bentley 1950-1965
Road & Track on Rolls Royce & Bentley 1966-1984
Road & Track on Saab 1955-1985
Road & Track on Toyota Sports & G T Cars 1966-1986
Road & Track on Triumph Sports Cars 1953-1967
Road & Track on Triumph Sports Cars 1967-1974
Road & Track on Triumph Sports Cars 1974-1982
Road & Track on Volkswagen 1951-1968
Road & Track on Volkswagen 1968-1978
Road & Track on Volkswagen 1978-1985
Road & Track on Volvo 1957-1974
Road & Track on Volvo 1975-1985
Road & Track Henry Manney at Large & Abroad

BROOKLANDS CAR AND DRIVER SERIES
Car and Driver on BMW 1955-1977
Car and Driver on BMW 1977-1985
Car and Driver on Cobra, Shelby & Ford GT40
  1963-1984
Car and Driver on Datsun Z 1600 & 2000
  1966-1984
Car and Driver on Corvette 1956-1967
Car and Driver on Corvette 1968-1977
Car and Driver on Corvette 1978-1982
Car and Driver on Corvette 1983-1988
Car and Driver on Ferrari 1955-1962
Car and Driver on Ferrari 1963-1975
Car and Driver on Ferrari 1976-1983
Car and Driver on Mopar 1956-1967
Car and Driver on Mopar 1968-1975
Car and Driver on Mustang 1964-1972
Car and Driver on Pontiac 1961-1975
Car and Driver on Porsche 1955-1962
Car and Driver on Porsche 1963-1970
Car and Driver on Porsche 1970-1976
Car and Driver on Porsche 1977-1981
Car and Driver on Porsche 1982-1986
Car and Driver on Saab 1956-1985
Car and Driver on Volvo 1955-1986

BROOKLANDS MOTOR & THOROUGHBRED & CLASSIC CAR SERIES
Motor & T & CC on Ferrari 1966-1976
Motor & T & CC on Ferrari 1976-1984
Motor & T & CC on Lotus 1979-1983

BROOKLANDS PRACTICAL CLASSICS SERIES
Practical Classics on Austin A 40 Restoration
Practical Classics on Land Rover Restoration
Practical Classics on Metalworking in Restoration
Practical Classics on Midget/Sprite Restoration
Practical Classics on Mini Cooper Restoration
Practical Classics on MGB Restoration
Practical Classics on Morris Minor Restoration
Practical Classics on Triumph Herald/Vitesse
Practical Classics on Triumph Spitfire Restoration
Practical Classics on VW Beetle Restoration
Practical Classics on 1930S Car Restoration

BROOKLANDS MILITARY VEHICLES SERIES
Allied Military Vehicles Collection No. 1
Allied Military Vehicles Collection No. 2
Dodge Military Vehicles Collection No. 1
Military Jeeps 1941-1945
Off Road Jeeps 1944-1971
V W Kubelwagen 1940-1975

CONTENTS

5	Alfa Sprint 1600 GT Road Test	Road & Track	Dec.	1964
9	Giulia Super & Giulia GT Cabriolet	Cars Illustrated	April	1965
11	Alfa Romeo Giulia Super & Sprint GTC	Autocar	March 12	1965
13	Alfa Romeo 1750 GTV Road Test	Motor	July 13	1966
19	Giulia Sprint GT Veloce Road Test	Autosport	Feb. 24	1967
20	Alfa Romeo GTA Road Test	Autocar	April 6	1967
24	Alfa Romeo GTV Road Test	Road & Track	July	1967
29	Alfa Romeo GT 1300 Road Test	Motor	July 22	1967
35	Alfa Romeo 1300 GT	Cars & Car Conversions	March	1968
37	Alfa Romeo 1750 GTV Road Test	Autosport	Aug. 16	1968
39	The Alfa That Scored	Sports Car World	Dec.	1968
42	Alfa Romeo GT 1300 Junior	Autocar	April 10	1969
47	The Alfa Romeo 1750 GTV	Motor Sport	Sept.	1969
48	Alfa Romeo 1750 Duetto Spider & 1750 GTV	Car & Driver	Oct.	1969
52	Alfa Romeo GT 1300 Long-term Assessment	Autocar	Oct. 9	1969
56	Alfa Junior GT Road Test	Motor Manual	March	1970
59	Alfa Romeo 1750 GTV vs. Lancia Flavia 2000 Coupé	Car	April	1970
64	Alfa Romeo 1750 GT Veloce Long-term Test	Autocar	June 17	1971
68	Alfa Romeo 2000 GTV Road Test	Road & Track	Aug.	1972
72	Alfa Romeo 2000 GTV Road Test	Autocar	July 6	1972
76	Alfa Romeo 2000 GTV Road Test	Modern Motor	Nov.	1972
82	Alfa Romeo 2000 GTV Brief Test	Motor	Dec. 30	1972
86	Alfa Romeo GT Junior 1600 Road Test	Sports Car World	Feb.	1973
90	Alfa Romeo 1750/2000 Buying Secondhand	Autocar	Sept. 6	1975
93	Alfa Allure	Autocar	Feb. 3	1979
95	Profile Alfa Romeo 2000 GTV	Classic and Sportscar	June	1982

BROOKLANDS BOOKS

ACKNOWLEDGEMENTS

There are now over 200 titles in the Brooklands series and not one of them has taken as long to compile as this work on the Giulia GT Coupés.

This marque is a veritable minefield for the uninitiated and if Richard Banks, the Alfa specialist, and Peter Nunn of Classic and Sportscar had not come to our aid there is no doubt that we would still be struggling with the subject. The car featured on our cover is in fact Peter Nunn's personal transport and our thanks go to Classic and Sportscar for supplying this attractive photograph.

We know before we go to press that there will be some frustrated Alfa owners who's favourite story has had to be omitted due to lack of space. We are therefore hoping that next year we will be able to produce a second collection for the avid enthusiasts that this model attracts.

We are indebted as always to the publishers of the world's leading motor journals. They have assisted us for many years and as a result made this series possible. In this instance our thanks go to the management of Autocar, Autosport, Car, Car & Driver, Cars Illustrated, Cars & Car Conversions, Classic & Sportscar, Modern Motor, Motor, Motor Manual, Motor Sport, Road & Track and Sports Car World for allowing us to include their valuable and informative copyright stories.

R.M. Clarke

ALFA SPRINT GT

A proper customer's touring machine—

a driver's car in the Alfa tradition

THE GRAN TURISMO car is a native product of Italy and Italian driving conditions, and one of the leading manufacturers of this type of vehicle is Alfa Romeo. It was therefore with considerable pleasure that we reacquainted ourselves recently with a genuine Gran Turismo car in the form of an Alfa Romeo Giulia Sprint GT.

The Sprint GT is the latest of a long line of Alfas, which commenced with the 1300-cc Giulietta and has since been updated on numerous occasions to take advantage of current trends and developments.

The heart of the Sprint GT is the Alfa Romeo twin-cam 4-cyl engine of 1570 cc which produces 122 bhp at 6000 rpm, and it is evident that the manufacturer has made little compromise in the design of this unit, either internally or externally. From a purely appearance standpoint, it has a strong appeal to the enthusiast because of the high standard of finish all the way from the camshaft covers to the intricate finning of the aluminum oil pan, which is typically Italian.

Internally it is evident that attention has been paid not only to the balance of the revolving and reciprocating parts, but also to the matching of the combustion chamber volumes and other points which contribute to smooth running throughout the range. The result is that the number of cylinders does not become apparent until one reaches about 4000 rpm, and even then the engine does not sound as though excessive demands

ALFA SPRINT GT
AT A GLANCE...

Price as tested	$4395
Engine	4 cyl, dohc, 1570 cc, 122 bhp
Curb weight, lb.	2200
Top speed, mph	112
Acceleration, 0–60 mph, sec	10.6
Passing test, 50–70 mph, sec	5.4
Average fuel consumption, mpg	25

DECEMBER 1964

ALFA SPRINT GT

are being made on it, unlike some of its pushrod contemporaries.

On the debit side, the idle is rather fast, with the tendency to "hunt" one associates with engines equipped with dual throat Weber carburetors. However, cold starting presents no problem and the carburetion is clean throughout the rest of the range. Although the output is now 122 bhp, the low speed torque does not seem to have suffered, and with 103 lb-ft @ 3000 rpm it is vastly more than the 79.61 lb-ft @ 4000 rpm of the 1300-cc Giulietta Sprint. While inspecting the engine we were pleased to note that the electrics are exclusively Bosch. Although Bosch equipment does tend to be expensive, it is at least reliable when compared with the even more expensive and often thoroughly unreliable Marelli components.

For those who are enamored of gear shifting, the *pièce de résistance* of the whole car is undoubtedly the 5-speed transmission. All forward speeds are synchronized and there is considerable spring loading in the 3rd/4th position to prevent accidental shifts from 2nd directly to 5th. In the past there has been some criticism of the sturdiness of the Alfa synchronizing mechanism, however, and only time can tell if there will be undue deterioration in the 5-speed version. Certainly, on our test car we were unable to find any fault at all.

For those who are unfamiliar with 5-speed transmissions,

it is necessary to accustom oneself to the gear positions until one's actions become automatic. From then on, full use can be made of all the ratios and the shift from 5th direct to 3rd can often be used to good effect.

The choice of ratios is good and, under fast touring conditions, there seems to be a ratio for any eventuality. Driving the car brings home the point that five speeds are a great asset to any car of limited engine capacity and torque, such as the Alfa, but tend to be an encumbrance on cars powered by large, flexible power units. Fifth gear on the Alfa is, of course, an overdrive (0.79:1), but without all the wizardry of epicyclic gear trains and electric controls of doubtful longevity which have come to be associated with the term "overdrive." If a manufacturer feels the need for a ratio of less than 1:1, a 5th gear in the transmission case selected by the shift lever would appear to be by far the most satisfactory method of achieving his purpose.

The clutch in the Sprint GT has a surprisingly short movement, and starts to take hold very early in its travel so that it is necessary to push the pedal all the way to the floor when engaging gears. However, its action is pleasantly progressive and it really bites when fully engaged. Starting in the 1st gear (15:1 ratio) we were able to spin the Pirelli Cinturatos for an appreciable distance, and a rapid change into 2nd would produce another squeal from the tires as the clutch took up the drive.

In keeping with the engine and transmission, the braking

ROAD TEST

ALFA SPRINT GT

SCALE: 10" DIVISIONS

PRICE

List price $4295
Price as tested $4395

ENGINE

No. cylinders & type . . . 4 cyl, dohc
Bore x stroke, in . . . . . . 3.07 x 3.23
Displacement, cc 1570
  Equivalent cu in 95.8
Compression ratio 9.0:1
Bhp @ rpm . . . . 122 @ 6000
  Equivalent mph 118
Torque @ rpm, lb-ft . . 103 @ 3000
  Equivalent mph 59
Carburetors, no. & make . 2 Weber
No. barrels & dia . . . . . 2-40 mm
Type fuel required . . . . . . premium

DRIVE TRAIN

Clutch type . . . . . . single plate, dry
  Diameter, in 7.9
Gear ratios, 5th (0.791) 3.603:1
  4th (1.000) 4.555:1
  3rd (1.355) 6.172:1
  2nd (1.988) 9.055:1
  1st (3.304) 15.049:1
Synchromesh . . . . on all 5
Differential type . . . . hypoid
  Ratio 4.555:1

CHASSIS & SUSPENSION

Frame type . . . . . . unit with chassis
Brake type . . . . disc
  Swept area, sq in 422
Tire size . . . . 155 x 15
Steering type . . . . . worm & sector
  Turns, lock to lock 3.25
  Turning circle, ft 32.8
Front suspension : independent with
  A-arms, coil springs, tube shocks.
Rear suspension : live axle, trailing
  arms, coil springs, tube shocks.

ACCOMMODATION

Normal capacity, persons 2
Occasional capacity 4
Seat width, front, in . . . . . 2 x 21.5
  Rear . . . . 2 x 23
Head room, front/rear 40/35
Seat back adjustment, deg 15
Entrance height, in 48
Step-over height 15
Door width 38
Driver comfort rating :
  For driver 69-in. tall 90
  For driver 72-in. tall 85
  For driver 75-in. tall 80
  (85-100, good ; 70-85, fair ;
    under 70, poor)

GENERAL

Curb weight, lb 2200
Test weight 2530
Weight distribution (with driver),
  front/rear, % 56/44
Wheelbase, in 93.0
Track, front/rear 51.5/50.0
Overall length, in 161.0
  Width 62.0
  Height 52.0
Frontal area, sq ft 17.9
Ground clearance, in 5.0
Overhang, front/rear 29/38
Departure angle (no load), deg . .18
Usable trunk space, cu ft 9.5
Fuel tank capacity, gal 12.2

INSTRUMENTATION

Instruments : 140-mph speedometer, 8000-rpm tachometer, oil
pressure, water temp., oil temp.
Warning lights : high beam, turn
signals, lights, heater fan.

MISCELLANEOUS

Body styles available : coupe as
tested.

ACCESSORIES

Included in list price : leather upholstery, heater, full instrumentation, seat belt anchors.
Available at extra cost : seat belts.

CALCULATED DATA

Lb/hp (test weight) 20.7
Cu ft/ton mi 66
Mph/1000 rpm (high gear) 19.6
Engine revs/mi 3063
Piston travel, ft/mi 1648
Rpm @ 2500 ft/min 4645
  Equivalent mph 91
R&T wear index 50.5

MAINTENANCE

Crankcase capacity, qt 6
  Change interval, mi 2500
Oil filter type . . . . paper
  Change interval, mi 2500
Chassis lube interval, mi 2500
Tire pressure, front/rear,
  psi 25/27

ROAD TEST RESULTS

ACCELERATION

0-30 mph, sec 4.4
0-40 mph 6.1
0-50 mph 8.2
0-60 mph 10.6
0-70 mph 13.7
0-80 mph 18.0
0-100 mph 31.8
Passing test, 50-70 mph 5.4
Standing ¼ mi 18.5
  Speed at end, mph 81

TOP SPEEDS

High gear (5700), mph 112
  4th (6200) 96
  3rd (6500) 75
  2nd (6500) 51
  1st (6500) 31

GRADE CLIMBING

(Tapley data)

5th gear, max gradient, % 6
  4th 10
  3rd 14
  2nd 21
  1st 28
Total drag at 60 mph, lb . . . 105

SPEEDOMETER ERROR

30 mph indicated . . . . . . actual 26
40 mph 35
60 mph 53
80 mph 70
100 mph 88

FUEL CONSUMPTION

Normal driving, mpg 24-27
Cruising range, mi 290-320

ACCELERATION & COASTING

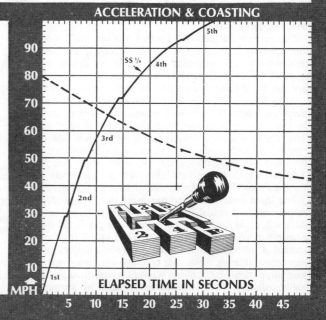

SS ¼   5th   4th

3rd

2nd

1st

ELAPSED TIME IN SECONDS

MPH

5   10   15   20   25   30   35   40   45

system is very highly developed. There are discs at all four wheels aided by a booster, and the results are exactly what we have come to expect from a well designed disc brake system. However, Alfa enthusiasts may regret the passing of those handsome aluminum finned drums which used to be one of the better features of the car.

On entering the car one finds that it is very well appointed, and correctly laid out for GT driving. There is sufficient seat movement to accommodate even the tallest driver, and the angle of the seat back can be adjusted, but the adjustment does not use the Reutter system and the movement is limited.

After a few minutes in the car, we noticed three minor but irritating faults. The first was an undue amount of distortion in the glass of both the windshield and the rear window. The second was an annoying engine vibration at about 2600 rpm which made itself felt through the accelerator pedal, and the third was the gross speedometer error which seems to be a feature of all Italian cars. However, the car made up for these shortcomings by the exhilaration of its performance.

For those people who are convinced that independent rear suspension is essential for fast driving, the handling of the Alfa will come as a surprise, because the car is an excellent example of what can be done with a live axle if it is correctly located. Under certain conditions, there is a suspicion of the rear wheel steering which one normally associates with swing axle suspensions, but it never becomes exaggerated and is normally indiscernible. It is presumably caused by movement of

the complete rear suspension in the big rubber bushes in which it is mounted.

In a fast corner, the car is basically neutral although the application of power in 3rd or 4th gears will cause it to understeer slightly. As one enters a turn at speed, there is a certain amount of roll oversteer initially, which seems to be accentuated by movement of the rear axle, but, as soon as the car is positioned, this changes abruptly and the car becomes extremely stable.

The strongest feature of the Sprint GT is its ability to cover ground quickly without effort, and it is sometimes necessary to remind oneself that the engine capacity is only a shade over a liter and a half. Obviously one must stay fairly busy with the gear lever, but shifting is a pleasure.

Second only to the transmission as a source of pleasure is the willingness of the engine. The tachometer goes to 8000 rpm with no red line and, due to the Webers, the manifolding and the exhaust system, there is little inclination for the engine to run out of breath. For maximum performance we shifted at 6500 rpm, but for normal fast touring 5000 rpm seems to be a good compromise.

The traditions of the Alfa Romeo company are long, and its racing experience is second to none. It is evident that a lot of this experience has been applied to the latest model, and for those people who doubt that racing improves the breed, the characteristics of the Alfa Romeo Giulia Sprint GT would seem to prove conclusively that it does.

two new alfa's

GIULIA SUPER

and

GIULIA G T Cabriolet

AT THE BEGINNING of March Alfa Romeo announced two new models to augment the Giulia range of 1,600 c.c. cars: both are high performance four-cylinder models and both will, in due course, be available in right-hand drive form in the United Kingdom: the words in due course are important, because the convertible, the Giulia G.T.C., will not be ready over here until June and the other new car, known as the Giulia Supèr, is expected "later on". When they do come, the Super will cost £1,547, tax, duty, surcharge and all that financial jazz paid, and the G.T.C. will set you back £1,937, also including all manner of taxes and duties. For comparison's sake, the standard Giulia T.I. (if you must know, this stands for Touring Internazionale) costs a little less than £1,500 in this country.

Well, that's the bad news. Now for the good. The Giulia Super is a further development of the Giulia T.I. saloon, the twin o.h.c. 1,570 c.c. power unit developing a net power output of 98 b.h.p. This power is produced at 5,500 r.p.m., the same crankshaft speed as that of the T.I. engine at maximum output, and there is, of course, that superb five-speed gearbox stuck on the end of it.

Bodily, the car looks little different from the outside. The basic shell is that of the T.I., a four-door five-seater saloon, but with improved interior fittings, better seats and re-arranged (and more complete) instrumentation. The gear-lever sits on the floor on the Super, whereas on the T.I., of course, it pokes out of the side of the steering column.

The engine is flexible and possesses a worthwhile torque value, so that using the five-speed box to good effect you can get it off the mark rather more briskly than is common on five-seater saloons of 1½-litres or so. Acceleration when on the move is useful, too, and from an indicated 100 m.p.h. there is still plenty of go before the maximum speed is reached.

We went to Monza to try both these new models, and the experience of trying new Alfa Romeos on Italy's principal racing circuit was well worthwhile. The Super's road holding, like that of most Alfas, is better than you give it credit for, and only rather low-geared steering reminds one that this isn't really a sports car, think what you might. Try and assume that every 1600 c.c. five-seater saloon has a maximum speed of well over the ton, a five-speed gearbox which is not only there to be used, but is worth using, disc brakes on the front and roadholding of the sort that only comes with sports cars in the usual way, and you will see the difficulty. That, nevertheless, is what the Giulia Super is.

Much of the credit for the car's likeable performance must obviously go to the twin-cam engine which nestles under the bonnet. The crankshaft runs, it almost goes without saying, in five main bearings, and the valves are sodium-filled for improved cooling. Disc brakes on the front wheels combine with drums at the back to take care of stopping the car. The suspension indicates that, provided the thing is properly done, there is nothing really against independent front and live-axle rear suspension on a car of this type: the Giulia Super, like the new G.T.C. and the rest of the Giulia range (except for the i.r.s. G.T.Z.) has wishbones at the front and a live axle, suspended on coil springs and located by "A" brackets, at the back. The answer is perfect controllability, and a willingness to be whistled in and out of corners on a wide variety of improbable lines without coming unstuck. "Our" car, actually, was shod with Pirelli tyres, but we heard equally good reports of those examples fitted with Michelin "X" boots.

The Super's interior is well laid-out in an attractive manner, with large matching rev-counter and speedometer set in a neat binnacle which looks as though it ought to be reflection-proof. There is a three-spoked steering wheel, off which the hand drops neatly and successfully to the traditionally stubby Alfa gearlever. The seats have fully-reclining backs

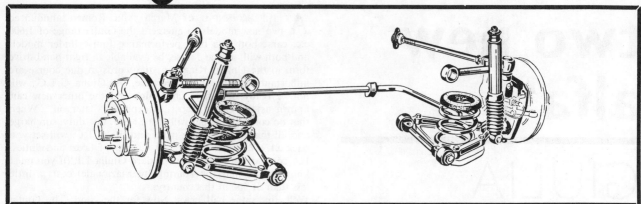

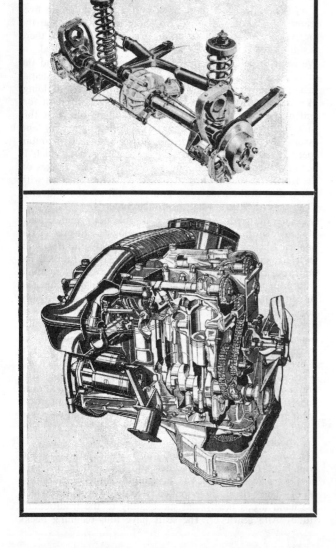

and are well-shaped for comfort and maximum support. It obviously wasn't possible at Monza to take proper acceleration and maximum speed figures, and a lap time would be pointless because of the inclusion of two extremely nasty little chicanes on the only two worth-while straights. But assuming that the speedometer was no more or less inaccurate than is usual on most cars, we see no reason seriously to dispute Alfas claims of over 110 m.p.h. for the Super, with a cruising speed of the ton—at which one has a thousand revs in hand, as it were.

The other new model, the Giulia G.T.C. is a drophead version of the Sprint G.T., which we have always considered to be the most attractive of the Giulia range anyway. This is much more of a sporting carriage, even by Alfa standards, and while it is possible to put adults in the rear seats this can only be done at the expense of everybody's comfort. With the hood closed Alfas claim a maximum speed of 112 m.p.h. for this model, and while, again, we had no opportunity to find out for ourselves we won't really argue. The power unit is more highly developed than that of the Super to give 106 b.h.p. net at 6,000 r.p.m.—a crankshaft speed which comes up on the rev-counter with remarkable swiftness, we may say. Once again the seats are comfortable, and offer slightly more fore-and-aft adjustment than those of the Super, so that one can more nearly approach the straight-arm driving position which this sort of car seems to insist on from the word go.

With the hood up or down the G.T.C. goes very fast and, what's more, does so round the corners as well. However, we were disappointed to notice rather vigorous scuttle shake on rough surfaces, which isn't the sort of thing one expects at all from an Alfa: to be fair, we compared notes with other drivers, who apparently had not found this on other cars. When cornering hard there is, as with most Alfas, pronounced body roll, but the important thing is that all the wheels appear to stay firmly on terra firma—a Good Thing. A good power-to-weight ratio gives the car lively acceleration, even when travelling three up, and it is occasionally difficult to remember that the engine is of only 1,570 c.c.

In common with most people we managed to run very short on brakes on the GTC, no doubt as a result of the car's sentence to be hammered round Monza all morning by the International Motoring Press (at least it sounds impressive). Even so, however, we felt that the brakes wouldn't have taken much less of a bashing on a journey from, say, London to the south of France, under which circumstances we would be disappointed to run out of stopping power.

Both cars are, however, extremely likeable and, like most Alfas, possess strong personalities which indicate from the word go that these are thoroughbreds.

While we were in Milan we took the opportunity to look round the new Alfa Romeo factory at Areze, just outside Milan. When this new plant is completed production is expected to be at the rate of around 100,000 cars a year—a striking illustration of the advance of mass-production in quality-constructed cars: in 1952, for example, the total production was only 4,500. Considerable pains are taken, however, to ensure that none of the quality is lost with the introduction of new methods, and this figure of 100,000 is is only an initial estimate—there is, it is pointed out, plenty of room for expansion.

Alfa Romeo Giulia Super and Sprint GTC

With hood up on the Giulia Sprint GTC there is hardly any loss of headroom compared with the closed coupé and vision is not impaired

LAST week we mentioned briefly that two new models had been added to the Alfa Romeo range of Giulia cars; since then we have been to Italy to inspect and drive the new Giulia Super and the Sprint GTC.

The Super is derived from the familiar TI saloon with a revised interior and a slightly more powerful engine, while the GTC (C for convertible) is an open-topped version of the angular Bertone Sprint GT coupé. It is a full four-seater, and is therefore almost unique as sports cars go. The Super is priced at £1,547 (£150 more than the TI) including tax, and the GTC costs £1,937 (£88 more than the coupé).

To increase the power of the TI engine for the Super, twin Weber 40DCOE4 carburettors replace the single twin-choke Solex, and the peak power is 98 b.h.p. net at 5,500 r.p.m.— 6 b.h.p. more than the TI and at 500 r.p.m. *fewer*. Engine breathing is improved substantially and maximum torque is 110lb. ft. at only 2,800 r.p.m. instead of 88 at 4,000. In fact the new engine develops over 90 lb.ft. torque all the way from 1,800 to 5,700.

To make the most of the extra pulling power the final drive ratio has been raised from 5·13 to 4·55 to 1. Since the engine now peaks at lower revs this change in gearing affects the speeds in the gears very little, but at the maximum of 110 m.p.h. or so, the revs are now just below the peak at about 5,400 instead of right over the top at 6,500. Cruising speeds are therefore significantly higher, with better fuel consumption and reduced engine wear.

Inside the car are new armrests-cum-door-pulls in line with lift-up release levers for the door catches, and a new

Left: Although the driving seat is a little far forward here for an average 5ft. 9in. man, it is not unbearably close to the controls and leaves adequate room for two adults in the back. Right: large circular instruments are used on both the new models

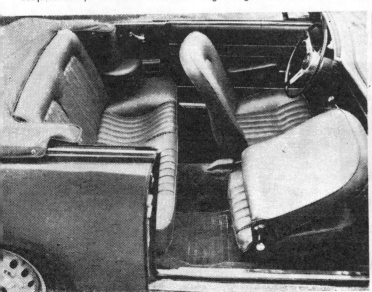

Alfa Romeo Giulia Super and Sprint GTC . . .

Pretty from every angle, the new convertible looks as smart and integrated as its closed forbear. The soft top is quicky and easily folded out of sight

facia lay-out. Replacing the previous ribbon-type speedometer with a circular rev counter styled in at one end of the scale, are two large round dials directly in front of the driver. The steering column is shorter, and a new, smaller wheel has three polished aluminium spokes instead of the black cross-bar and horn ring of the TI. The rest of the dashboard is covered with simulated wood veneer capped with matt black crash padding. Long toggle switches replace piano keys for the auxiliaries.

Driving the car for three laps round the Monza road circuit showed how much quicker is the Super than the TI. The engine pulls lustily from very low revs and the five-speed gearbox has well matched ratios. It was very easy to reach an indicated 100 m.p.h. on the two long straights, and in characteristic Alfa fashion the handling gave every confidence through the turns. At arms' length from the wheel one can drive in true Grand Prix style, although once or twice the outside rear suspension seemed to bottom as the body heeled over accurately toward the limit.

The Giulia saloon body is unusually efficient aerodynamically (only 46 b.h.p. are needed to propel it at 88 m.p.h.), so it was not surprising to find the con-vertible GTC with its hood folded down hardly any faster than the Super. Even so, we were still able to take the fast left-handed Curva del Vialone at an indicated 160 k.p.h. (100 m.p.h.) and accelerate to around 175 (109 m.p.h.), before braking hard for an artificial chicane Alfa had wisely built to slow the cars before the South Turn. After a couple of hours of fast lapping, some of the cars began to show signs of brake fade, but given a little respite they were quick to recover.

With the same engine as the coupé Sprint GT, the GTC can reach about 112 m.p.h. with the hood up. Peak power is 106 b.h.p. at 6,000 r.p.m., torque 102 lb.ft. at 3,000, and the same gearing is used as in the Super.

The convertible roof folds quickly and simply after two clamps are released from the top of the windscreen rail. There are small rear quarter-windows which wind down out of sight, as does the glass in each door. Travelling in the back with the hood down and neatly hidden under a tonneau cover, we found the car surprisingly quiet but rather draughty round the back of the neck. The rear seats are comfortably shaped and there is enough room for legs and feet if those in the front are prepared to compromise a little.

The car we drove did not feel entirely rigid, and there was some scuttle shake when travelling over the rougher parts of the track. Like the Super, however, it handled impeccably with all the precision and predictable behaviour that have kept Alfa models so well established in sports car markets throughout the world.

After driving the cars we took a quick peep at the new 330-acre site Alfa are developing at Arese, nine miles north of Milan. Body pressing, welding, painting and trim shops are already operating, and initial production when the plant is completed will be 100,000 cars a year. In the old factory at Porto-bello, severely damaged during the war, production was only 352 cars in 1950, since when it has risen progressively to 87,000 in 1963. Despite these high rates of manufacture, all Alfas are still largely hand-built, and every engine is stripped for examination after it has been run at the factory before being passed to the assembly lines.

G. P. H.

News Briefs

Regulations permitting motorists to place red triangles on the road, warning others of a stationary vehicle ahead, are expected next month.

Bond Equipe and GT4S models will be fitted in future with the new Triumph Spitfire engine (pages 524-528). Both models have been increased in price by £12 including tax.

According to the A.A. there are now 26,502 parking meters operating in the U.K., 15,000 in central London, 11,030 in 12 provincial cities and towns, and 472 in Edinburgh.

Flight International's Private and Executive Flying number, on sale on 18 March price 1s 6d, contains comprehensive tables of all light aircraft in production with technical data, performance figures, weights, dimensions, and accommodation. Details of every flying club and group in Britain, and information on all United Kingdom manufacturers and agents are also included.

Giulia Supers can be identified only from the TI by the name plate on the boot and facia. New instruments are fitted into a simulated wood veneer panel (right) capped with matt black crash padding

Flair for speed

Stylish high performance two-door coupé with superb handling and roadholding; economy excellent

TESTING the Alfa Romeo 1750 GT Veloce was rather like meeting an old friend—a friend improved in status and prosperity. This is not so much due to familiarity, although it is the fifth Alfa to come under our scrutiny in four years, but because once more the general excellence of these Italian cars has been brought home to us. The engineers at Arese might be accused for wearing permanently smug I-told-you-so smirks on their faces, for this excellence derives from the far-seeing adoption many years ago of three main design features which several rival manufacturers are still struggling to perfect: a light-alloy twin-overhead-camshaft engine, a five-speed gearbox and a good suspension system which includes a properly located rear axle. From the first feature Alfas get their unusually good performance relative to capacity; from the second the ability to use it under a wider variety of conditions than is possible with other cars; and from the third, handling and roadholding that can only be surpassed by an all-independent suspension layout of exceptional design.

Having refined the gearbox and suspension almost to perfection, only the power unit remained capable of much further improvement; accordingly, Alfa Romeo announced early this year a bigger and more powerful engine. This new power unit is now the standard fitting for the Spider, and for the sporting 1750 GTV reported on here; it is also available in the new 1750 saloon whose bodyshell is a larger version of the Giulia Super—which remains in production as before.

By increasing the capacity of their existing 1,570 c.c. four-cylinder unit to 1,779 c.c., power output has been raised from 125 (gross) b.h.p. at 6,200 r.p.m. to 132 b.h.p. at 5,500 r.p.m., and maximum torque from 114 lb.ft. at 2,500 r.p.m. to 137 lb.ft. at 2,900 r.p.m. Although the stroke has been increased by a greater amount than the bore (the stroke/bore ratio is up from 1.05 to 1.1) increased wear seems unlikely if the moderate oil consumption is anything to go by, and the ability of the engine to rev freely and smoothly to 6,200 r.p.m. remains unchanged.

Already a fast car in its earlier form, the new engine makes the GTV even faster. Compared with our best available yardstick, the Duetto—which probably has a lower frontal area but a higher drag factor than the GTV—the top speed is 115.5 m.p.h. instead of 111.1 m.p.h. and the 0-60 m.p.h. acceleration time 9.3s. instead of 11.2s. The important points are the quietness with which this

PRICE: £1,758 plus £490 8s 5d purchase tax equals £2,248 8s 5d
INSURANCE: AOA group rating 7: Lloyd's, On application

Alfa Romeo 1750 GTV

performance is achieved (sound insulation has been improved) and the superb handling and roadholding that go with it. In a week spent on give-and-take Belgian and French roads in company with an American sports car of four times the capacity and over three times the power (Chevrolet Corvette Sting Ray) the Alfa was seldom left far behind, and on rough, twisty roads it could often go faster. A flat spot at around 2,000 r.p.m. and a tendency for the inside rear wheel to lift and spin were the only minor criticisms we could find in what many of our test staff came to regard as their ideal car.

Unfortunately, in this country the 1750 GTV costs £2,248, which means that it competes on more or less level terms with other foreign performance cars like the Peugeot coupe and the Porsche 912, or even our own Lotus Elan +2, but is drastically undercut by such cars as the Lotus Cortina which is almost as fast but costs only £1,162. Alternatively there is the E-type 2 + 2 (not shown in our comparison chart because we have not tested it in

manual gearbox form), which is available for about the same price but has considerably superior performance. Nevertheless, the outstanding qualities of the Alfa should still guarantee it a reasonable market.

Performance and economy

High performance car though the Alfa undoubtedly is, it does not give this impression to the driver (although driving pleasure is in no way diminished in consequence) because of the smoothness and reticence of the engine. Were it not for the flat spot around 2,000 r.p.m.—which we suspect could be cured without much reduction in economy by attention to the accelerator pump or fitting slightly richer jets—the engine would pull cleanly, albeit a little weakly at first, all the way from around 1,500 r.p.m. up to the maximum of 6,200. There is, however, a slight resonant period at around 4,800 r.p.m. which is noticeable in third and fourth. At these high r.p.m. there is a muffled bellow of pleasing tone from the exhaust. During the start-up period there is a little mechanical clatter before the aluminium block has expanded to its working dimensions.

The rear seats are well shaped but there is little legroom.

Wing nut adjusts headrest height. Lower knob is for rake adjustment.

The front seats—grooved and cut away for ventilation—can be reclined and have a good range of fore and aft adjustment. The front passenger's seat has a built-in headrest.

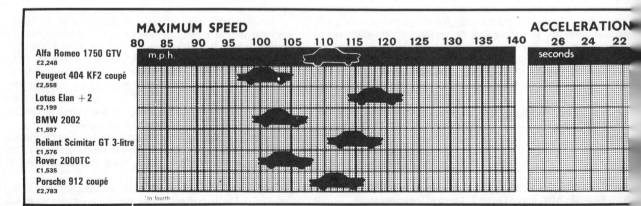

	MAXIMUM SPEED													ACCELERATION		
	80	85	90	95	100	105	110	115	120	125	130	135	140	26	24	22
Alfa Romeo 1750 GTV £2,248	m.p.h.													seconds		
Peugeot 404 KF2 coupé £2,558																
Lotus Elan +2 £2,199																
BMW 2002 £1,597																
Reliant Scimitar GT 3-litre £1,576																
Rover 2000TC £1,535																
Porsche 912 coupé £2,783																

In fourth

MOTOR ROAD TESTS

It would take a very keen eye to distinguish between the GT 1300 and the road test Alfa shown here.

Performance

Performance tests carried out by *Motor's* staff in Belgium.

Test Data: World copyright reserved; no unauthorised reproduction in whole or in part.

Conditions

Weather: Warm and dry, wind 5 m.p.h.
Temperature approx. 65°F.
Surface: Dry tarmacadam.
Fuel: 98 octane (RM). 4-star rating.

Maximum speeds

	m.p.h.	k.p.h.
Mean opposite runs	115.5	185.5
Best one-way kilometre	118.0	189.9
4th gear	107.0	172.0
3rd gear	80.0	129.0
2nd gear	54.0	87.0
1st gear	33.0	53.0

"Maximile" speed: (Timed quarter mile after 1 mile accelerating from rest)

Mean	. . . .	109.7 m.p.h.
Best	. . . .	112.3 m.p.h.

Acceleration times

m.p.h.	sec.
0-30	3.0
0-40	4.8
0-50	6.8
0-60	9.3
0-70	12.7
0-80	16.7
0-90	22.3
0-100	29.7

m.p.h.	5th sec.	4th sec.	3rd sec.
10-30	—	—	6.8
20-40	13.6	8.6	5.7
30-50	13.2	8.1	5.8
40-60	11.1	7.5	5.5
50-70	11.5	8.0	6.1
60-80	13.3	9.0	6.8
70-90	17.0	10.0	—

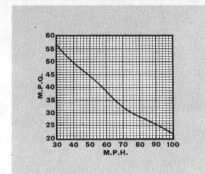

Fuel consumption

Touring (consumption midway between 30 m.p.h. and maximum less 5% allowance for acceleration) . . . . 29.5 m.p.g.
Overall . . . . 23.4 m.p.g.
(= 12.1 litres/100km)
Total test distance . . . . 1,713 miles

Brakes

Pedal pressure, deceleration and equivalent stopping distance from 30 m.p.h.

lb.	g	ft.
25	0.48	62½
50	1.02	29
Handbrake	0.30	100

Fade test

20 stops at ½g deceleration at 1 min. intervals from a speed midway between 40 m.p.h. and maximum speed (= 78 m.p.h.)

	lb.
Pedal force at beginning	25
Pedal force at 10th stop	25
Pedal force at 20th stop	25

Steering

Turning circle between kerbs:	ft.
Left	36¾
Right	34½
Turns of steering wheel from lock to lock . .	3½

Steering wheel deflection for 50 ft. diameter circle . . . . 1 turn

Clutch

Free pedal movement . . . . = 1 in.
Additional movement to disengage clutch completely . . . . = 4 in.
Maximum pedal load . . . . =42 lb.

Speedometer

Indicated	30	40	50	60	70
True	27½	37	47½	57½	67
Indicated		80	90	100	110
True		76	85	93	102

Distance recorder . . . . 3.5% fast

Weight

Kerb weight (unladen with fuel for approximately 50 miles) . . . . 20.0 cwt.
Front/rear distribution 57/43
Weight laden as tested . . . . 23.8 cwt.

Parkability

Gap needed to clear 6ft wide obstruction parked in front:

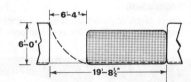

6'-4"
6'-0"
19'-8½"

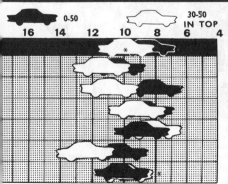

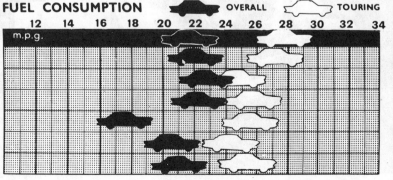

FUEL CONSUMPTION

The elegant Bertone body is identical to the one used for the less powerful GT 1300, the main external differences being a badge at the rear, fatter wheels and four headlamps instead of two in a slightly different frontal treatment.

Alfa Romeo 1750 GTV

Despite the exceptionally hard driving of our road test in France and Belgium, the overall fuel consumption was as good as 23.4 m.p.g., and like most Continental fast cars the Alfa runs well on second best fuel. The constant-speed consumption figures are also excellent, more than 20 m.p.g. (22 m.p.g. in fact) being obtained at a steady 100 m.p.h., while the touring fuel consumption which is calculated from these values is at 29.5 m.p.g. better than all the other cars in the comparison chart including the aerodynamic Elan +2 and the fuel-injected Peugeot. British driving gave a consumption of 26-27 m.p.g., and thus a range of more than 250 miles from the 10-gallon tank.

Transmission

Decades of participation in racing and other forms of motor sport are apparent in such details as the smooth, progressive action of the throttle and clutch. And the clutch did not slip on our test car as has happened on several Alfas tested previously. By ordinary standards the gearchange was light, precise and a pleasure to use, but compared to those of other Alfas we have tried it was a little stiff and sometimes obstructive, particularly when selecting bottom.

The five ratios offered by the gearbox provide for almost every conceivable contingency. Apart from those lucky enough to do their motoring in such places as the Scottish Highlands or the Welsh mountains, the rest of us in Britain mainly require of a gearbox that it should have a ratio well chosen for overtaking on main roads. This requirement is completely satisfied by third gear

The fair-sized boot accepted 6.8 cu.ft. of our test boxes.

14" X 11" X 5"

17½" X 13" X 6"

24" X 18" X 8"

1, main beam warning light. 2, horn buttons. 3, speedometer. 4, mileometer. 5, trip mileometer. 6, heater fan warning light. 7, charge warning light. 8, rev counter. 9, oil pressure gauge. 10, lights tell-tale. 11, air distribution control. 12, heater volume control. 13, wiper switch. 14, panel light switch. 15, heater fan switch. 16, water temperature gauge. 17, fuel gauge. 18, headlamp control switch. 19, indicator stalk. 20, cigarette lighter. 21, trip reset. 22, washer button (foot-operated). 23, ignition/starter lock. 24, choke. 25, hand throttle.

MOTOR ROAD TESTS

in which the engine will pull very strongly from, say, 40 m.p.h., yet maintain good acceleration right up to nearly 80. Equally, the gearbox is well equipped to fulfil the generally more complex demands of Continental driving. Thus, first gives a quick getaway without being too low; second is for the very twisty sort of mountain road, negotiated in the 30-50 m.p.h. speed range; third is for the less twisty bits, mountainous but with longish straights between the corners; fourth is for fastish main roads; and fifth is for the motorway or very fast and open ordinary roads. Even in fifth, however, there is enough acceleration for a fairly rapid return to a 100 m.p.h. cruising speed after an autostrada baulking.

Handling and brakes

Although the new GTV retains the classic Alfa suspension layout, some detail changes go with the bigger engine. At the front the geometry of the wishbones has been altered to raise the roll centre height, the resultant tendency towards reduced roll and increased front-end weight transfer being partly counteracted by the use of softer front springs to improve the ride. The remainder of the tendency is balanced out by the addition of an anti-roll bar at the rear where, as usual, the live axle is suspended on coil springs and located by lower trailing arms and an upper A-bracket. Wider wheels with 5½J rims instead of 4½J, are fitted all round.

The net result of these changes has been to leave the handling characteristics of the Alfa unchanged in essentials: as before, it has superb—perhaps better—roadholding and takes corners in a stable, mild understeer. There is less roll than on the earlier cars, but the Michelin XAS tyres squealed rather easily, though with a thin, cage-of-mice cheeping rather than a full-blooded howl. The curious Alfa lurching movements when near the limit have also been diminished.

Specification

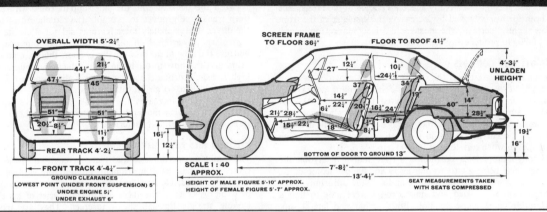

Front engine (1,779 c.c.) with rear wheel drive; independent front suspension and live rear axle.

Engine

Block material	Aluminium
Head material	Aluminium
Cylinders	4 in line
Cooling system	Water
Bore and stroke	80 mm. (3.15 in.) x 88.5 mm. (3.48 in.)
Cubic capacity	1,779 c.c. (108.4 cu. in.)
Main bearings	5
Valves	Twin overhead camshafts
Compression ratio	9.5 : 1
Carburetters	Two twin-choke Weber 40 DCOE 32
Fuel pump	Fispa mechanical
Oil filter	Full-flow
Max. power (gross)	132 b.h.p. at 5,500 r.p.m.
Max. torque (gross)	137.4 lb. ft. at 2,900 r.p.m.

Transmission

Clutch	Fichtel and Sachs s.d.p. diaphragm
Top gear	0.79 : 1
4th gear	1.00 : 1
3rd gear	1.35 : 1
2nd gear	1.99 : 1
1st gear	3.30 : 1
Reverse	3.01 : 1
Synchromesh	On all forward ratios
Final drive	Hypoid bevel 4.1:1
M.p.h. at 1,000 r.p.m. in:—	
Top gear	21.9
4th gear	17.3
3rd gear	12.8
2nd gear	8.7
1st gear	5.3

Chassis and body

Construction	Unitary

Brakes

Type	ATE discs, servo-assisted
Dimensions	10.7 in. dia. front; 10.5 in. dia. rear.

Suspension and steering

Front	Independent by double wishbones and coil springs with an anti-roll bar
Rear	Live axle on coil springs located by lower trailing arms and an upper A-bracket. Anti-roll bar fitted

Shock absorbers:	
Front } Telescopic	
Rear }	
Steering type	Recirculating ball
Tyres	165 x 14 Michelin XAS
Wheels	Steel 14 in.
Rim size	5½J

Coachwork and equipment

Starting handle	None
Tool kit contents	Wheelbrace, plug-spanner, screwdriver, Philips screwdriver, pliers
Jack	Screw pillar
Jacking points	Two each side under sills
Battery	12-volt negative earth, 60 amp hour capacity
Number of electrical fuses	10
Headlamps	Four Carello 45/40W
Indicators	Self-cancelling flashers
Reversing lamp	Yes
Screen wipers	Electric two-speed self-parking
Screen washers	Foot-operated electric
Sun visors	Two
Locks:	
With ignition key	Ignition only
With other key	Doors, boot, glove compartment
Interior heater	Fresh air
Upholstery	PVC
Floor covering	Carpet
Alternative body styles	Saloon and Spider

Maintenance

Fuel tank capacity	10.1 galls
Sump	12 pints SAE 20W/40
Gearbox	3 pints SAE 90 EP
Rear axle	2½ pints SAE 90 EP
Steering gear	½ pint SAE 90EP
Coolant	17 pints (2 drain taps)
Chassis lubrication	Every 3,750 miles to 3 points
Minimum service interval	3,750 miles
Ignition timing	3° ± 1° b.t.d.c.
Contact breaker gap	0.014-0.016 in.
Sparking plug gap	Preset
Sparking plug type	Lodge 2HL

Tappet clearances (cold)	Inlet 0.0187-0.0197 in.; Exhaust 0.206 -0.216 in.
Valve timing:	
Inlet opens	37° b.t.d.c.
Inlet closes	61° a.b.d.c.
Exhaust opens	55° b.b.d.c.
Exhaust closes	30° a.t.d.c.
Rear wheel toe-in	None
Front wheel toe-in	3 mm.
Camber angle	0° 20' ± 30'
Castor angle	1° ± 30'
Tyre pressures:	
Front	20 p.s.i.
Rear	24 p.s.i.

Safety Check List

Steering Assembly

Steering box position	Well back
Steering column collapsible	No
Steering wheel boss padded	No
Steering wheel dished	Yes

Instrument panel

Projecting switches	Some on central console
Sharp cowls	No
Padding	Above and below facia

Windscreen and visibility

Screen type	Laminated
Pillars padded	Yes
Standard driving mirrors	Interior
Interior mirror framed	Yes
Interior mirror collapsible	No
Sun visors	Crushable

Seats and harness

Attachment to floor	On slides
Do they tip forward?	Backrests only
Head rest attachment points	Headrest built-in on passenger's seat
Back of front seats	Unpadded
Safety harness	Lap and diagonal
Harness anchors at back	Yes

Doors

Projecting handles	Yes
Anti-burst latches	Yes
Child-proof locks	No, but only two doors

Alfa Romeo 1750 GTV

When trying really hard, however, as on a circuit, the inside wheel will lift and spin at speeds up to 70 m.p.h., producing a mildly disconcerting oversteer. This very seldom occurs during normal driving on the public roads except at low speeds or when accelerating round a corner from a standstill: the tail is then easily provoked but as easily corrected. Such action is facilitated by the light, precise steering which gives good feel as became apparent during our brief period of wet-road running. Over the years this has become a little more direct, now being 3.5 turns for a rather poor lock.

A ball-and-ramp pressure-limiting valve is fitted to the rear brake circuit with the result that the maximum retardation achieved was over 1g. Strong servo assistance allows this to be attained with a pedal pressure of only 50lb., and a little practice is needed to get used to the lightness of the brakes, especially for heeling and toeing. The already adequate margin of fade resistance has been further improved by increasing the diameter of the front brakes slightly; certainly the most rapid driving along Continental roads failed to produce any loss of efficiency.

Comfort and controls

A remarkable feature was the comfortable ride provided even on some of the worst roads to be found in Belgium: concave in cross-section and covered with ruptured pavé, these make the roughest surfaced British roads seem as flat as plate glass by comparison. Nor was much effort ever needed to hold the nearside wheels of the car accurately in the gutter to clear the oncoming camion, even when travelling at 90-100 m.p.h.

Although the driving position is a trifle Italian in layout, the steering wheel being a little too far away and the pedals too close, there is an excellent range of fore-and-aft seat adjustment, the backrest can be reclined and most drivers were able to find a comfortable compromise position. Both lumbar and lateral support are good, but the side supports could be a little closer together. The rear seats are well shaped, but legroom is very limited—almost non-existent on the driver's side when the front seat is pushed most of the way back.

Pedals that are perfectly laid out for heeling and toeing match the well located gearlever, steering wheel and handbrake. Most of the minor functions are controlled by separate indicator and lights control stalks, augmented by a wiper switch at the base of the central console and a wash/wipe button on the floor. Forward visibility is good, and the wipers clear right to the edge of the heavily curved windscreen; but the boot is not visible, even to a tall driver. The four headlamps provide a good blaze of light.

Brake and accelerator are well located for heeling and toeing

As in our recently tested Lancia, the front seats have cut-outs between the backrest and the side-support rolls, with additional deep transverse grooves to promote the circulation of air round the driver. Unfortunately these features did not eliminate perspiration of the lower back in the hot weather of our test, perhaps because the flow of air into the car is poor: there are no face-level vents and the flow through the heater ducts is moderate even at high speeds. Adequate cooling requires the front windows to be opened a little to let air in, with the rear quarterlights also open to let it out. This increases the already considerable wind noise. Engine noise is very moderate, but some thump and buzz from the tyres is transmitted to the interior.

Fittings and furniture

The matching speedometer and tachometer fitted to the Alfa are probably the best set of instruments fitted to any modern car: they are well located, pleasant to look at and of such a splendid size that the driver can read them out of the corner of his eye when looking straight through the windscreen. They are spoilt by a pair of stops which, with an infuriating disregard for the science of measurement, stick out of their dials at 10 m.p.h. and 500 r.p.m., preventing the needles from reaching zero. The fuel and water temperature gauges at the top of the console are difficult to see when on the move and would be better located on either side of the speedometer and rev-counter.

Oddments can be stowed in a lockable front glove compartment, and on a rear parcel shelf, while the boot will take 6.8 cu.ft. of our test boxes—good for a car of this kind. A cigarette lighter is provided, and there is a single ashtray on the front console with two others at the rear. A particularly ingenious and useful fitting is the wind-up headrest which forms part of the front passenger's seat and allows the occupant to doze comfortably with supported head when the backrest is reclined.

Servicing and accessibility

Servicing is required every 3,750 miles (6,000 km.) at which the main job is a change of engine oil; chassis lubrication is required only for the propeller shaft. Despite a rather crowded bonnet, most of the important service points are easy to get at. Since there were, in 1968, 100 dealers throughout the country, few owners should have difficulty in getting such work done. The pillar type jack is easy to use, but the spare wheel lives under the floor of the boot and could be tedious to remove when fully loaded. **M**

1, brake servo. 2, brake and clutch fluid reservoir. 3, air cleaner. 4, oil filler cap. 5, dipstick. 6, distributor. 7, overflow reservoir cap. 8, radiator cap.

Maintenance summary

Every 3,750 miles (6,000 km.): Change engine oil, check fan belt and timing chain tensions, check sparking plugs, check distributor and crankcase ventilation valve, clean carburetter gauzes and jets; Check level of gearbox, differential and steering box oils, grease propeller shaft.

Every 11,250 miles (18,000 km.): Change gearbox and differential oils, change brake fluid, replace air filter element, check steering geometry.
Every 30,000 miles: Adjust front wheel bearings and repack with grease.

MAKE: Alfa Romeo. **MODEL**: 1750 GTV. **MAKERS**: Alfa Romeo S.p.A., via Gattamelata 45, Milan, Italy. **CONCESSIONAIRES**: Alfa Romeo (GB) Ltd., 164 Sloane St., London, S.W.1.

Road Test by PATRICK McNALLY

THE ALFA ROMEO GIULIA SPRINT GT VELOCE

ABOUT this time last year Alfa Romeo invited journalists from all over the world to Lake Garda to try out their latest creation, the Veloce or high-performance model of their well-established Giulia GT. It was very well received and I immediately put my name down for a full road test.

The GTV employs the same body shell, suspension and transmission as the Giulia GT, but the power output has been increased by 3 bhp (theoretically—it certainly feels more). Yet surprisingly there is simply no comparison between the GT and the GTV, for the very minor alterations make the Veloce a much better car. Around Lake Garda the improvements were not that noticeable but the cars were brand new with only a few hundred kilometres on the clock—not even run-in. The car I have just tested, by courtesy of Alfa Romeo GB in Sloane Street, SW1, had covered some 10,000 miles and was sufficiently loose to give it of its best. The GTV is the latest and the best of the current range of Alfa Romeos I have driven, the Giulia TI Super being my previous favourite.

Alfa's well-tried 1570 cc four-cylinder twin overhead-camshaft design is still the driving force. This engine has gone from strength to strength and in the GTV produces 109 bhp DIN on a compression ratio of 9:1, the increase in horsepower coming from various alterations in porting, increased valve lift and revised timing. Despite being slightly under square, with a bore/stroke ratio of 78 mm to 82 mm, the all-alloy engine revs happily to well over 7000 rpm, sounding really strong at the top end like all the best Italian machinery. However, as maximum power is developed at 6000 rpm, although exceeding that figure can make a marginal improvement in the 0-60 time where it can save a gear change, for general purposes it is a waste of time. One of the most outstanding features of the Veloce is that the increase in horsepower has been obtained without a detrimental effect on flexibility. The new valve timing makes the most of the refined twin-Weber

carburation induction system and, if anything, the engine is just as flexible as that of the ordinary Giulia. The Weber trumpets are housed within a very elaborate cold air filter system and the intake hiss is barely detectable. Just to make sure that I remembered what a Giulia GT was like, I tried one in the middle of the test, but maybe our test car was in better tune.

Along with the rest of the Alfa Romeo range, the gearbox is a five-speed unit with ZF-type synchromesh on all forward gears. When the first of this type of five-speed box appeared—I think it was on the Giulia 1600 —the synchro was notoriously weak especially on second gear. This is now all past history; the present baulk system is exceedingly powerful and changes can go through like lightning. There is a spring biasing the gear lever towards the centre of the gate in the same horizontal plane as third and fourth speeds. This enables the driver to change up and down in the correct sequence automatically as soon as one realises that for first and second gear pressure to the left is required. When fifth speed is required the lever must be pulled slightly to the right to counteract the spring bias. It all sounds very difficult, but within a very few miles one finds oneself gear-perfect, so to speak. Top gear, fifth, is in fact an overdrive ratio of 0.79:1, fourth gear being direct drive. The ratios are well-chosen and reflect Alfa Romeo's racing heritage.

The gear lever itself is very substantial, with a sprung knob which has to be compressed before reverse gear can be selected —as it is opposite fifth this is rather important. The lever comes perfectly to hand. Often on foreign cars which have been designed primarily for left-hand drive markets the gear shift and the whole selection mechanism is on the driver's side of the gearbox, and when the cars are built RHD the lever tends to be that fraction too far away. Power is transmitted to the gearbox by a single eight-inch dry plate clutch with mechanical actuation. The prop-shaft is a two-piece affair with a central bearing

and a rubber doughnut effecting union with the gearbox output shaft. This has a cushioning effect on the drive without giving the car an elastic feeling. The rear axle is of a hypoid bevel type with a copiously finned aluminium casing.

The front suspension is by a pair of wide base wishbones with coil springs and separate spring damping units; there is also a fairly substantial anti-roll bar. At the rear is the usual elaborate live axle system with coil spring/damper units, a pair of very substantial trailing arms and an equally robust top mounted A bracket controlling axle movement. The upward movement of the axle is limited by rubber pads, with rebound restricted by fabric rubber straps. The fully floating rear end of the Alfa is as sophisticated a live axle design as one sees, and is certainly preferable to a mediocre all-independent design.

The braking system is fundamentally a Dunlop design built under licence by ATE. It consists of four wheel disc brakes mounted outboard, operated by a single master cylinder through a vacuum servo. The front calipers are fairly conventional, but the rear brake pads are actuated through a pair of pressed steel levers by push rods; these are connected to the remote operating cylinders which are mounted on a rear axle—ingenious. Along with other foreign manufacturers, Alfas have not got the message about wide-rim wheels and the ventilated pressed steel wheels have only 4.5-inch rims. Worm and roller steering is used and great pains have been taken to get good geometry.

The engine fires instantly whether it be hot or cold, by courtesy of the Weber carburation. It is inadvisable to use the choke even in extreme cold for more than a few seconds, as it is all too easy to wet a plug. The little twin-cam engine warms up quickly and settles down to idle smoothly at about 750 rpm. The gearbox is far stiffer when the oil is cold and care must be taken over engagement of second to avoid snicking the gears. When cold there is a slight squeak from the central prop-shaft bearing, but this vanishes as soon as the prelubricated bearing has warmed a little.

Without doubt the best feature of the car is the *rapport* which exists between car and driver. This feeling of being part of the car enables the driver to throw the car about with much abandon, especially with

CONTINUED ON PAGE 28

ALFA ROMEO GTA

GIVEN THE WORKS 6

By GEOFFREY HOWARD

Right: Lamps ablaze we drove on and on into the dusk.

Below: Successful outing for the GTA at Spa when after 24 hours this car driven by Pinto and Demoulin finished second overall

THE MUSIC of a racing car is like a symphony. Ahead it is a smooth and subdued whine superimposed on a commotion, not a noise, of a shape parting streamlines fast. As it passes the full blast of the exhaust strikes, blood vessels throb and the faint whiff of racing oil thrills the senses. Inside it is a sensation, the echo of power rattling round the box of the body and a thrust in the back whenever the accelerator is pressed.

Just three laps at Silverstone last June in a works group 2 Alfa GTA were enough to give me the taste. Watching a full works team and some private entries for 24 hours at Spa a few weeks later whetted my appetite even more; and when another works car came to England to sit on the Mangoletsi stand at the Racing Car Show, I started all the string-pulling I knew.

Friendly Dr. Tassan of Alfa Romeo (G.B.) is an enthusiast, so when I explained my desire and how I had to leave for the Brussels Show the Monday after the Racing Car Show closed on Saturday night, he arranged to have the exhibit delivered to me just for the Sunday. So by 10.30 in the morning I was behind the wheel and pulling out of the Toddington Service Area on M1, with 160 b.h.p. on tap.

This GTA is a rally car prepared by Autodelta to group 2 specification and owned by the Belgian Alfa distributors. Compared with the circuit racer it is much more docile and pulls well from as low as 2,000 r.p.m. in 5th gear. The clutch is not fierce and it can be eased away from rest quite gently. The rally car has a full-length exhaust system and not the flat megaphone under the driver's door of the racer, so it is not so noisy. But it's just as exciting.

In place of the usual rev counter, a chronometric instrument reading to 10,000 r.p.m. had been fitted, complete with red tell-tale needle. At about 3,000 the engine would go flat until 4,000, when it would suddenly clear and scream on to whatever the works allow. The needle read 7,500 when I took the car over, so I tried to respect this limit. Overall gearing is low, for rallying, and a special top gear of 0·86 instead of 0·79 to 1 is one of the Autodelta mods (GTAs all have a special close-ratio set compared with the Sprint GT anyway, except for 5th). As a result we found we had to back off the throttle at about 114 m.p.h. in 5th to prevent over-revving, and the snag was that this speed came up in about ¾ mile from rest.

To get the feel of the car with its competition suspension, quick-steering, Kléber-Colombes V.10 radial tyres and limited-slip differential, I took the A50 from Newport Pagnall to Lutterworth, which is a fast and twisty main road largely through farmland. The grip in the wet was quite astonishing, and even on muddy patches I was able to turn on the power very early in the bends without snaking. Obviously with such performance, public roads, even on a wintry Sunday, are not the place to learn about the car, so we headed straight for the M.I.R.A. test track.

Somehow by the time we arrived, the tell-tale was up to 8,000 r.p.m., so I groped my way through the facia wiring to find the re-set button. First things first, and we set to work with fifth-wheel and stopwatch to record the acceleration before the real fun of the day started on the inner road circuit. Somehow, by the time we had finished all this the tell-tale was again on 8,000 r.p.m. so I groped through the wiring again to get at the re-set button.

On the Circuit

Then I was away, into the double bend by the tunnel under the banked track, and down the main straight which is just over a half-mile long. Before the next turn 7,500 was showing in 5th and I was lifting off. Then hard on the brakes, and heel-and-toe down through 4th to 3rd, lift off, another dab and into 2nd for that nasty tight bend with all the big red-and-white striped barrels. Surprisingly the tail stayed right in line when I opened up before the apex, and I was away again —up through the box to 5th, then down to third for the next double left-hander at the start of the control tower straight.

As I came out of this, accelerating hard in 4th, the rev counter showed 7,000 (about 95 m.p.h.) and I was using the full width of the track and getting a bit of a twitch on the tail. And so I went on lapping, feeling more and more at home in the snug bucket seat and enjoying each corner more and more. Soon I was having to lift off at 7,500 in second all the way through the bottom bend, so I took it in third next time round. That was my undoing for without the same torque at the rear wheels, the front of the car ran wide and I found myself understeering straight for a barrel. I managed to tweak it round enough to clear, but by then I was off the asphalt and sliding wildly on the gravelly shoulder.

I collected myself and proceeded with more restraint. It was then, with great reluctance, I remembered the others who were standing in the cold waiting their turn. First Ted Eves spluttered off, gaining song and confidence very rapidly and finding it all just as much fun. We dragged him out and let Mike Scarlett take the wheel. He too was most reluctant to stop circulating, but now it was getting dark. Standing there on the edge of what was once a war-time airfield, listening to the exhaust wailing and growling, crackling on the over-run and blasting forth with renewed strength at every gearchange, it took me back to Spa and the

excitement of an endurance ordeal.

Still flushed from it all, we gathered up the equipment and turned to the motorway and home. The car never missed a beat all day—which, considering it had been on show since last season and had not been attended to in any way since its last outing, was all the more amazing. It had been driven to Olympia from Brussels and, after 10 days on the stand, started on the second turn of the key without even the battery being charged. And we never even looked at the plugs.

About the GTA

The GTA is a production car and is listed in England at £2,898, compared with £1,950 for a Sprint GTV. It has an aluminium body, but still looks just like any Sprint GT. Engine power is boosted from 109 b.h.p. net to 115, both at 6,000 r.p.m. by fitting a new cylinder head with dual ignition. From then on Autodelta will do the rest if you pay them, and add another 40-50 b.h.p. at about 7,500 or so. Standard on the GTA are pressed steel 14in. wheels in place of the 15in. of

the Sprint GT, which enable much bigger section tyres to fit in the wheel arches. Close-ratio gears and a special final drive complete the set up.

When Autodelta get to work they fit a limited-slip differential, oil cooler, special exhaust, modified starter and dynamo. Then special competition suspension is added, plus 7in. wide alloy wheels, rear anti-roll bar and extra lateral axle location, long-range 20-gallon fuel tank, heavy-duty clutch, double roll-over bar inside the roof and modified seats.

The result is the car that won its class in the 1966 European Touring Car Championship and the Transamerican Championship. In rallying, the Alfa GTA won the 1966 Alpine driven by Frenchman Jean Rolland, who also finished second in the Tour de Corse. The test car had a rather vague history as it apparently began its racing career in the hands of de Adamich at Zolder and was then converted for rallying. On the circuits it has had the legs of the Lotus-Cortinas nearly without exception, but the rallying performance has not been very serious.

▶

ALFA GTA

PERFORMANCE DATA

Figures in brackets are for the Alfa-Romeo Giulia Sprint GTV tested in AUTOCAR of 16 Dec. 1966.

Acceleration Times (mean): *Speed range, gear ratios and time in seconds.*

m.p.h.	Top	4th	3rd	2nd	1st
	4·62 (3·58)	5·38 (4·56)	6·78 (6·20)	9·13 (9·08)	13·62 (15·03)
10–30	—	—	—	3·7 (4·2)	2·6 (3·0)
20–40	—	(8·3)	4·5 (5·4)	3·8 (5·4)	1·8 (—)
30–50	— (11·6)	6·0 (7·8)	5·3 (5·5)	3·7 (4·0)	—
40–60	7·5 (11·6)	6·9 (7·7)	5·3 (5·9)	—	—
50–70	9·3 (13·0)	7·3 (8·5)	4·4 (6·2)	—	—
60–80	9·9 (14·7)	6·0 (9·5)	— (8·0)	—	—
70–90	9·1 (18·9)	6·6 (10·8)	—	—	—
80–100	9·6 (25·6)	9·1 (16·0)	—	—	—
90–120	11·2 (—)	—	—	—	—

From rest through gears to:

30 m.p.h.	3·4 sec	(3·7 sec)
40 „	4·6 „	(5·5 „)
50 „	6·4 „	(7·8 „)
60 „	8·8 „	(11·1 „)
70 „	11·0 „	(14·2 „)
80 „	14·1 „	(19·2 „)
90 „	17·3 „	(25·5 „)
100 „	23·9 „	(35·4 „)
110 „	30·9 „	(— „)

Standing quarter-mile 16·7 sec, 89 m.p.h. (17·7 sec, 77 m.p.h.)
1 km 29·9 sec, 108 m.p.h. (32·7 sec, 97 m.p.h.)

Maximum speeds on gears:	m.p.h.	k.p.h.	r.p.m.
Top (mean)	114 (113)	186 (182)	7,500 (5,780)
(best)	114 (115)	186 (185)	7,500 (5,880)
4th	105 (100)	169 (161)	7,500 (6,590)
3rd	77 (80)	124 (129)	7,500 (6,500)
2nd	56 (54)	89 (87)	7,500 (7,100)
1st	40 (30)	64 (48)	7,500 (6,500)

Overall fuel consumption for 203 miles:
15·5 m.p.g. 18·2 litres/100km
(21·9 m.p.g. 12·9 litres/100km)

Left: A twin-plug head is fitted to the GTA and the snake-like pipe leads to an oil catch tank

Below left: The test car was Belgian registered but fully-prepared by Autodelta. Wide-rimmed cast wheels with Kléber Colombes radial tyres were fitted

Right: Alpine winner, Jean Rolland at the Cannes control

Below right: Tailpiece. On the road, the Alfa has impeccable manners

ALFA ROMEO GTV

*Grace, style and excitement in
an (occasional) 2+2 sports sedan*

CRASH! THE ENTRANCE of our Alfa Romeo Giulia Sprint GTV was undeniably dramatic. The scene: A fog-smothered coast highway intersection, where the Alfa waited apprehensively before a red signal, surrounded by darkness and things that go bump in the night. The heavy: An on-coming full-size native sedan, secure in self knowledge and pride of home turf. The action: Predictable and disastrous. Nuccio Bertone would have wept.

Taken squarely up the back by two tons at 30 mph, the rear bodywork was crushed, but with superb progressive reluctance; to such good effect that our driver emerged physically unharmed, though with a bombed-out psyche. Crumpling extended forward to the front of the rear wheel well, popping loose the rear window and distorting the rear vent frames. Surprisingly, however, the doors could be opened after the collision, and even the chassis and rear axle geometry remained undistorted. All of which rounds out to high marks indeed for the craftsmen of Milano, plus a concomitant hint to the legislators of Washington that there may be even more to automotive safety than lap belts and hazard lights.

Three weeks later, after corrective ministrations by Alfa Romeo's Long Beach, Calif., facility, we were once again entrusted with the same GTV. Barring a high-speed wind whistle from the vent window and a rattle from the rear package shelf the car seemed as new, and once again we began to experience that rare, easy Italian charm with which nearly any Alfa Romeo progressively disarms, beguiles and finally enchants us.

Very few test cars have been flattered by the instant acceptance and sustained interest the GTV commanded during its reign over the *Road & Track* parking lot. Our tenure with the very similar Giulia Sprint GT (R&T, December 1964) had been enthusiastic but brief, and this time most staff members managed to find impeccable reasons either to renew their acquaintance or to see what they had missed three years ago. As testing proceeded, nearly every driver had praise for the car; a rather startling unanimity of opinion.

For example, even a Porsche owner ungrudgingly approved the entire Alfa *gestalt,* and spoke highly of its quick, precise handling and instant recovery through a badly chuckholed stretch of dirt road. And a former Chrysler engineer tried a brief test ride, returned wondering "how the devil do they do that with a live rear axle," then forthwith demanded more time for a really thorough examination.

On analysis, the reasons for this broad spectrum of appeal are both simple and complex. They boil down to a machine carefully designed to become an extension of the human body, satisfying its wishes and amplifying its physical actions with a minimum of mechanical interference. This is no uncommon goal for automobile designers, of course, but the scarcity of such vehicles indicates the extreme difficulty of execution.

An Alfa Romeo GTV in full flight down a winding back road is considerably more than the sum of its parts, but an examination of some important components at least partially describes the whole car. The engine, a 1570-cc, dohc, inline 4, is basically the same power source Alfa has used in previous 1600 models, including the Sprint GT, Sprint Speciale and the Duetto. In the Giulia GTV (Grand Touring Veloce) carburetion is by a pair of horizontal twin-choke Webers.

Engine performance is flexible but not mechanically smooth. It is quite possible to lug from 2000 rpm, and if the owner does this judiciously at the appropriate times the engine's longevity will be enhanced. The engine starts quickly, idles quietly and outside of a tendency to foul plugs in easy running it is remarkably vice-free for a unit with a power output of over 1.2 bhp/cu in. Alfa tests each engine for over two hours on the bench before installation.

At cruising speeds of 70-80 mph, where the car would otherwise be in its element, a peculiar resonance appears— apparently a heterodyning beat between the dual exhaust system and another noise element. This annoyance could, and

should, be tuned out. Also, this engine has the standard Alfa trait of running "too cool"; at less than 175° F. A long-time Alfa owner's ploy has been to partially block the radiator, especially in cold weather, but a 195° thermostat would be a better solution. A higher operating temperature should reduce wear, corrosion, and hydrocarbon emission, and certainly should improve performance of the minimal Alfa heating system.

The fuel-gauge needle is supplemented by a red warning light which flashes intermittently as low fuel sloshes from side to side in the tank; then the light settles down to a baleful, accusing glare as the last few gallons are reached. The early blinking can cause an inexperienced driver to make over-frequent gas stops, but the progressive action of the system soon becomes useful.

Our great enjoyment of the superb Alfa Romeo transmission has brought forth encomiums in the past and undoubtedly will again. This all-but-faultless unit gives the driver a control of gear ratios very nearly as flexible, swift and effortless as the thought of shifting itself. All five forward gears are synchromesh, with first and second on the lefthand leg of a "double-H" gate, third and fourth in the center, and fifth and a telescoping lockout reverse at the right. A double spring action urges the lever toward the center from either side, and as soon as the driver learns to let it seek its own position there is no excuse whatever for confusion in either up- or downshifting.

Gear ratios are evenly spaced, from the very low 3.30:1 first gear up through the overdrive 0.79:1 fifth. Most abouttown puttering centers around third gear, however, to the det-

ALFA ROMEO GTV
AT A GLANCE

Price as tested............................$4448
Engine..........4-cyl inline, dohc, 1570 cc, 125 bhp
Curb weight, lb..............................2230
Top speed, mph.................................112
Acceleration, 0-¼ mi, sec.....................17.6
Average fuel consumption, mpg..................23
Summary: Traditional Alfa virtues and vices: superb handling, gearbox, finish; minimal heating & ventilation . . . redesigned front seats, improved rear seating area.

ALFA ROMEO GTV

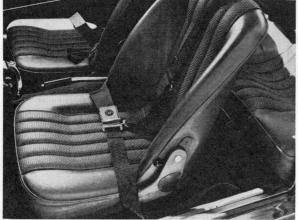

New vinyl-clad bucket seats give firm support, have seatback adjustment. Lever lets back fold forward for rear-seat entry.

Veloce arrangement requires cross-top air duct leading to two side-draft Webers. In line 4-cyl engine produces 125 bhp.

Hooded console cuts reflections; is well instrumented, but needs ammeter. Redline-less tachometer reads to 8000 rpm.

riment of the fuel supply but the benefit of the engine. The sharp, eager clutch bite recorded in our test of the Sprint GT was missing in the GTV. Acceleration tests, and even the reasonably fierce street driving this car invites, produced unmistakable indications of slip when completing shifts, along with doubts regarding the adequacy and longevity of the 7.9-in. dia. clutch plate. At this time, this is speculation.

Comfort appraisals were oddly varied, and we could arrive at no clear pattern of agreement. Most drivers, ranging through both extremes of the height scale, could find excellent accommodation for operating the car easily and with long-haul comfort. Others decided that their arm and leg length apparently were outside the Italian norm, requiring some to adopt an indecorous knee-spraddle around the steering wheel and a few to resort to an unstylish elbow-cock.

The new Alfa swept-around bucket seat, however, earned complete—or nearly complete—approval. (One right-side entrant attempted too-hasty ingress, came afoul of the seat's outer wing, and later made piteous claims of having been rendered rump-sprung.) The configuration of the front seats is very good, giving complete lateral support during brisk driving, yet freedom for necessary body action. Seat travel is long and seat-back rake is variable through a considerable arc by use of a large, positive-acting control knob at the side. The rear compartment is comfortable and large enough for occasional occupancy by two adults, with the lower seat cushions hollowed somewhat to make better use of headroom.

The instrument panel design is almost identical with the clean, readable layouts of the GTV's forebears. Dials and gauges, including an oil-temperature gauge, are set well down into the console, eliminating all but occasional sidelight reflections from their faces. The manual controls are grouped close to the driver's hands in natural, logical positions, though a row of three identical toggle switches is unlabeled and unnecessarily confusing. Operation of the light switch will be unusual to most new drivers—it consists of a knobbed stalk projecting leftward out of the steering column and is twisted forward to turn on the headlights, then lowered for high beams.

The interior of the GTV is luxurious and impressive, yet not overdone. All the amenities are functional, not merely decorative, and taken together they give an overall feeling of invitation, comfort and purpose. Both the seats and the side panels are upholstered in soft, padded vinyl, which is both firm and agreeable to the touch. The steering wheel is large and properly substantial, yet simple and attractive, as are the other major controls. Rather than attempting to camouflage them—the parking brake lever is prominently, and conveniently, right out in the open between the front seats—Alfa took the opposite course and made them important features of the interior design.

Vision from within the car is particularly good, and the large glass area and unobtrusive pillars also help give the exterior an airy, sporting look. The rear-quarter *quadrifoglio* badges are a reminder of the days when great racing Alfas carried this symbol, which, incidentally, has begun to appear again on the new 2-liter, rear-engine prototype.

Alfa Romeo brakes have always been a matter of considerable pride to their owners, from the impressive-finned-aluminum drums of yesteryear down to the present vacuum-servo-assisted discs. With 11.3-in.-discs in front and 9.7-in. at the rear, the GTV can be slowed or stopped quickly, without undue effort, and under perfect control. A series of hard stops from 60 mph showed exactly the result we expected from a well-designed disc system: sustained braking power with very little increase in pedal effort, and no loss of control.

As one of the last sporting redoubts of the live rear axle, Alfa maintains its position with powerful ammunition indeed. The combination of light, precise steering and controllable understeer through almost any road condition makes it an easy, safe and enjoyable car for the novice, as well as a source of continuing exhilaration to the skilled driver.

ROAD TEST
ALFA ROMEO GTV

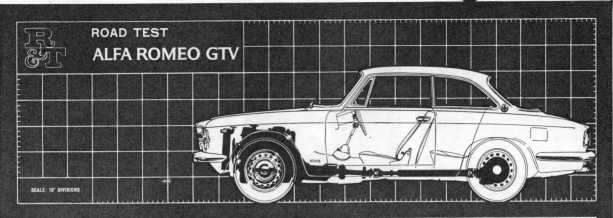

SCALE: 10" DIVISIONS

PRICE

Basic list................$4200
As tested................$4448

ENGINE

Type.........4 cyl inline, dohc
Bore x stroke, mm........78 x 82
Equivalent in.......3.07 x 3.23
Displacement, cc/cu in..1570/95.8
Compression ratio.........9.0:1
Bhp @ rpm.........125 @ 6000
Equivalent mph...........116
Torque @ rpm, lb-ft...115 @ 2800
Equivalent mph...........54
Carburetion..2 Weber 40 DCOE 27
Type fuel required.......premium

DRIVE TRAIN

Clutch diameter, in..........7.9
Gear ratios: 5th (0.79).....3.60:1
4th (1.00)..............4.56:1
3rd (1.36)..............6.21:1
2nd (1.99)..............9.08:1
1st (3.30)..............15.0:1
Synchromesh...........on all 5
Final drive ratio..........4.56:1

CHASSIS & BODY

Body/frame............steel unit
Brake type: ATE disc with vacuum
assist, drum parking brake
Swept area, sq in.........368
Wheel type & size, in......15 x 4.5
Tires....Pirelli Cinturato S 155-15
Steering type.....worm & sector
Overall ratio.............15:1
Turns, lock-to-lock........3.75
Turning circle, ft.........32.8
Front suspension: independent with
unequal-length A-arms, coil
springs, tube shocks, anti-roll bar.
Rear suspension: live axle, trailing
arms, coil springs, tube shocks.

OPTIONAL EQUIPMENT

Included in "as tested" price: AM/
FM/SW radio, 2 seat & shoulder
belts, outside mirror.
Other: cast alloy wheels, rear seat
belts, rear window defroster.

ACCOMMODATION

Seating capacity, persons...2 + 2
Seat width, front/rear
................2 x 21.5/2x23.0
Head room, front/rear...40.0/35.0
Seat back adjustment, deg.....30
Driver comfort rating (scale of 100):
Driver 69 in. tall...........85
Driver 72 in. tall...........80
Driver 75 in. tall...........75

INSTRUMENTATION

Instruments: 140-mph speedometer, 8000-rpm tachometer; oil
pressure, oil temp, water temp
& fuel level gauges.
Warning lights: generator, directional signals, lights on, high
beam, heater on, low fuel.

MAINTENANCE

Crankcase capacity, qt........6.0
Change interval, mi.......3600
Filter change interval, mi....3600
Chassis lube interval, mi....3600
Tire pressures, psi........24/26

MISCELLANEOUS

Body styles available: coupe as
tested.
Warranty period, 6 mo/unlimited
mileage.

GENERAL

Curb weight, lb..........2230
Test weight................2625
Weight distribution (with
driver), front/rear, %....53/47
Wheelbase, in............93.0
Track, front/rear.......51.5/50.0
Overall length............161.0
Width................62.0
Height................52.0
Frontal area, sq ft.........17.9
Ground clearance, in.........5.0
Overhang, front/rear...30.4/37.6
Usable trunk space, cu ft.....9.5
Fuel tank capacity, gal......14.0

CALCULATED DATA

Lb/hp (test wt).............21.0
Mph/1000 rpm (5th gear)....19.6
Engine revs/mi (60 mph)....3060
Piston travel, ft/mi........1645
Rpm @ 2500 ft/min........4645
Equivalent mph...........91
Cu ft/ton mi.............64.4
R&T wear index...........50.4
Brake swept area sq in/ton....280

ROAD TEST RESULTS

ACCELERATION

Time to distance, sec:
0–100 ft....................3.7
0–250 ft....................6.3
0–500 ft....................9.6
0–750 ft...................12.5
0–1000 ft..................14.9
0–1320 ft (¼ mi)..........17.6
Speed at end of ¼ mi, mph...77
Time to speed, sec:
0–30 mph....................3.4
0–40 mph....................5.5
0–50 mph....................7.2
0–60 mph...................10.5
0–70 mph...................14.2
0–80 mph...................19.2
0–100 mph..................35.5
Passing exposure time, sec:
To pass car going 50 mph......7.4

FUEL CONSUMPTION

Normal driving, mpg.......21–25
Cruising range, mi.......295–350

SPEEDS IN GEARS

5th gear (5700 rpm), mph.....112
4th (6800)................104
3rd (6800).................77
2nd (6800).................53
1st (6800).................31

BRAKES

Panic stop from 80 mph:
Deceleration, % g..........78
Control.............excellent
Fade test: percent of increase in
pedal effort required to maintain
50%-g deceleration rate in six
stops from 60 mph.........11
Parking brake: hold 30% grade..no
Overall brake rating.....very good

SPEEDOMETER ERROR

30 mph indicated.....actual 26.8
40 mph.................36.0
60 mph.................54.6
80 mph.................73.2
100 mph................91.4
Odometer, 10.0 mi....actual 9.62

ACCELERATION & COASTING

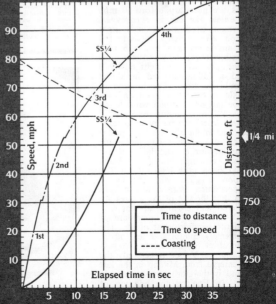

Time to distance
Time to speed
Coasting

Elapsed time in sec

CONTINUED FROM PAGE 19

the right-hand-drive model, where the gearbox tunnel provides a great deal of support for the left leg. When driving fast it is very necessary to have the maximum body support so that the hands can be used not to brace oneself but to twiddle the wheel—which is the idea anyway.

The suspension, considering it is the combination of a live rear axle and fully independent front suspension, is exceptionally good and the Veloce goes through corners sitting down well on the road with the minimum of the characteristic Alfa body roll. The roadholding in the dry is excellent and for a production car the understeer is minimal. Although the GTV could never be described as an oversteerer, the lock over direction has been reduced considerably. Most cars which have near-neutral handling tend to be very twitchy and lack straight line stability, but this is not the case with the Veloce.

Flattery is always pleasing and driving the GTV does wonders for you—it is like playing with a toy, it is so responsive. The steering could be a little higher-geared considering this is meant to be a high-performance car, and the castor return action feels unnecessarily strong. Nevertheless it is sufficiently sensitive to enable the driver to use the car to its maximum, for it has plenty of feel with virtually no kickback. In the wet, with Cinturato tyres on the tiny 4.5-inch rims, the adhesion is disappointing; but at least the car is controllable, so it's more fun than a problem—even if it doesn't get you anwhere very quickly. By changing to 5½J rims with SP41 tyres or something similar, the cornering could be improved out of all recognition, particularly in the wet.

At high speed the stability is really first class, and side winds have very little effect. The Veloce takes changes of road surfaces in its stride, the ride being firm without being too hard. The brakes are extremely powerful and very little pressure is needed to stop the car. The vacuum servo is to my mind too powerful, and it is all too easy to lock up the front wheels, especially in the wet. However, one does get used to the small amount of pressure that is required and the complete absence of fade is very reassuring.

The 109 bhp when coupled to the extremely close ratio gearbox make for promising performance figures; 60 mph can be reached in just over 10 secs, a very respectable time by any standards. Two gear changes are necessary before 60 mph is reached unless the car is over-revved. The acceleration continues strongly right up to 90 mph, after which it tends to fall off. Maximum speed is a true 116 mph but it is possible to get one-way times some 2 mph faster, and with a slight downhill gradient and a following wind no doubt 120 mph could be seen. The location of the back axle is extremely good and the power can be got on the road without too much fuss. When cornering really hard the inside rear wheel can be made to leave the ground, and in the absence of a power lock diff this can have some interesting effects. The interior is well laid out but the dashboard, although finished in black leather, could be a little less utility. The instrumentation is good, with the tachometer and speedometer immediately in front of the driver, but the rest of the gauges are a little cluttered and are not all that easy to read, and there is a certain amount of reflection on the windscreen at night. The seats are extremely comfortable and afford very good location for the driver.

The Alfa Romeo Veloce is certainly the best car to emerge from Milano in the last few years and is therefore not surprisingly selling well. In England the addition of import duty as well as purchase tax puts it into the luxury market at £1,950, almost the price of a Jaguar E-type. Nevertheless the thoroughbred upbringing of the Veloce makes it an attractive proposition.

SPECIFICATION AND PERFORMANCE DATA

Car Tested: Alfa Romeo Giulia Sprint GTV fixed head 2+2 coupé. Price as tested: £1,950 including PT.

Engine: Four cylinders, 78 x 82 mm (1570 cc). Twin overhead camshafts. Compression ratio 9 to 1. 109 bhp DIN at 6000 rpm. Twin 40DCOE Weber carburetters. Bosch coil and distributor ignition.

Transmission: Fichtel & Sachs 8-inch single dry plate clutch. Five-speed all-synchromesh gearbox with central change, ratios top 0.79, fourth 1.0, third 1.36, second 1.99, first 3.30, reverse 3.01 to 1. Two-piece open propeller shaft. Hypoid bevel final drive, ratio 4.56 to 1.

Chassis: Integral body-chassis unit. Independent front suspension with wishbones, helical springs and anti-roll bar. Worm and roller steering. Live rear axle with trailing arms and A bracket, coil springs and telescopic dampers. 11.3 ins diameter front disc brakes with 9.75 ins rear discs. Bolt-on disc wheels with 4.5J rims and Pirelli Cinturato SR tubed tyres.

Equipment: 12-volt lighting and starting. Speedometer, tachometer, water temperature, oil temperature, oil pressure and fuel gauges. Heating and demisting. Single speed self-parking wipers and windscreen washer. Flashing direction indicators. Reversing lamp.

Dimensions: Wheelbase: 8 ft 7 ins. Track (front): 4 ft 2 ins, (rear): 4 ft 3.6 ins. Overall length: 13 ft 5 ins. Width: 5 ft 2.2 ins. Turning circle: 35 ft. Weight (dry): 18 cwt 3 qtrs.

Performance: Maximum speed: 116.25 mph. Speeds in gears: fourth: 100 mph, third: 80 mph, second: 55 mph, first: 31 mph. Standing quarter-mile: 17.3 secs. Acceleration: 0-30 mph: 3.25 secs; 0-50 mph: 7.0 secs; 0-60 mph: 10.3 secs; 0-80 mph: 17.9 secs.

Fuel Consumption: 23 mpg.

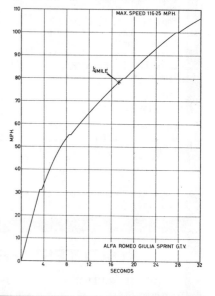

Gent's natty GT

. . . body by Bertone . . . reasonable seating for three or four people . . . not particularly fast . . . highly desirable piece of machinery. . . .

IT MUST be a source of considerable concern to the technicians in the motor industry when market research proves that attractive lines and a good name are such highly rated selling points, frequently over-ruling other more substantial merits. With the Alfa Romeo GT 1300 you get the lot—a respected name, a body by Bertone, an efficient twin overhead cam engine with five-speed gearbox and quite reasonable seating for three or four people. On those counts alone it has many of the ingredients to satisfy a wide range of owners of either sex with a taste for the striking and different and with £1,649 to pay for it.

Until now, *Motor* has never put this shape of Alfa through a full road test, although we have driven similar ones with different power units at the Total Test Days at Silverstone where they have always impressed us as being splendid circuit cars. The Sprint GT feels better than the boxy saloons as it rolls less and doesn't develop the same lurches on full roll at its high cornering limit; of course the racing version, the GTA, is particularly successful and won last year's European Touring Car Championship.

The 1300 is a light and easy car to drive, and fun too. If you want to keep ahead of the larger cars you have to use the gearbox, but mostly the engine pulls sufficiently well throughout its wide range to keep going at a very respectable rate; good roadholding keeps average speeds up on cross-country trips. The test figures for our car are not particularly startling—0–50 m.p.h. in 9.4s. and a maximum of 102.3 m.p.h. Rather are they an indication of the efficiency of both engine and wind tunnel testing that 19 cwt. of car can be pulled along so well by 1,300 c.c. If you want more performance, the Sprint Veloce 1600 will do nearer 115 m.p.h. and provide slightly more interior refinement for an extra £300. The intermediate Sprint GT 1600 is no longer available on the British market.

There are lots of cars on the market which cost less, go faster and have more room, but an Alfa is a highly desirable piece of machinery and the GT 1300 would appear to offer the best value of this connoisseur's range.

Performance and economy

The 1600 Giulia appeared in the summer of 1962, replacing the 1300 Giulietta series. In its hottest form, in the bulbous Giulietta SS, it had given 100 b.h.p. (net), but the more popular Giulietta Sprint Veloce produced 90 b.h.p. (net) at 6,500 r.p.m. with twin Webers and it was mated to a four-speed gearbox. The 1300 engine (actually 1,290 c.c.) fitted in the Giulia Junior series is not strictly a reversion to the Giulietta engine, but embodies subsequent production developments for strength and reliability as well as the ability to produce more power at lower r.p.m.—in other words, torque. Still with twin Webers, this now gives 103 b.h.p. (gross) at 6,000 r.p.m.

PRICE: £1,340 plus £308 16s. 1d. equals £1,648 16s. 1d.

Alfa Romeo GT 1300

In mild weather it is quite easy to start the car in the morning without the choke: just a couple of squirts on the accelerator pumps and it fires, although it is best to use a bit of choke to get even pulling during the mile or so necessary for warming up. You are recommended to run the engine at fast idle on the hand throttle for a bit before moving off, but mainly to ensure that the gearbox oil has circulated sufficiently.

Once warm, the unit impresses with its remarkably wide torque band; although it is not really the thing to do with an Alfa with its delightful gearbox, we found it could pull smoothly and without juddering from less than 20 m.p.h. in fifth, preferably by feeding in the throttle until it reached around 2,000 r.p.m. Power increases steadily to about 5,000 r.p.m. in top, or 91½ m.p.h. In the lower gears it is easy to reach the red line at 6,500 r.p.m.

Front seats are well shaped and have good adjustment. Facia is covered in imitation wood. Rear seat passengers have head room but not much for knees unless front seat is moved forward.

at which the engine feels perfectly happy; for normal motoring on the road, just 4,000 r.p.m. and five speeds give quite good performance and keep the engine below the noisy level—quiet in fact. Beyond this, noise increases to an intake/exhaust hum, rather than the thrash of a less well insulated Giulia engine as in the SS, for example; the noise is not unpleasant and is part and parcel of the feeling of the driver being in harmony with the car.

In performance the GT 1300 is about as fast as the Giulia TI saloon which is no longer available in this country, having given way to either the Giulia Super or the 1300 TI. The TI's extra ¾ cwt. is more than offset by a 12½% lower final drive ratio; at maximum speed it is geared to reach 103 m.p.h. at 6,000 r.p.m. while the 1300 falls slightly short of the peak with 102.3 m.p.h. at 5,600 r.p.m. Very few 1,300 c.c. production cars can top 100 m.p.h.—the Lotus Elite and Renault Gordini being two that spring to mind—and it is quite a tribute to the Alfa, which is essentially a fast tourer, that it can do this quite easily. On motorways the comfortable cruising speed is around 85-90 m.p.h. which can be maintained up hill and down dale all day without the oil temperature rising further than 170° F.

For 1,250 miles of Continental driving on roads which were mostly either twisty and hilly or motorways, we averaged 25.3 m.p.g.; a 450-mile local spell with traffic and short sprints returned 21 m.p.g. giving an overall average of 24 m.p.g. Most owners will probably get around this mark since the touring consumption is only 27.7 m.p.g. Three pints of oil were used in just over 1,500 miles.

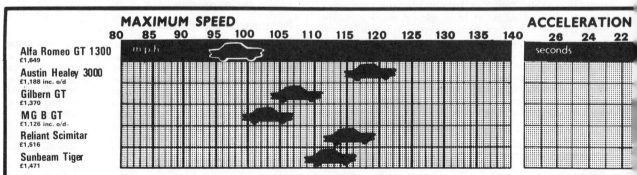

	MAXIMUM SPEED	ACCELERATION
	80 85 90 95 100 105 110 115 120 125 130 135 140	26 24 22
Alfa Romeo GT 1300 £1,649	m.p.h.	seconds
Austin Healey 3000 £1,188 inc. o/d		
Gilbern GT £1,370		
MG B GT £1,126 inc. o/d		
Reliant Scimitar £1,516		
Sunbeam Tiger £1,471		

Transmission

One of the main reasons why everyone enjoys Alfa Romeos on test tracks is that with five gears they have a ratio suitable for almost every corner you can meet; on the road this is particularly noticeable with the 1300 since you need to use the gearbox frequently when in a hurry. First gives a reasonable getaway but the car cannot quite manage a clean start on a 1-in-3 hill, being defeated by clutch slip; 1-in-4 is easily surmounted. Top gear, a geared up fifth, is good for fast cruising without the engine obtruding. The remaining three gears are neatly spaced in between to give one of the nicest boxes in production. The gate is a normal four-speed H-pattern with fifth forward in its own plane nearest the driver.

The substantial lever is conveniently placed for the left hand and is spring loaded in the 3-4 plane; thus the frequent change from fifth to fourth only needs a two-finger pull from the forward fifth and the lever slides into the adjacent plane on the spring loading. Into third is more two finger stuff, but it is rather harder work to push over into second and first. Reverse is opposite fifth—to the right and back—and you need a fairly substantial push down on the knob to overcome the stop.

With a maximum required pressure of 42 lb. the clutch is fairly heavy but you don't really notice it with the rampant pedals at a comfortable angle; the combined movements of clutch and gear lever are pleasantly firm and conducive to smooth changes. This, coupled with brake and accelerator pedals ideally spaced for heel-and-toeing, makes the Alfa particular fun for the keen driver.

Handling and brakes

Although the ride of sporting Italian cars like the Alfa is not particularly soft, they all seem to transmit a splendid feel of the road which is immediately reassuring and you find it much easier to drive fast than with some of the more remote but more comfort-

Performance

Performance tests carried out by *Motor's* staff at the Motor Industry Research Association proving ground, Lindley.

Test Data: World copyright reserved; no unauthorised reproduction in whole or in part.

Conditions

Weather: Dry with light winds 5-15 m.p.h.
Temperature 58°-70°F. Barometer 29.4-29.38 in. Hg.
Surface: Dry concrete and tarmacadam.
Fuel: Premium 98-octane (RM), 4-star rating.

Maximum speeds

	m.p.h.
Mean of opposite runs	102.3
Best one-way ¼-mile	105.9
4th gear ⎫	102.0
3rd gear ⎬ at 6,500 r.p.m.	75.0
2nd gear ⎭	51.5
1st gear	31.0

"Maximile" speed: (Timed quarter mile after 1 mile accelerating from rest)

Mean	97.1
Best	100.0

Acceleration times

m.p.h.	sec.
0-30	4.3
0-40	6.7
0-50	9.4
0-60	13.8
0-70	18.5
0-80	26.8
0-90	40.2
Standing quarter mile	19.6

m.p.h.	Top sec.	4th sec.	3rd sec.
10-30	—	—	7.5
20-40	14.5	10.6	7.5
30-50	14.0	10.4	7.4
40-60	14.6	11.1	8.1
50-70	16.9	12.7	9.1
60-80	23.6	15.2	—
70-90	—	20.8	—

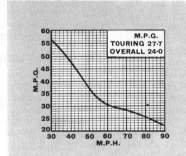

Fuel consumption

Touring (consumption midway between 30 m.p.h. and maximum less 5% allowance for acceleration) .... 27.7 m.p.g.
Overall .... 24.0 m.p.g.
(=11.8 litres/100 km.)
Total test figure .... 1,630 miles
Tank capacity (maker's figure) ..... 10 gal.

Brakes

Pedal pressure, deceleration and equivalent stopping distance from 30 m.p.h.

lb.	g	ft.
25	0.15	200
50	0.33	90
75	0.47	64
100	0.66	45½
125	0.92	32½
130	0.95	31½
Handbrake	0.36	83½

Fade test

20 stops at ½g deceleration at 1 min. intervals from a speed midway between 30 m.p.h. and maximum speed (=66.1 m.p.h.).

	lb.
Pedal force at beginning	78
Pedal force at 10th stop	57
Pedal force at 20th stop	57

Hill climbing

At steady speed

		lb./ton
Top	1 in 12.0	(Tapley 185)
4th	1 in 9.5	(Tapley 235)
3rd	1 in 6.5	(Tapley 340)
2nd	1 in 4.7	(Tapley 470)

Steering

Turning circle between kerbs:

	ft.
Left	31¼
Right	33⅓
Turns of steering wheel from lock to lock	3.5
Steering wheel deflection for 50 ft. diameter circle	1.0 turns

Clutch

Free pedal movement	= 1½ in.
Additional movement to disengage clutch completely	= 3 in.
Maximum pedal load	=42 lb.

Speedometer

Indicated	20	30	40	50	60	70	80	90	100
True	17½	26½	35½	44½	54	63	73	82	91

Distance recorder .... 3½% fast

Weight

Kerb weight (unladen with fuel for approximately 50 miles) .... 18.9 cwt.
Front/rear distribution 57½/42½
Weight laden as tested ...... 22.7 cwt.

Parkability

Gap needed to clear a 6 ft. wide obstruction parked in front:

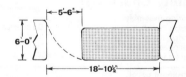

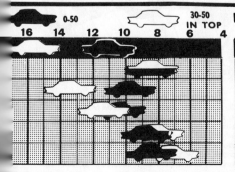

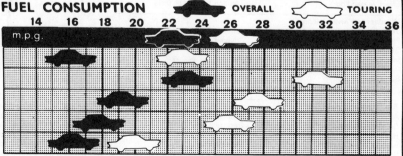

Alfa Romeo GT 1300

able set-ups. The Alfa Giulias all use conventional wishbone front suspension but the live rear axle is located by twin lower trailing arms and an upper, slightly offset, A-bracket which gives a fairly high roll centre. However, there is little tendency for the inside rear wheel to spin on tight turns with the modest output of the 1300 engine, despite the quite high roll angles.

The steering ratio did not appear to be as low as on the saloon models and all direction changing except side-street turns could be done without shuffling hands. Little kickback is felt at the wheel and plenty of wet road feel is transmitted as the car starts to slide gently on its Cinturato S tyres; these are a special Milan brew for Alfas which have a slightly higher speed rating than the standard tyre—not that it's necessary on the 1300—traded for slightly lower wet road grip than the standard Cinturato. On dry roads they hang on very well with some squeal and it is difficult to break adhesion unless you throw the car round; it understeers through most of the range and only occasionally do you reach the oversteer condition, when you are going very fast, but it doesn't leap sideways on bumpy corners and doesn't have the rocking motion which the saloons develop at track speeds. Even if you ease up on corners there is no sudden directional change and, in fact, the handling is very safe and predictable. On wet roads it is much easier to lose adhesion but it is not sudden and you can feel the front wheels beginning to run wide before they eventually break away; if you do feed too much power in on wet roads, which is difficult on the 1300, the tail comes round but you can still catch it from surprisingly high attitude angles, although you might have to take another bite at the wheel, thus increasing the danger of over-correction. But, whatever happens, it is safe, fun and controllable.

Initially, we were surprised by the brakes; they felt very heavy at town speeds and a $\frac{1}{2}$ g stop required 80 lb. pedal pressure. But during the fade test they rapidly became lighter as they warmed up and at the end the same stop required only 55 lb.—an average figure. The pads thus appear to be quite hard and to resist fade completely; they needed only a single stop after the water splash to restore them to their normal cold pressures. There is some logic in this: for occasional use they are not too heavy for normal stopping up to $\frac{1}{2}$ g but, for a panic stop, their heaviness reduces the danger of premature wheel locking since it needs around 130 lb. for the best stop. On the other hand, for frequent use around the Alps when heavy brakes would be rather tiring, the required pressure is some 30 lb. less.

Despite the high sill and slightly narrow boot opening we managed to get a good 6.8 cu.ft. of our test luggage inside. The spare wheel lives under all the luggage. Toolkit is surprisingly versatile.

With a strong pull the handbrake can lock the wheels for a 0.36 g stop and hold the car on a 1-in-3 hill; we had to use two hands for this on the test car, but it is possible that one having less slack would allow better leverage and less effort.

Comfort and controls

Firm suspension breeds a firm ride; the Alfa follows the surface fairly faithfully but it is sufficiently well damped not to jerk the occupants unpleasantly. On typical French roads, the worse bumps generate a rocking motion and you can sense that the car is moving on a highish roll axis, but on the generally better English roads this is fairly rare and the car can be driven quickly over any surface with no rattles. At low speed there are some radial ply thumps on ridges, but the mounting points do not excite any body vibrations.

Much of the slightly restless ride is absorbed in the excellent seats; although they are not quite as sumptuous as those in the bigger-engined cars and are a little short in the thigh, they are very comfortable with good side support and can give an ideal long-armed position to all sizes. Taller people may find their knees fouling the steering wheel while "heel-and-toeing". The seat slides over such a range that an average 5 ft. 9 in. driver still has two notches left over; a simple cam controls the backrest angle, giving 10 positions over quite a small angle so the adjustment is unusually fine for this system. There are lap-and-diagonal seat belts at the front; the shoulder strap passes over at a good angle and grips the driver well with no tendency to slip off the shoulder. Once you are strapped in, however, choke and hand throttle

Safety Check List

Steering assembly

Steering box position	On bulkhead
Steering column collapsible	No
Steering wheel boss padded	No
Steering wheel dished	No

Instrument panel

Projecting switches	Three on facia
Sharp cowls	None
Effective padding	Top and bottom of facia

Windscreen and visibility

Screen type	Laminated pop-out
Pillars padded	Covered
Standard driving mirrors	Interior only
Interior mirror framed	Yes
Interior mirror collapsible	Yes
Sun visors	Soft padding

Seats and harness

Attachment to floor	Sliding runners
Do they tip forward	Back rest only
Head rest attachment points	No
Back of front seats	Well padded
Safety harness	Lap and diagonal well placed
Harness anchors at back	No

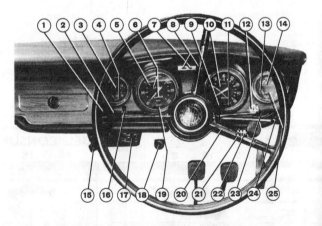

1, fan. 2, panel light. 3, water temperature gauge. 4, oil temperature gauge. 5, speedometer. 6, total and trip mileage recorders. 7, dynamo warning light. 8, indicator tell-tales. 9, main beam tell-tale. 10, rev. counter. 11, lighting tell-tale. 12, ignition/starter key. 13, fuel reserve tell-tale. 14, oil pressure gauge. 15, heater temperature. 16, wiper switch. 17, heater direction control. 18, washer/wiper plunger. 19, heater fan tell-tale. 20, horn spokes. 21, choke. 22, hand throttle. 23, indicator stalk. 24, lighting stalk. 25, fuel gauge.

One of Bertone's most attractive designs, kicking up the dust. You can just see the rear deck if you stretch your neck.

Specification

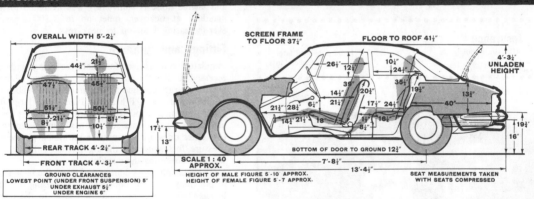

OVERALL WIDTH 5'-2½"

44½" 21½"
47½" 45½"
51½" 50½"
8½" 21½"
10½" 51½"

REAR TRACK 4'-2½"
FRONT TRACK 4'-3½"

GROUND CLEARANCES
LOWEST POINT (UNDER FRONT SUSPENSION) 5"
UNDER EXHAUST 5½"
UNDER ENGINE 6"

SCREEN FRAME TO FLOOR 37½" **FLOOR TO ROOF 41½"**

26½" 12½"
10¼" 24½"
39 35½"
14½" 20½" 19½" 13½"
21½" 21½" 17½" 24½" 40"
21½" 28½" 6½"
14½" 21½" 18 1½" 16½"
8½"

4'-3½" UNLADEN HEIGHT

17½"
13"
19½"
16"

BOTTOM OF DOOR TO GROUND 12½"

SCALE 1 : 40 APPROX.
HEIGHT OF MALE FIGURE 5·10 APPROX.
HEIGHT OF FEMALE FIGURE 5·7 APPROX.

7'-8½"
13'-4½"

SEAT MEASUREMENTS TAKEN WITH SEATS COMPRESSED

Engine

Cylinders	4
Bore and stroke	74 mm. x 75 mm.
Cubic capacity	1,290 c.c.
Valves	Twin overhead camshafts
Compression ratio	9:1
Carburetters	2 Weber 40DCOE28
Fuel pump	Fispa 4033/01
Oil filter	Fram
Max. power (gross)	103 b.h.p. at 6,000 r.p.m.
Max. torque (gross)	101 lb. ft. at 3,200 r.p.m.

Transmission

Clutch	Fichtel and Sachs 8 in. dia. s.d.p.
Top gear (s/m)	0.86
4th gear (s/m)	1.00
3rd gear (s/m)	1.355
2nd gear (s/m)	1.988
1 gear (s/m)	3.304
Reverse	3.01
Final drive	Hypoid bevel 4.555:1

M.p.h. at 1,000 r.p.m. in:—

Top gear	18.3
4th gear	15.7
3rd gear	11.6
2nd gear	7.9
1st gear	4.7

Chassis

Construction	Unitary

Brakes

Type	Hydraulic disc brakes
Dimensions	11¼ in. dia. front, 9¾ in. dia. rear

Friction areas:

Front:	16.1 sq. in. of lining operating on 227 sq. in. of disc
Rear:	11.8 sq. in. of lining operating on 139 sq. in. of disc

Suspension and steering

Front	Independent—double wishbones and anti-roll bar; coil springs
Rear	Live axle—two lower trailing arms and upper A-bracket; coil springs

Shock absorbers:

Front:	Girling telescopic
Rear:	
Steering gear	Burman cam and peg
Tyres	Pirelli or Michelin 155-15
Rim size	4½J x 15

Coachwork and equipment

Starting handle	None
Jack	Side lift
Jacking points	Two either side under door sill.
Battery	12 volt negative earth, 40 amp. hour capacity
Number of electrical fuses	8
Indicators	Self-cancelling flashers
Screen wipers	Electric single speed
Screen washers	Foot plunger
Sunvisors	Two

Locks:

With ignition key	Ignition/starter only
With other keys	1 for doors, boot and glove locker
Interior heater	Fresh air type
Extras	Radio
Upholstery	Elasticated leatherette
Floor covering	Rubberized carpeting
Alternative body styles	None

Maintenance

Sump	10 pints SAE 20W/40
Gearbox	3.2 pints SAE 90
Rear axle	2.5 pints SAE 90 EP
Steering gear	SAE 90 EP
Cooling system	13¼ pints (drain taps 2)
Chassis lubrication	Every 3,750 miles to 2 points
Minimum service interval	3,750 miles
Ignition timing	2-4° b.t.d.c.
Contact breaker gap	0.014-0.016 in.
Sparking plug gap	Preset non-adjustable
Sparking plug type	Lodge 2 HL
Tappet clearances (cold)	inlet 0.019 in.; Exhaust 0.021

Valve timing:

Inlet opens	18½° b.t.d.c.
Inlet closes	42½° a.b.d.c.
Exhaust opens	42½° b.b.d.c.
Exhaust closes	18½° a.t.d.c.
Front wheel toe-in	0.08—0.16 in.
Camber angle	0° 50'
Castor angle	0° 30'-1° 30'
Kingpin inclination	Not given

Tyre pressures:

Front/Rear:	24/26 p.s.i. (normal) 26/30 p.s.i. (high speed)

Alfa Romeo GT 1300

Hand throttle and choke concealed under the facia. Pedals sprout from the floor; water came in through here in our water splash test. (Right) Release for the boot is concealed in the door lock pillar. It can be locked.

become inaccessible so you have to prod them with a gentle right foot, although if you follow the instructions the engine should be warm before moving off.

Access to the rear seat is quite good when the front backrest has been folded forward; there is plenty of head and shoulder room for people up to 5 ft. 10 in. but the one behind the driver will have to sit with knees askew, while the other one will have to push the front passenger forward to get his knees either side of the seat back. Once arranged like this, the Alfa is a fairly reasonable four-seater for short journeys; for long distances it is better termed a three-seater.

From the driver's seat the view is good in all directions with thin pillars all round, and it is possible to see the rear end if you reach upwards slightly when parking. The single-speed wipers overlap in the centre and sweep up parallel to the screen pillar to maintain good wet vision and there is a foot-operated wash-and-wipe button. The lights are well up to the car's performance, although the dipped beam is rather short.

Controls for the heater are kept to a simple minimum with two levers and one flap to control temperature, volume and direction very effectively. There is no separate face level ventilation, but it is not unpleasant to drive with the side window open on a hot day; with the rear quarter-lights open there is little useful increase in air throughput but some increase in noise.

On the whole the noise level is untiringly low; there is little

Seat back rest angle is controlled by simple cam with good fine adjustment. Quarter lights have their own wing nuts (right).

wind noise—a slight whistle through poor quarter-light sealing—and engine noise is sufficiently well insulated to make it almost inaudible at tickover, quiet up to 3,500 r.p.m. and just an ever-increasing hum up to peak revs.

Fittings and furniture

Simulated wood is used for a facia covering, with the instruments recessed. Unlike the classically simple layout of the Giulia Super, with two large dials and a clock in between visible through the top of the wheel, the GT has four dials—two large flanked by two small—giving you oil temperature in exchange for the time. The centre two instruments still fall easily in the line of sight but the two outer ones are just outside the quick glance line and the oil pressure/fuel gauge on the right reflects the light from the side window, obscuring the markings.

There is only one oddment locker on the facia and nowhere else to put things, but the boot takes a surprising 6.8 cu.ft. of our test luggage. The lid is released by a lever in the rear door upright and needs a good slam to shut it. One ashtray is provided on the transmission tunnel and two in the rear compartment.

Servicing and accessibility

Although the under bonnet area is rather cluttered with the short, wide engine, you can reach all the items required for running maintenance, like distributor, fuel pump, plugs, etc., but since an oil change is required every service at 3,750 miles it is probably better to have all the work done by a dealer—there are 66 of them, well spread throughout the country. **M**

1, coil. 2, dipstick. 3, oil filler cap. 4, radiator filler cap. 5, battery. 6, washer reservoir. 7, fuse/terminal box. 8, brake fluid reservoir.

MAKE: Alfa Romeo. MODEL: GT 1300. MAKERS: Alfa Romeo S.p.A., via Gattamelata 45, Milan, Italy.

Routine service

Every 3,750 miles: Change engine oil and filter; check gearbox, back axle and steering box oil levels; grease distributor and prop. shaft joints; clean air filter and carb. jets; check fan belt, plugs, contact breaker gap and timing, battery level and brake pads; top up brake fluid reservoir.
Every 7,500 miles: Check valve clearances and clutch pedal play;

clean fuel filter, check headlamps and change over wheels.
Every 11,250 miles: Change gearbox and differential oils; check water pipes and hoses; check steering linkage, front wheel toe-in and camber, adjust front wheel bearings, change brake fluid, replace air filter element.
Every 22,500 miles: Inspect brake system, tighten all nuts and bolts. General: grease all linkages and hinges.

ALFA ROMEO 1300 GT

WE fell in love with this car the moment it arrived—mainly because of its splendid colour scheme, which was a sort of tangerine yellow, if you follow. Probably you don't, but no matter—it appealed to us no end. Alfas have made a lot of nice motor cars in the last few years—and a lot before that—and the 1300 Junior represents a sort of amalgam of some of the nicest. The power unit is derived from the 1290 c.c. "four" fitted to the dear departed Giulietta, the bodyshell is the pretty Pininfarina coupe normally worn by the 1600 Sprint GT, and the transmission includes the 1600's five-speed gearbox. Throw in front and rear disc brakes, the latter having integrally-machined drums for the handbrake, and the usual Alfa suspension, independent at the front, live axle—but VERY positively located —at the rear, and you end up with a pretty nice little motor car by any standards. A nice, pretty car, too . . . Like most Italian cars, the Alfa is a classic example of "If it looks right, it is right", and there aren't many better-looking small cars on the road these days. It is beautifully proportioned and very properly furnished inside unless you are strong on the liking for carpets, which you don't get on the Junior. What you do get is full

Our photographer must like bird-watching—can't get him o' those damn woods.

No carpets, but otherwise everything you need to make the thing march.

instrumentation, dominated by large, easily-read speedometer and rev-counter, plus oil pressure, oil temperature and water temperature gauges; the oil pressure shares a dial with the fuel gauge at the extreme right-hand end of the dashboard, and reflections through the side window mean that it is totally illegible unless you shade it with a spare hand during the daylight hours. It also has a hand-throttle control for warming-up in the mornings, an efficient heating/demisting system and two outstandingly comfy seats with adjustable back-rests. Rising phallically out of the centre of the transmission tunnel is a great girder of a gear lever which selects any one of five gears (the right one, too) forward or one to go astern with, and what's more it does so precisely, quickly and cleanly.

The go-box is the usual Alfa twin-overhead camshaft four-cylinder job, with cylinder dimensions in this case of 74 mm. x 15 mm. to give 1,290 c.c. and out of this they get 103 b.h.p. by benefit of Weber carburation, alloy

high-compression heads and all that sort of go-faster jazz. There is not a lot of low-speed torque and the power starts to happen at about two-five, but with five near-perfectly spaced gear ratios at your command who the hell cares about torque? The great thing about the Alfa is that it has to be driven all the time, and This Is Fun, to put it mildly. You can thrash about the countryside to your heart's content even in these benighted, restricted days, using the gear lever to chase the rev-counter needle up and down the dial; try it on quiet but interesting country lanes and you get maximum effect—particularly if you happen to be motoring in East Anglia at sugar-beet time, when the roads tend to accumulate a nice layer of slime!

The Alfa suspension isn't exactly daring about innovation: they made the independent front, live axle rear arrangement work properly years ago and have seen no good reason to change it since. The Junior, admittedly is a shade tail-happy on wet or greasy surfaces if you happen to be trying a bit hard, but the thing is so controllable that, rather than being a snag, this is really a plus-point which all adds to the fun and to the spirit of the thing. All you have to do is to sit there, reclining in the best Clark (or should we say Farina?) fashion. Every so often the old left hand flashes across to the well-placed gearstick, moves it as fast as the eye can see, and flashes back to the steering wheel, which you then proceed to twirl from lock to lock. It helps a bit, of course, if you flex the wrists and incline the head from side to side, and if some happy laughing bird can admire you at the same time it's perfect. . . . This way you travel quite quickly from A to B and control is maintained. Mind over matter. Man over machine. 'Smarvellous.

Actual performance tends to reflect

the fact that this is, after all, a mere 1300, and even an Alfa of only 1300 c.c. has to be worked pretty hard to give the brush-off to determined Cortina GTs and Cooper "S"s. Top whack is pretty close to the ton, and from a standing start you can reach 60 in just over 11 seconds if you use the full six-two in all the lower gears to make sure of it. Seventy comes up in 16 seconds, which is of course quicker than the Cortina GT (we're talking about the 1500 now, of course, and not the cross-flow which we haven't yet had a go at) and roughly the same as that of the 1275 Cooper "S". The advantage of the smallest of the Alfa engine range comes in the petrol bill—driven hard, you can get 28 m.p.g. out of the Junior, and if you do the thing like a gentleman you can get better than 30.

We also had a go at the Junior GT's big brother, with the same body but with the 1570 c.c. engine. This does all that the Junior does, only there's more of it; we couldn't unfortunately get any performance figures because the car had only done a couple of hundred miles when we got it, and time prevented us from putting on sufficient extra miles to free it all off. But we were able to notice a worthwhile improvement in torque for the extra capacity, with the larger-engined car doing in fifth what the Junior would do in fourth when it came to accelerating for overtaking purposes or summat. We could very cheerfully make room in the garage for either of 'em. Or both. . . .

PERFORMANCE DATA

Alfa Romeo 1300 GT Junior

Maximum speed 98 m.p.h. approx.

Acceleration: 0-30 3.0 seconds
           0-40 4.3   ,,
           0-50 7.9   ,,
           0-60 11.4   ,,
           0-70 16.0   ,,

Watkins—at it.

Photographs by Spencer Smith

A faster and more flexible Veloce

ALFA ROMEO have certainly been making twin overhead camshaft production engines for longer than any other manufacturer in the world, now that the Salmson is regrettably no more. The four-cylinder unit is still a light-alloy five-bearing job, but it has now had its bore and stroke stretched to give a capacity of 1779 cc. The car is called the 1750, in memory of a famous model of the past, though the earlier machine was a small "six" and its faster versions were supercharged.

This larger engine is mated to the celebrated five-speed gearbox and, though the front suspension geometry has been altered, with slightly quicker steering, there is still a rigid rear axle on trailing arms and an A-bracket. However, there is now a torsional anti-roll bar at the rear as well as in front, and broader rims carry Michelin XAS tyres.

The Bertone body is not new, and is also found on the smaller model, but in the case of the 1750 it is identified by four extremely powerful headlamps. The interior is truly delightful, with high-quality round instruments, and the seats are cut away to avoid perspiration, the top of the squab of the passenger's seat winding up to form a headrest—very neat, this. It goes almost without saying in the case of an Alfa Romeo that the driving position is excellent, and that the pedals are ideally placed for heel-and-toe.

Reverting for a moment to the original 1750, the greatest change is in ease of handling. The old supercharged car had to be steered with sensitive fingers and the gear-change demanded extreme precision. The latest model, in spite of having one carburetter choke per cylinder, is quite remarkably flexible and will pull hard at very low speeds. For this reason it is an ideal dual-purpose car, handling impeccably in the hands of a fast driver yet proving just as

satisfactory when his wife uses it for shopping.

The new engine gives a lot more performance, with improved acceleration right through the range and a maximum speed within two mph of the magic 120. The longer stroke is noticeable, the unit being obviously busy at 6000 rpm, and one would certainly not attempt to emulate the 8000 rpm of the early Giulietta. The extra punch is so great that this is a much better engine for touring, though it would be sacrilege not to make proper use of the delectable five-speed gearbox.

It would be fair to say that the GTV has typical Alfa Romeo roadholding. There is less roll than with previous models but the tyres emit a loud whistle during fast cornering, which rather gives the game away. Fundamentally the car understeers, but during fast cornering it may tend to spin the inside rear wheel, at which point oversteering sets in. This is a very highly developed chassis and certainly remarkable results are achieved with a conventional design. The ride feels pleasantly firm but the riding comfort is very satisfactory.

High praise must be given to the steering, which gives a fine sense of control, though the turning circle is rather large for a car of moderate size. The brake pedal is almost too light to operate for a sports car, but the power is very great with good resistance to fading. The hand brake has a rigid lever but the teeth of the ratchet are rather too coarse, which means that one must sometimes exert a fair amount of force to secure the vehicle on a steep gradient.

When the Alfa is used by the less experienced members of the family, it may be treated as an ordinary four-speed car and it will still exceed 100 mph. By pushing the lever to the right against a spring and then forward, the overdrive comes into play, and this gives very easy high-speed cruising. The movement from fifth to fourth is a sheer

unusual pleasure, the lever merely being pulled back and allowed to centre itself. The gearbox of the test car was not quite as light in action as those of previous Alfas, which was probably something that would correct itself at a greater mileage.

The engine and gearbox are not mechanically noisy, though the power unit has the functional sound of efficient machinery in action. The exhaust is well silenced and the two twin-choke carburetters are unusually well subdued. When most people are in

ROAD TEST
by John Bolster

Alfa Romeo 1750 GTV

Seating position of the Alfa Romeo 1750 GTV is excellent, and the pedal controls are ideally placed for heel-and-toe gear-changes.

For the driver who enjoys doing his own maintenance the engine compartment allows easy access to the uncomplicated motor.

Body styling by Bertone remains unchanged from that used on the smaller model. The 1750 can be identified by the four headlamps.

bed, the Alfa Romeo can be driven safely at very high speeds on the deserted roads, the four headlamps literally making their own daylight. The difficult task of insulating engine and transmission heat from the passengers has been well done, but the ventilation is rather inadequate. In spite of the clean shape of the body there is some wind noise at high speeds.

The rear seats are comfortable in themselves but the lack of leg room makes them more suitable for children or dogs than fully grown human beings. In contrast, the luggage boot holds more than would be expected as it extends well forward. The under-bonnet accessibility is good, and the car would suit the expert driver who enjoys doing his own maintenance. The machine would be easy to service and there is nothing difficult or complicated to do.

The 1750 GTV is a car with a remarkable performance for its engine size. It would be possible to obtain a bigger and more powerful car for the same purchase price, but that is not the point. The Alfa Romeo appeals particularly because of its moderate size, and because it goes so much better for a good driver. No car could be easier to handle, but the full performance is only available to the man who enjoys using all five speeds.

To the connoisseur, it is so satisfactory that this new model is, above all, a typical Alfa Romeo. All the characteristics that one expects to find in this *marque* are more pronounced than ever, which means that this is a car of character and not just another automobile. It is, of course, very costly if one takes its size into account, yet its air of quality, its standard of engineering and its patrician style are things that are simply not available among cheaper cars. Those of us who are old enough to have drooled over the original 1750 must admit that the new model is worthy to carry those very special numerals.

SPECIFICATION

Car tested: Alfa Romeo 1750 GTV coupé, price £2248 including PT.

Engine: Four cylinders, 80 mm x 88.5 mm (1779 cc). Twin overhead camshafts. Compression ratio 9.5:1. 132 bhp (gross) at 5500 rpm. Two twin-choke Weber carburetters.

Transmission: Single dry plate diaphragm spring clutch. 4-speed all-synchromesh gearbox with central lever, ratios 0.79, 1.00, 1.35, 1.99, and 3.30:1. Hypoid rear axle, ratio 4.1:1.

Chassis: Combined steel body and chassis. Independent front suspension by wishbones, helical springs, and anti-roll torsion bar. Recirculating ball steering gear. Rigid rear axle on helical springs with trailing arms, A-bracket, and anti-roll torsion bar. Telescopic dampers all round. Bolt-on disc wheels fitted 165 x 14 Michelin XAS tyres. Disc brakes all round with servo assistance.

Equipment: 12-volt lighting and starting. Speedometer. Rev-counter. Oil pressure, water temperature, and fuel gauges. Heating, demisting and ventilation system. 2-speed windscreen wipers and washers. Cigar lighter. Radio (extra).

Dimensions: Wheelbase 7 ft 8.75 ins. Track (front) 4 ft 4.25 ins, (rear) 4 ft 2.25 ins. Overall length 13 ft 4.5 ins. Width 5 ft 2.25 ins. Weight 1 ton.

Performance: Maximum speed 118 mph. Speeds in gears: fourth 104 mph, third 77 mph, second 53 mph, first 32 mph. Standing quarter-mile 17.2 s. Acceleration: 0-30 mph 3 s. 0-50 mph 6.9 s. 0-60 mph 9.4 s. 0-80 mph 16.5 s. 0-100 mph 28.8 s.

Fuel consumption: 23 to 29 mpg.

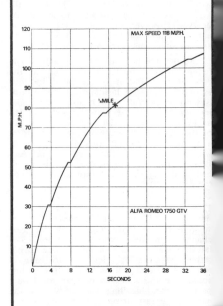

PERFORMANCE GRAPH

MAX SPEED 118 M.P.H.

¼MILE

ALFA ROMEO 1750 GTV

M.P.H.

SECONDS

THE ALFA THAT SCORED

It's not built as a race car, but it certainly doubles well as one. Kevin Bartlett reports on the track behavior of the Alfa Romeo 1750 GTV . . . just for your astonishment.

"I RECKON we're good for 10-12 secs a lap quicker than the last Giulia Super and slightly quicker than the current Falcon GT. The car sits much flatter than the Giulia and is even more predictable — if that's possible," said Kevin Bartlett, the professional half of our track test team after practice for the Surfers Paradise 6-Hour Sports Car Race this year.

With most of the Alfa Romeo 1750 GTV units which had any sort of miles on the clock either in pieces being prepared for a coming race meeting or out on the Surfers Paradise International Motor Circuit practising for the marathon event, we decided that a race-track test under the utmost realistic conditions would be the highest compliment we could pay the car, regardless whether it won or lost.

Naturally, it's easy to discuss Alfa Romeo with Kevin, an Alec Mildren works driver. But it's also easy to realise the professionalism he puts into his work, and his test reporting is in no way biased simply because he knows Alec Mildren is going to be reading this test with a magnifying glass over a chicken dinner down at the club.

This test, written before the Hardie-Ferodo 500 where the GTV was up against the Australian V8 sedans, nevertheless points out some obvious advantages of the car over its rivals. Two races were planned prior to the "500", the Surfers 6-Hour, and the Sandown 3-Hour, both not critically important to the Alfa entrants from a point of winning, but designed to point out factors which would come into consideration during the gruelling, mountainous 500-miler at Mt Panorama on October 6.

The 1750 GTV has a lot in common with the smaller-engined machines of the make. First and foremost, it is a luxurious high performance car of outstanding beauty built to the highest standards of Alfa Romeo engineering, from its superb twin ohc engine right down to the smallest detail. Nothing has been spared to ensure the maximum comfort of driver and passenger, without detracting in any way from its appeal as a high performance Gran Turismo vehicle.

Such has been the progress in normally-aspirated engines that this 1779 cc (80 mm x 88.5 mm) light-alloy unit develops a comfortable 132 bhp at 5500 rpm — or some 37 bhp more than the pre-war six-cylinder 1750 Zagato with its supercharger. As regards all-round performance, there is scarcely any comparison, both in acceleration and maximum speed. The modern 1750 has it all the way and must be as exciting to drive as any

A varying range of tyres and sizes of tyres were used in practice, along with a selection of anti-roll bars to try and bring times down. Finally, the car was run absolutely standard during the race.

of the best-maintained 17/95s, albeit with a measurably superior ride. Somehow or other, Alfa Romeo has managed to impart a great deal of charm — evident in the pre-war machine — to what is basically a high performance sporting closed car. However, fresh-air enthusiasts can, as an alternative, plump for the attractive Duetto Spyder, which has identical mechanical specifications.

The 6-Hour event told us much about the GTV under racing conditions. The car brakes better and with a shade more stability. Bartlett was braking for Dunlop Bridge at the 175 yard mark (as against 225-250 yards with the Giulia) with the

speedometer gently fluctuating between 105-110 mph. The car required heavy braking only twice on each lap of the two-mile circuit, once for Dunlop Bridge and once for Lukey Corner. Only occasionally would gentle braking pressure be required for Firestone and Lucas before pushing on through the Esses.

Doug Chivas took charge of our test Alfa for the first three-hour stint of the marathon, with Bartlett finishing the final three. Times between the two were similar, with Chivas coming out on top with 1 m 33.2 secs — 0.2 secs ahead of Bartlett. Both drivers limited the engine range to 6000 rpm, with the occasional run-over to 6100 when

Tyre wear, running Firestone racing rubber, was no problem to the Alfa team. At the finish of the race, the left front tyre was almost bald, and the right tyre still had five percent of tread left.

Through a well-planned race, the Mildren Alfa came through to the front of its class by 4.30 pm, two and a half hours after the start. Despite two blown tyres, it still finished the race two laps up on the second Alfa in the class.

the engine was running better later in the race when, rather than change a gear for a very brief run, they let the engine run out a little further in that gear.

The handling is typical Alfa with initial understeer, which is easily corrected with the throttle breaking the car into very slight oversteer — again easily controlled with the right foot. Overall handling is little changed from full tanks to empty — which totals 18 gal — 12 in the regular tank plus the optional/delete (homologated) 6-gal tank fitted for Australian conditions.

During the 6-Hour race, the test car consumed one half pint of oil over 438 miles, and returned 12.5 mpg — naturally recorded under hard useage. Therefore, the tanks give the GTV a hard-driving range of some 300 miles! good enough for only one pit stop at Mt Panorama. The bonnet wasn't opened during the race.

It was interesting to note tyre wear during the 6-Hour race. Wide-rim mag wheels were tried in an effort to get more tyre contact, but the idea didn't pan out as expected. The mag wheels came from the GTA, but the GTV wheel arches proved slightly smaller and the tyres were scraping on the inside of the wheel arch. With the wide-rim wheels on, the left hand front tyre was almost bald after some laps at racing speed, while the right hand front still had five percent tread left. Once the standard wheels were refitted there

were no tyre problems, although two of the Firestone racing tyres used for the race blew — costing the car extra time it could ill-afford in the pits.

During practice, various tyres, anti-roll bars and tramp rods were fitted, but the end result was that the car was run strictly stock standard.

In closing, we've recorded the progress of the GTV in the Surfers Paradise 6-Hour race. The event got under way at 2 pm, and by 3.30 pm the Alfa was running fourth in its class, one lap down on another Alfa, a Fiat and a Volvo. By 4 pm, it was sitting second to the Bill Goode Alfa, still one lap down, but now on the same lap as the Volvo of Seldon/Kearns and two laps ahead of the Basile/Vasta Fiat 125. Half an hour later, the Alfa was one lap ahead of the Seldon/Kearns Volvo, two laps up on the Goode Alfa and three on the Fiat. At 5.30 pm the Goode Alfa was still one lap down, the Fiat five laps down, and the Seldon/Kearns Volvo had retired. Six-thirty pm, the Alfa was three laps ahead of Bill Goode's similar car, six laps up on the Fiat with a Morris 10 laps down in the class. As the flag fell, the Alfa figured sixth in the outright placings, two laps ahead of the Goode Alfa, 11 ahead of the Fiat and on the same lap as the Foley/Stewart Alfa. The 1750 GTV Alfas came first and second in Improved Production Touring, and second in Series Production Sports.   #

Bartlett heads for the inside of Howie Sangster in the Don O'Sullivan Cooper as he prepares to lap the Cooper in the early stages of the race. The Cooper finished 30 laps down after six hours of racing on the Alfa.

Above: Junior Sprint GT Alfas can be recognized by their single headlamps and matt black grilles. The 1750 Veloce version has a paired headlamp system. Below: Big dials, clearly marked and turned to bring their business ends uppermost, are features of the GT Junior. Carpets are normally fitted on the floor. Inset: Twin cams and double-choke Weber carburettors look impressive under the bonnet

Autotest

Alfa Romeo GT 1300 Junior (1,290 c.c.)

2233

AT-A-GLANCE: Economy coupé in expensive range now with improved suspension. Much more refined and quieter. Excellent handling and brakes. Good open-road performance from small engine, lacking bottom-end punch only.

MANUFACTURER
Alfa Romeo S.p.A., Via Gattamelata 45, Milan, Italy.

UK CONCESSIONAIRES
Alfa Romeo (GB) Ltd., Edgware Road, London, N.W.2.

PRICES
Basic	£1,338	0s	0d
Purchase Tax	£411	10s	6d
Seat belts (approx)	£9	0s	0d
Total (in GB)	£1,758	10s	6d

PRICE AS TESTED	£1,758	10s	6d

PERFORMANCE SUMMARY
Mean maximum speed	102 mph
Standing start ¼-mile	19.1 sec
0-60 mph	13.2 sec
30-70 mph through gears	14.5 sec
Typical fuel consumption	27 mpg
Miles per tankful	280

Introduced in September 1966, the 1300 GT Junior is the least expensive of the Alfa Romeo coupés. Externally, there is little to distinguish it from the 1750 GT Veloce, the main difference being two headlamps instead of the more expensive model's four. Less luxurious interior trimming is used and the central console is dispensed with.

MECHANICALLY, apart from engine size, the two models are also very similar. Bore and stroke of the GT Junior are the same as were used in the Giulietta (74 by 75mm respectively, giving a capacity of 1,290 c.c.), whereas the dimensions of the 1750 are 80 by 88.5 mm, giving 1,779 c.c. The smaller engine requires lower gearing (4.55 to 1 axle ratio, that of the larger-engined car being 4.10 to 1).

The front brakes are slightly smaller than those of the 1750. Earlier models had no servo, but the standard specification now includes one. Introduced at the same time as the brake servo were hydraulic clutch operation, revised suspension with an anti-roll bar at the rear as well as the front, 165-14in. wheels and tyres (formerly 155-15in.) and a number of other detail refinements.

There is, however, a great deal of difference in the price. The GT Junior sells for £1,749,

Above: Lamps are made by Carello and the front-end design is simple and effective

whereas the price of the 1750 GT Veloce is £2,300. As the difference of £551 would buy a Fiat 600D (£543), it makes good sense to consider very carefully before choosing.

Performance

The Giulia coupé range started life with an engine capacity of 1,570 c.c. When we tested the 1750 GT Veloce last autumn, we found that the additional 209 c.c. made surprisingly little difference to the car's performance. In fact, the lower geared 1600 Sprint GT Veloce tested two years earlier had a slight edge so far as performance was concerned but was less economical.

Alfa Romeo claim a maximum of 103 bhp (gross) at 6,000 rpm for the GT Junior. This we estimate to be around 90 bhp net, compared with the 1600 Sprint GT Veloce's 109 bhp and the 1750 GT Veloce's 122 bhp.

The GT Junior returned a mean maximum speed of 102 mph, compared with 113 and 116 mph for the 1600 and 1750 equivalents. Its best one-way was 104 mph, at which the speedometer reads fractionally over 110 mph.

New to Alfa Romeo is a red sector on the tachometer which on the GT Junior starts at 6,000 rpm. We chose to exceed this for performance measurements, changing gear at an indicated 6,600 rpm—a true 6,200 rpm. From rest to 50 mph took only 9.3 sec, which for a solidly built, fully equipped car of this size is very creditable. However, the extra muscle of the 1600 and 1750 GTV models tells, their respective times being 7.8 and 7.9 sec. From rest to 60 mph—a useful yardstick—takes the GT Junior 13.2 sec. Equivalent times for the 1600 and 1750 GTV are 11.1 and 11.2 sec.

Present-day traffic conditions often require a car which has good instant-acceleration qualities—that Jekyll and Hyde personality which allows it to trickle along gently, but have brisk acceleration "on-tap" without having to recourse to a great deal of gear-changing. This is where the GT Junior falls short of its larger-engined stable-mates, as the in-the-gears acceleration times illustrate. From 50 to 70 mph in top (fifth) gear takes 18.1 sec, compared with the 13.0 and 12.9 sec taken by the 1600 and 1750. Using fourth gear, it takes 14.8 sec—still slower than the larger-engined models in fifth. One is only aware of these deficiencies in congested traffic, or when one is feeling lazy or tired. On the open road, the GT Junior is a real delight. The engine is incredibly smooth and the handling absolutely superb. Ideally spaced gearbox ratios and overall gearing which allows near flat-out cruising add to one's enjoyment. It really does feel every bit the thoroughbred it is.

As frequently happens, the use of a smaller engine does not result in significant gains in economy. The overall figure of 24.4 mpg, although good in relation to the car's performance and the way we drove it, is little better than the 23.9 mpg of the 1750 GT Veloce. The 1600 was rather thirstier, returning 21.9 mpg. Even the steady-speed figures tell the same story, generally falling somewhere between those of the 1600 and the more economical 1750. Oil consumption worked out at 500 miles per pint—much the same as on the larger-engined models.

Engine and Transmission

Unlike many previous Alfas, the GT Junior prefers the use of full choke, in conjunction with a whiff of throttle, for cold starting. Using the hand throttle, it immediately settles down to a smooth and quiet fast-idle. It pays to observe the handbook's recommendation to run the engine at 1,500 rpm for a short spell before driving off, as otherwise the gearbox is unpleasantly stiff. Apart from the initial start, very little choke is required and the engine is soon completely flexible. Carburation generally, in fact, seems unusually clean.

Although the gearbox soon warms up, the change never quite loses a slight trace of stickiness. It is very good, but not quite amongst the best. The gears are very quiet, but one can sometimes detect a trace of axle whine—presumably one of the penalties of really adequate location. Reverse, opposite fifth on the right of the gate, now has a spring loaded guard—a much more convenient arrangement than the previous one, which necessitated telescoping the knob.

Hydraulic operation of the clutch has greatly improved its feel, but effort and travel (48lb and 5.7in.) both leave scope for improvement. The clutch always behaves well and is capable of coping with a re-start on a 1-in-3 gradient without difficulty.

Ride and Handling

Although all the Giulia variants have been very pleasant to handle, the ultimate cornering power of earlier examples was not in any way exceptional. Such traits as body roll, steering fight, tyre squeal and wheelspin were also quite evident but, oddly enough, detracted little from the pleasure of driving them—all Alfas are very much driver's cars. The latest suspension changes (shared, incidentally by the Spider and other coupé models, as well as the Giulia Super) have eliminated these idiosyncrasies without in any way detracting from the typical Alfa character; Alfa enthusiasts will enjoy it even more. The GT Junior "hangs-on" remarkably well on slippery corners. The larger section tyres are loath to squeal—possibly the result of a higher synthetic rubber content than hitherto. The steering retains its precision and feel but has lost all traces of fight. It is still a shade on the heavy side at low speeds but represents an almost ideal compromise.

The ride, on the other hand, seems firmer than in the past, but is by no means uncomfortable. One is mainly aware of the suspension's comparative stiffness when driving slowly over "nobbly" surfaces. As the speed rises, the firmness disappears and a very good, level ride results.

Brakes

The brakes always feel most reassuring and the pedal effort is quite low (0.8g requires only 60lb). In wet conditions, a best of 0.97g was obtained, using an effort of 80lb—a highly creditable performance.

Fade resistance is most impressive, the pedal effort remaining at 30lb throughout the test. This performance was borne out by their behaviour during hard driving, both on the road and on closed circuits. Only a thin film of pad

Above: The back seat is strictly for occasional use, or for kids. There is an acute shortage of legroom in the rear if those in the front take their full share of space

Below: Smaller wheels and fatter Cinturato tyres are features of the latest GT Junior

PERFORMANCE

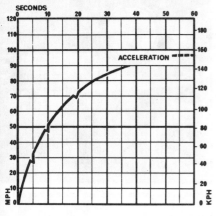

ACCELERATION ---

MAXIMUM SPEEDS

Gear	mph	kph	rpm
Top (mean)	102	164	5,600
(best)	104	168	5,700
4th	97	156	6,200
3rd	71	114	6,200
2nd	49	79	6,200
1st	29	47	6,200

Standing ¼-mile 19.1 sec 72 mph
Standing kilometre 35.7 sec 90 mph

MOTORWAY CRUISING

Indicated speed at 70 mph	74 mph
Engine (rpm at 70 mph)	4,000 rpm
(mean piston speed)	1,970 ft/min
Fuel (mpg at 70 mph)	27.4 mpg
Passing (50-70 mph)	9.5 sec
Noise (per cent silent at 70 mph)	70 per cent

TIME IN SECONDS

TIME IN SECONDS	4.3	6.6	9.3	13.2	18.8	25.3	36.3
	0						
TRUE SPEED MPH	30	40	50	60	70	80	90	100
INDICATED SPEED	31	42	53	63	74	85	95	106

Test distance 1,483 miles.
Mileage recorder 1.7 per cent over-reading.

SPEED RANGE, GEAR RATIOS AND TIME IN SECONDS

mph	Top (3.91)	4th (4.55)	3rd (6.37)	2nd (9.05)	1st (15.0)
10-30	—	—	—	5.3	—
20-40	15.6	11.9	6.9	4.4	—
30-50	14.4	10.7	7.4	—	—
40-60	15.1	12.2	8.0	—	—
50-70	18.1	14.8	9.5	—	—
60-80	25.6	16.9	—	—	—
70-90	—	20.7	—	—	—

CONSUMPTION

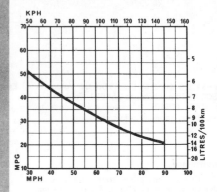

FUEL

(At constant speeds—mpg)

30 mph	52.0
40 mph	44.0
50 mph	37.7
60 mph	32.2
70 mph	27.4
80 mph	23.6
90 mph	20.8

Typical mpg	27.0 (10.5 litres/100km)
Calculated (DIN) mpg	24.9 (11.4 litres/100km)
Overall mpg	24.4 (11.6 litres/100km)
Grade of fuel	Super premium, 5-star (min 100RM)

OIL

Miles per pint (SAE 20W/40) 500

HOW THE CAR COMPARES

Maximum speed (mph)

80 90 100 110

- Alfa Romeo GT Junior
- Lancia Fulvia 1.3 Rallye
- MG 1300
- BMW 1600
- Fiat 124 Sports Coupe

0-60 mph (sec)

20 10

- Alfa Romeo GT Junior
- Lancia Fulvia 1.3 Rallye
- MG 1300
- BMW 1600
- Fiat 124 Sports Coupe

Standing start ¼-mile (sec)

30 20

- Alfa Romeo GT Junior
- Lancia Fulvia 1.3 Rallye
- MG 1300
- BMW 1600
- Fiat 124 Sports Coupe

MPG OVERALL

20 30

- Alfa Romeo GT Junior
- Lancia Fulvia 1.3 Rallye
- MG 1300
- BMW 1600
- Fiat 124 Sports Coupe

PRICES:

Alfa GT Junior	£1,749
Lancia 1.3 Rallye	£1,698
MG 1300	£931
BMW 1600	£1,399
Fiat 124 Sports	£1,438

TEST CONDITIONS Weather: Dry and cloudy. Wind: 5-15 mph. Temperature: 1 deg. C (34 deg. F). Barometer 29.80 in. Hg. Humidity: 90 per cent. Surfaces: Dry concrete and asphalt (wet for brake test).

WEIGHT Kerb weight 19.9 cwt (2,224lb-1,015kg) (with oil, water and half full fuel tank). Distribution, per cent F, 56.0; R, 44.0. Laden as tested: 23.1 cwt (2,584lb-1,172kg).

TURNING CIRCLES Between kerbs L, 36ft 7in.; R, 34ft 4in. Between walls L, 37ft 11in.; R, 35ft 8in. steering wheel turns, lock to lock 3.6.

Figures taken at 4,000 miles by our own staff at the Motor Industry Research Association proving ground at Nuneaton.

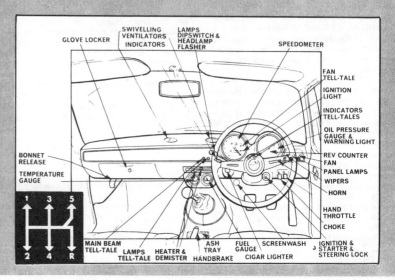

Alfa Romeo GT 1300 Junior (1,290 c.c.)

BRAKES

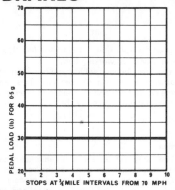

RESPONSE (from 30 mph in neutral)

Load	g	Distance
20lb	0.30	100ft
40lb	0.67	45ft
60lb	0.80	38ft
80lb	0.97	31ft
Handbrake	0.30	100ft

Max. Gradient 1 in 3

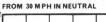

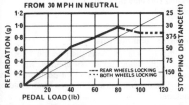

CLUTCH

Pedal 48lb and 5.7in.

SPECIFICATION

FRONT ENGINE, REAR WHEEL DRIVE

ENGINE

Cylinders	4 in line
Main bearings	5
Cooling system	Water; pump, fan and thermostat
Bore	74mm (2.91 in.)
Stroke	75mm (2.95 in.)
Displacement	1290 c.c. (78.6 cu. in.)
Valve gear	Twin overhead camshafts
Compression ratio	9.0-to-1 Min. octane rating: 100RM
Carburettors	Two Weber twin-choke
Fuel pump	Fispa mechanical
Oil filter	Fram full flow
Max. power	103 bhp (gross) at 6,000 rpm
Max. torque	101 lb. ft. (gross) at 3,200 rpm

TRANSMISSION

Clutch	Fichtel and Sachs single plate 8in. dia.
Gearbox	5-speed all synchromesh
Gear ratios	Top 0.86
	Fourth 1.0
	Third 1.36
	Second 1.99
	First 3.30
	Reverse 3.01
Final drive	Hypoid bevel 4.55-to-1

CHASSIS and BODY

Construction	integral with steel body

SUSPENSION

Front	Independent, coil springs, wishbones, anti-roll bar, telescopic dampers
Rear	Live axle, trailing arms, A-bracket, coil springs, telescopic dampers

STEERING

Type	Cam and peg
Wheel dia.	15.0 in.

BRAKES

Make and type	ATE discs front and rear
Servo	Vacuum
Dimensions	F. and R. 10.5 in. dia.
Swept area	F. 184.5 sq. in.; R. 166.9 sq. in. Total 352 sq. in. (305 sq. in./ton laden)

WHEELS

Type	Pressed steel disc, 4-stud fixing. 5.5 in. wide rim
Tyres—make	Pirelli
—type	Cinturato radial ply tubed
—size	165-14 in.

EQUIPMENT

Battery	12 Volt, 50 Ah
Generator or Alternator	Bosch 27.5-amp a.c.
Headlamps	Sealed beam 80/90-watt (total)
Reversing lamp	Standard
Electric fuses (number)	8
Screen wipers	Two-speed, self-parking
Screen washer	Standard, foot pedal
Interior heater	Standard, water-valve
Heated backlight	Not available
Safety belts	Extra
Interior trim	Elasticated leatherette seats, vinyl head-lining
Floor covering	Carpet
Jack	Screw pillar
Jacking points	2 each side, under sills
Windscreen	Zone-toughened
Underbody protection	Bitumastic on all surfaces exposed to road

MAINTENANCE

Fuel tank	10.1 Imp. gallons (low level warning light) (46 litres)
Cooling system	13.3 pints (including heater)
Engine sump	11.5 pints (5.2 litres) SAE 20W/40. Change oil every 3,750 miles. Change filter element every 3,750 miles.
Gearbox and overdrive	3.2 pints SAE 90. Change oil every 11,250 miles.
Final drive	2.5 pints SAE 90EP Change oil every 11,250 miles.
Grease	3 points every 3,750 miles
Tyre pressures	F. 24; R. 26 psi (all conditions)
Max. payload	770 lb. (350 kg)

PERFORMANCE DATA

5th gear mph per 1,000 rpm	18.2
Mean piston speed at max. power	2,953 ft/min
Bhp per ton laden (gross)	89

STANDARD GARAGE 16ft x 8ft 6in.

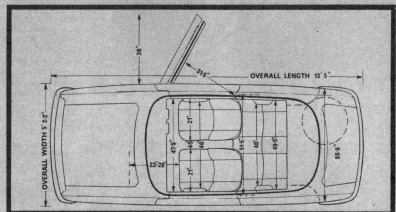

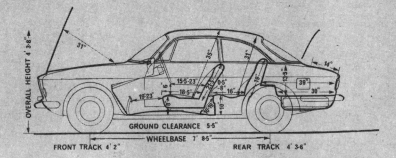

SCALE 0.3in. to 1ft
Cushions uncompressed

ALFA JUNIOR SPRINT GT...

Above: This wide-angle shot distorts the interior but shows the controls and finish well. Horn push bars are set within the wheel spokes

Right: Bertone's styling of the Alfa GT body is perfect from any angle. Rear quarter windows are hinged

Below: Although the boot opening is small, there is a deep compartment inside lined with rubber mats

dust on the front rims betrayed the fact that the brakes had been working hard.

The handbrake, which utilizes miniature drums in the naves of the rear discs, easily holds on a 1 in 3 and is capable of producing 0.30g retardation on a dry surface.

Noise

The latest GT Junior is a remarkably quiet and refined car with none of the raucous exhaust boom periods of the earlier models. The exhaust note itself, although crisp and business-like, is in no way obtrusive either.

Tyre roar is well insulated but there is some bump thumping, which is accentuated by the generally quiet background.

Wind noise is only average. It is a pity that Alfa Romeo haven't provided air extraction and face-level ventilation—a car of this calibre should certainly be so equipped.

Furniture and Fittings

Although less luxurious than on the 1750 GT Veloce, the seats are nicely shaped. Rake adjustment is by means of eight-position cams but no safety catches are provided for the folding backrests.

A higher seating position is used than hitherto. Although this affords the driver a commanding view along the bonnet, it accentuates the shortcomings of the wiper pattern. Extending the blades would improve the view upwards, but this would still leave quite large unwiped areas at the lower corners and outer edges of the screen.

The general fit and finish are very good. Door closure is no longer a problem and the whole car is completely free from rattles and squeaks. In fact, the body structure feels remarkably rigid.

The GT Junior lacks only the sheer performance of the 1750. Compared with lesser cars it offers unusually rapid, satisfying and inherently safe transport at a realistic price.

THE ALFA ROMEO 1750 GTV

Another Thoroughbred from Milan

ALFA ROMEOS are irresistible! I am sure Barry Needham, who looks after Alfa Romeo publicity in this country, will not mind me making this observation. He reminded me of the truth of it recently by lending me a 1750 GTV coupé for test.

All modern Alfa Romeos offer you a light-alloy twin-overhead-camshaft four-cylinder engine, the camshafts driven by a duplex chain and the tappets set by the racing method of shimming them, a five-speed gearbox, all-disc servo-assisted ATE brakes, a lightweight, properly located back axle and a very high-quality interior. They appeal to those who can drive by reason of a sense of life and real performance which relieves dull routes of tedium and makes open-road motoring a real delight, and because they possess especially responsive recirculatory ball steering, suspension which, although lively, rides road irregularities well yet keeps the wheels glued to the surface, and the ability to corner very quickly without emotion. This cornering is perhaps Alfa Romeo's greatest asset, for it is so effortlessly fast, with no sliding, or undue understeer. But smooth, quick steering and the excellent braking run it very close. The three, combined, are superb.

The little GT Veloce, a 2+2 coupé, *disegno di Bertoni*, made by

An Alfa Romeo stands out beside lesser motor cars!

Alfa Romeo and good if the latter "2" are children or one small grown-up sitting athwartwise, is typically Alfa in all the just-mentioned respects and a fast car in its own right, with recommended top speeds in the gears of 29, 48, 71, 99 and 118 m.p.h., and 32 m.p.h. in reverse if you feel like it. Moreover, there is acceleration to match, such as 0 to 60 m.p.h. in 9.3 sec., from an $80 \times 88\frac{1}{2}$ mm., 1,779-c.c. engine carburetted by twin 40 DCOE32 Webers and poking out 132 b.h.p. in S.A.E. trim, at a modest 5,500 r.p.m.

The interior of this plainly-handsome coupé is beautifully appointed, with some nice items, such as a cigarette-lighter which accepts a cigarette and lights it, instead of just becoming a detachable lighter (alas, stupidly-located on r.h.d. cars), and rather special seats, in which there is more workmanship than in most complete cars—or has that been said of another make? Anyway, the squabs adjust easily by turning knobs, the seats slide easily, have shaped and deeply-ventilated p.v.c. upholstery, and by using a small knob on the passenger's a headrest can be wound up into position, so much nicer than having it always there. In fact, I found the upholstery too hard and ridged when wearing summer clothes and the lively ride tiring at first, after Rover luxury.

But very soon I was again an Alfa Romeo addict. It is impossible not to be, after a few miles of using that splendid five-speed gearbox giving ratios of 13.54, 8.15, 5.55, 4.10, and 3.24 to 1, and enjoying the responsive "thrummy" engine and the great sense of security which accurate steering ($3\frac{1}{2}$ turns, lock-to-lock, plus some sponge), wonderful road-holding and light powerful braking impart.

The engine likes 3rd gear to help it get away sharply from low speeds, although it is surprisingly flexible; it will run smoothly at 1,500 r.p.m. but flat-spots ruined the pick-up below 3,000 r.p.m. The wood-rimmed steering wheel of the 1750 GTV is too thick and slippery for my liking, the doors lack "keeps", the hand-brake held only on the last notch on the test car, and the dip-stick is rather hidden and tended to trap a coil wire when put back into its tube. The pedals are set rather far from the floor and biased to the right.

The GTV has some interesting features. Thus the big 140-m.p.h. speedometer and tachometer have neat white needles which move at first across the bottoms of the dials. The latter is lightly straked from 5,700 r.p.m. on to an impressive 8,000 r.p.m. At times 2nd gear seems too low but it is necessary to remember that the engine seldom needs to be taken much above 5,000 r.p.m. in ordinary driving (the handbook does not specify maximum safe r.p.m., which are 6,200) and there is consequently plenty in hand for holding on to 2nd. In 5th gear an indicated 70 m.p.h. is 3,000 r.p.m. below peak revs. There is a narrow central console from which the substantial gaitered gear-lever, working very smoothly and splendidly positioned, protrudes.

CONTINUED ON PAGE 85

CAR and DRIVER ROAD TEST

Alfa Romeo 1750 Duetto Spider and 1750 GTV

Has Alfa gone conservative? You bet your sweet customs permit.

All right, Mrs. Robinson, your late-model, wide-eyed, stud-service-turned son-in-law is a year older, and armed with that magic password to everlasting happiness in the business world, has—once he returned to his senses—joined a plastic dishware manufacturer; where he soared through the ranks to enviable respectability once again.

And let's be honest, Mrs. R., you *did* have a bit to do with the metamorphosis of that naive twist into a substantive breadwinner. What did you see in him anyway? Tongue-tied, acne-scarred, the only thing he had going for him was that darling little red car. What was it again? An Alfa Romeo, Oh that's *Ro-may-o,* anything you say, dear. Whatever happened to that darling little car?

Well, darling little car fans, we're here to tell you that Benjamin isn't alone in conforming to what the world expects—demands even. It's not quite a dehumanized, plastic transportation module yet but it isn't the Alfa of old, either. A dead giveaway as to what's happening is the fact that the engine has been increased in displacement from 1570 cc to 1779 but the model designation is only "1750." Alfa would have you believe that the new name is meant to bring back memories of the fabulous 1750 racers of the Thirties—a few years back a displacement of 1779 would have been more than ample justification to christen the car "1800"—more likely it would have been "2000."

But there are other things to the good. All electrical system trauma is forgotten, the slate wiped clean. Still, have *they* forgotten that it used to be once a car was sold it was treated like the bastard son of a leprous cousin—totally disavowed, condemned to go through life curing whatever maladies might befall it with chewing gum and J.C. Whitney parts?

And then, there's that SPICA fuel injection system on all '69 models. Any dealer/bon vivant/disenfranchised prince/former member of the Alfa Formula One Team (which is to say *every* used-to-be Alfa Dealer) could have told you that fuel injection, *iniezione,* has but one function—to allow the car to go faster, make it more of a racer. But, again, that's the old Alfa dealer, and this is 1969, remember.

The new breed—these marketing guys who actually seem worried about the government restrictions, image, service, repeat sales—is more interested in telling you how the fuel injection allows the 1750 to pass the U.S. anti-emission regulations.

Smog laws, fog laws, what the hell is all this? Has Alfa gone conservative?

You bet your sweet customs permit Alfa has gone conservative.

Earlier this year we tested the 1750 Berlina (*C/D, May*) a pleasant sports sedan that, for all intents and purposes, is simply a practical manifestation of the Duetto Spider and Sprint GTV we are considering this month. Our only unfavorable comment with that model was the lack of engine response caused by the fuel injection. And, if anything, the sportier nature and appearance of both the GTV and Duetto Spider makes this problem more noticeable. If there was one thing that the pre-injection Alfa sports car had in abundance, it was engine response. Kick down the throttle and you were greeted by immense sucking noises as the big 2-bbl Weber carburetors took a deep breath for the extra exertion. It was immediate, it was soul-satisfying and, with a good driver behind the wheel, it permitted dramatic handling corrections at the last minute—an instantaneous power reserve that (provided proper gear selection was made) was available at all legal, and most illegal speeds. And, while it's true that the increased torque of the 1750s (137 lbs.-ft. @ 2800 rpm vs. 115 @ 2800) makes the cars easier for *anyone* to drive in a competent manner—thanks in large part to the long, almost flat torque curve stretching from 2500 to 5000 rpm—the precise and instantaneous throttle responses of the Weber carbureted "1600" engines make those cars immeasurably more pleasurable for really good drivers.

But darling little car-wise, which is the unfortunate impression left with much of *The Graduate's* audience, the Alfa 1750 Duetto Spider, and to a less extent the 1750 GT Veloce, comes on strong. The Duetto's mini 1959 Buick side sculpturing and flat, tapered overall appearance sent a shock wave through the purists when it first appeared in late 1966, but esthetics are a matter of habit as well as personal

PHOTOGRAPHY: JIM McGUIRE

ACCELERATION standing ¼ mile, seconds

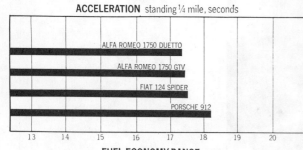

ALFA ROMEO 1750 DUETTO
ALFA ROMEO 1750 GTV
FIAT 124 SPIDER
PORSCHE 912

13 14 15 16 17 18 19 20

BRAKING 80-0 mph panic stop, feet

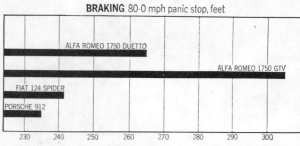

ALFA ROMEO 1750 DUETTO
ALFA ROMEO 1750 GTV
FIAT 124 SPIDER
PORSCHE 912

230 240 250 260 270 280 290 300

FUEL ECONOMY RANGE mpg

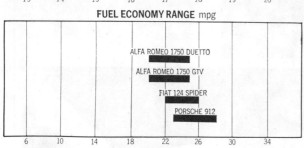

ALFA ROMEO 1750 DUETTO
ALFA ROMEO 1750 GTV
FIAT 124 SPIDER
PORSCHE 912

6 10 14 18 22 26 30 34

PRICE AS TESTED dollars x 1000

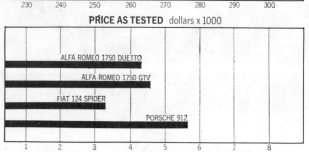

ALFA ROMEO 1750 DUETTO
ALFA ROMEO 1750 GTV
FIAT 124 SPIDER
PORSCHE 912

1 2 3 4 5 6 7 8

ALFA ROMEO 1750 DUETTO SPIDER AND(1750 GTV VELOCE)

Importer: Alfa Romeo Inc.
231 Johnson Ave.
Newark, New Jersey

Vehicle type: Front-engine, rear-wheel-drive, 2-passenger convertible (coupe)

Price as tested: $4,283.00 ($4,531.00) (Manufacturer's suggested retail price, including all options listed below, Federal excise tax, dealer preparation and delivery charges, does not include state and local taxes, license or freight charges)

Options on test car: None; dealer preparation, $85.00

ENGINE
Type: Four-in-line, water-cooled, aluminum block and heads, 5 main bearings
Bore x stroke..3.15 x 3.49 in, 80.0 x 88.5 mm
Displacement............108.4 cu in, 1779 cc
Compression ratio....................9.0 to one
Carburetion.........SPICA, timed, port-type fuel injection
Valve gear........Double overhead camshaft
Power (SAE)............132 bhp @ 5500 rpm
Torque (SAE)........132 lb-ft @ 2900 rpm
Specific power output.........1.22 bhp/cu in, 74.2 bhp/liter
Max recommended engine speed...6000 rpm

DRIVE TRAIN
Transmission............5-speed, all-synchro
Final drive ratio...................4.56 to one

Gear	Ratio	Mph/1000 rpm	Max. test speed
I	3.30	5.0	30 mph (6000 rpm)
II	1.99	8.2	49 mph (6000 rpm)
III	1.35	12.1	72 mph (6000 rpm)
IV	1.00	16.3	98 mph (6000 rpm)
V	0.79	20.0	104 mph (5200 rpm)

DIMENSIONS AND CAPACITIES
Wheelbase.....................88.6 (92.5) in
Track, F/R....................52.1/50.1 in
Length.......................167.9 (160.6) in
Width.........................64.2 (62.2) in
Height........................50.8 (51.8) in
Ground clearance..................6.0 in
Curb weight.............2320 (2380) lbs
Weight distribution, F/R..........53.5/46.5% (56.4/43.6%)
Battery capacity..........12 volts, 60 amp/hr
Alternator capacity.............420 watts
Fuel capacity......................12.0 gal
Oil capacity.......................7.1 qts
Water capacity.....................10.0 qts

SUSPENSION
F: Ind., unequal length control arms, coil springs, anti-sway bar
R: Rigid axle, trailing arms, coil springs, anti-sway bar

STEERING
Type.......................Recirculating ball
Turns lock-to-lock....................3.75
Turning circle curb-to-curb...........33.9 ft

BRAKES
F:..........10.6-in solid disc, power assisted
R:..........10.5-in solid disc, power assisted

WHEELS AND TIRES
Wheel size....................14 x 5.5-in
Wheel type............Stamped steel, 4-bolt
Tire make and size........Pirelli Cinturato H 165HR14
Tire type....Rayon, radial-ply, tube type
Test inflation pressures, F/R.......24/26 psi
Tire, load rating.....1200 lbs per tire @ 36 psi

PERFORMANCE
Zero to	Seconds
30 mph	2.7
40 mph	4.6
50 mph	7.2
60 mph	9.9
70 mph	13.3
80 mph	17.5
90 mph	22.5

Standing ¼-mile........17.3 sec @ 79.7 mph (17.4 sec @ 79.0 mph)
Top speed (estimated)..............115 mph
80-0 mph........265 ft (0.81 G) [305(0.70G)]
Fuel mileage......20–25 mpg on premium fuel
Cruising range...................240–300 mi

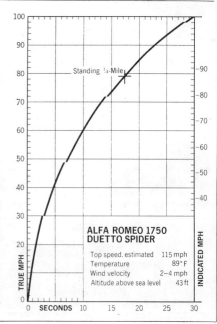

100
90
80 — Standing ¼-Mile — -90
70 — -80
60 — -70
50 — -60
40 — -50
30 — -40
20
10
TRUE MPH
INDICATED MPH

ALFA ROMEO 1750 DUETTO SPIDER

Top speed, estimated   115 mph
Temperature   89°F
Wind velocity   2–4 mph
Altitude above sea level 43 ft

0 5 SECONDS 10 15 20 25 30

taste and the Pininfarina design has been in production long enough to gain its measure of acceptance from the same purists. This does not preclude it from being perhaps the most impractical body envelope ever sold in the American market. It has an pristine life expectancy of about three minutes in any supermarket parking lot you care to choose and considerably less in a parallel parking slot.

The older GTV is a less dramatic-looking car but infinitely more capable of defending itself. The Bertone creation was introduced in 1965, and the only change since that time has been to the interior, where a roof insert has been cut into the headliner to meet FIA Group II sedan specifications. The rear two seats are still a cruel joke for anyone seriously contemplating using the GTV as a 4-seater sedan, but who's to dispute the FIA?

The drivetrain in both the GTV and Duetto (and for that matter, the Berlina) is identical, right down to the same gear ratios in the 5-speed transmission. The same can be said of the basic suspension design concept and hardware; however there is a significant difference which gives each car an individual personality. The Duetto's wheelbase (88.6 inches) is 3.9 inches shorter than the GTV's, but the open car has an overall length (167.9 in.), 7.3 inches *longer*. How 'bout that overhang, fans. Need some more? The Duetto has a *front* overhang of 37.4 inches (8.7 in. more than the GTV) and a rear overhang of 41.9 inches (2.5 inches longer); keep in mind that this is on a shorter wheelbase. Okay, we've got all that sheet-metal dangling out in space so you figure the car should handle something like a half-loaded, double-trailer milk rig. In point of fact, the opposite is the case. The Duetto's more equal weight distribution actually makes it the better handling.

The 1750 series Alfa models have had several suspension changes with the net result being a smoother ride and somewhat less understeer. For 1969 the front suspension utilizes softer rate springs and has a higher roll center. In the rear an anti-sway bar has been added. In addition, the previously-used 14-in. wheels have been replaced by wider (5.5-in. vs. 4.5-in.) stamped steel wheels—but still wider wheels and tires would be desirable for more precise handling. Ride comfort in both cars is noticeably improved. Unit body construction is used for both cars and, somewhat surprisingly, the Duetto transmits less suspension and radial-ply tire noise into the passenger compartment.

Of course, the *raison d'être* for the 1750 series Alfa Romeo models is the new engine. Well, not really new. The all-aluminum, 5-main bearing, double overhead camshaft unit actually began life over a decade ago as a 1290 cc, and this latest enlargement (bore from 3.07 in. to 3.15, stroke from 3.22 to 3.48) probably represents the end of the line. The fuel injection system (described in the May issue of

Despite the deceptively easygoing nature of the fuel-injected Alfa Romeo 1750 Duetto Spider and GTV, both are significantly quicker than their predecessors

C/D) is made by Alfa's subsidiary SPICA and has its origin as an injection system for diesel trucks. Alfa has made a number of adaptations to improve its suitability for passenger cars, but a possible indication of Alfa's opinion of the unit is that only cars sold here in the U.S. are not equipped with Weber carburetors (Alfa engineers are still working on the emission problem, and it appears probable that both carbureted and injection versions will be offered).

Although the fuel injection system has a manually adjustable cold start enrichment valve the 1750s are reluctant to get down to the job at hand, and until the water temperature reaches its standard 190° F operating range, engine response is poor.

Once warmed up and under way everything falls into place, and you discover that the 1750s are among the easiest cars in the world to drive smoothly. Despite the implication of a 5-speed transmission, gear selection need not be as precise and demanding an art as it was with the 1600s. It's a lot more pleasurable—but not crucial —to keep the engine revving in or above the 4000 rpm range where response is best and the muffler's sporty exhaust note announces that you are a force on the road to be reckoned with.

The weight differential between our two test cars was only 60 lbs., so as might be expected, acceleration figures were nearly

CONTINUED ON PAGE 89

AUTOCAR, 9 October, 1969

● **LONG TERM ASSESSMENT**

JUST WILLUM

10,000 miles in an Alfa Romeo GT 1300

By Geoffrey Howard and Michael Scarlett

SOMEHOW the mixed feelings of sadness and nostalgia battled incompatibly with excitement as I trickled up the Edgware Road towards Alfa's new London centre. I was parting with our long-term Giulia 1600 Super and collecting a new 1300 GT Junior. The Super had been a delightful car which had taken me safely and reliably through several months and over 12,000 miles. The Junior was to be a 1969 model (with all the latest improvements) in yellow ochre. As soon as I saw the WLM 39G registration, this Alfa became "Willum".

Immediately I drove it I noticed lots of differences compared with the Super. It was a much tauter car with a firm, joggly ride and near-neutral instead of understeering characteristics. But I fitted it better than the Super and I liked its many differences.

Willum was barely 200 miles old when an odd thing happened at the back end. I reversed out of my garage one cold dark morning and set off through the London suburbs. I was surprised when the wheels spun briefly on the loose gravel of the drive and I was alarmed to hear a deep rumble from the rear axle on the over-run. Somehow I thought the differential was breaking up, so I parked near the station and prepared to catch a train. Then I saw that one rear tyre was flat and kicked myself for being so stupid. In defense I should perhaps add that the Alfa was singularly unaffected by this disturbance. At least it served as a good demonstration of the excellent jacking system. Fortunately I remembered from the Super that the left-hand wheels on Alfas have left-handed threads for some inexplicable reason.

These early days in Willum's life seemed fated and before even the first service, at 350 miles, the windscreen shattered on the way to Rob Walker's Corsley Garage in Wiltshire. Prior to this there had been ominous creaks from the scuttle, so it looked like a stress failure. Anyway, the easiest thing was to continue without a screen, raincoat buttoned to the neck and eyes screwed tight to keep out the flying mud and glass splinters emerging from the cracks and crannies. Being official Alfa distributors, Rob Walker's people made light work of fitting a GTV screen (laminated!) at my request and performing the first service.

When I returned to collect it a few days later, I can pay the Alfa no greater compliment than to say it was no disappointment after the Ferrari 365 GTC I had been driving in the meantime. Some say the Ferrari is just like a big Alfa; I prefer to think of the Alfa as a mini-Ferrari.

From then on we built up miles without incident, and our little twin-cam ran like a train getting freer and faster with every yard which passed under its wheels. Obviously with only 1,290 c.c. the performance could never be startling, but with five gears and a fairly wide rev range it was always easy to keep the engine singing sweetly and with such delightfully balanced handling journey times were always brisk.

Partly because of the "with it" colour, partly because of the chic shape, and partly because Willum was the kind of car which deserved affection, I always liked to drive it clean. The colour lightened several shades between dirty and clean, and the paint always shone without the aid of a polish. Even dirty, Willum still looked smart.

Such had been the excellence of Rob Walker's service (no-one had ever set up twin Webers to idle so smoothly as the mechanics at Corsley), that we sent the car back for its second service. With so many of the staff so keen to get behind the wheel, the mileometer clicked happily up to 3,500-odd miles in no time at all, or so it seemed. To stop myself getting too conditioned, I then passed Willum over to Michael Scarlett, as compensation for suffering 10,000 in his Honda N.600. **GPH**

BEING. like *Iolanthe's* Lord Chancellor, highly susceptible to attractive things, I had hardly looked at the car for fear of becoming too envious; it was a delightful surprise to be given charge of it at 3,480 miles. Without knowing that the Technical Editor had permitted himself a little untechnical wallow in anthropomorphism, I saw WLM 39G and straightway called him William. About 5,000 miles later Geoff and I discovered each other's guilty secret—test drivers, like that peer, should not grow fond of their wards—and in mutual embarrassment agreed to stop confusing the animal; we settled on Willum. Which just goes to show what sentimental fools these journalist mortals be.

First impressions were a strong mixture of immediate likes and dislikes. Dealing with bad points first, Willum certainly did not fit the 6ft of me. He had been made for a particularly deformed specimen of the Darwinian ape who is Italian Standard Man for most Latin car interior designers; thanks to Lancia, Fiat and Alfa, one has grown familiar with, if not friendly towards, this unfortunate chap, who normally has very short legs, a stocky trunk, and long arms. He is at least symmetrical. The GT1300 Junior one is not so lucky, having his right leg considerably shorter than his left; the accelerator pedal is therefore some way back from the brake and clutch. He is a strong enough fellow however, happily applying nearly 50lb of pedal effort over 6in. every time he de-clutches. Not being as healthy, I found this tiring in traffic. Not being the same shape, my right leg had to remain partly unsupported and there wasn't enough rearward seat movement by about 2in. My head brushed the roof. If I reclined the seat enough to clear, then I could hardly reach the wheel or gearlever. (It was a great relief to find that by about 5,000 miles, the seat had settled just enough to cure this.) The ride seemed rather jerky, there was quite loud bump-thump, you had to keep the revs up to get any performance —which made it fussy—the flat interior mirror wasted the car's excellent rear view and I was glad that I hadn't as part of the long-term test been made to lay out such a lot of money for a 1.3-litre car.

On the other hand, every important control moved with superb smoothness and precision; this is common to all Alfas—nothing felt even slightly rough or grating as on so many other cars—there were no sharp-edged nuts under gear-knobs, no sticky-fingered handles, no gooey-rimmed steering wheel. The steering and handling were much better than before, the servo-assisted brakes worked beautifully, the seat held me well round corners, it made a lovely subdued hum as you revved it—overlaid, as the revs rose, with a fascinating quiet crackle like a chuckle to itself in its throat—it went quite fast, incredibly so remembering its 19.9cwt kerb weight, and it looked absolutely perfect in my opinion. The shape was of course familiar before I met Willum, and until the sad day when I watched him being driven away was an almost daily sight (assuming I'd selfishly managed to keep him to myself, always a running fight). Yet every time I set eyes on it and no matter from what angle, it always looked "right"—exactly right. Bertone has made many wonderful shapes, but I think that the Giulia Sprint GT

Alfa in various settings. Opposite, close-up in Richmond Park; above from top, in Connemara, County Galway, watching the evening tide rise near Cloonisle, at Roundstone with the Twelve Pins behind, overlooking Bertraghboy Bay from Bunnahown, and under Derryclare and Bencorr. Modom (the Peugeot) is included because, though Willum's senior, she rides Irish roads more comfortably, like most other French cars

AUTOCAR, 9 October, 1969

JUST WILLUM . . .

body is one of his masterpieces. Perhaps he thinks so too, if that pardonable swagger of a motif *"disegno di Bertone"* is anything to go by.

The colour certainly made it stand out. It was the source of several picturesque comments. I was asked on one occasion if I'd come "in that vulgar yellow car again". Many people thought it "soopah". Others suggested it was derived from canine sources. Another person said she thought it was "a very nice little car but I'm not sure about the paint". One man was reminded of his godson's nappies, and one other of stale mustard. Fiat, whose "Positano yellow" is very close to the Alfa shade, were wrongly credited by many with starting to make the colour popular—Porsche actually are the culprits with their "Bahama yellow". Whether it was the colour I'm not sure, but I was rarely baulked on motorways—slower cars in the fast lane nearly always seemed to see Willum coming well in advance. I loved it unashamedly; it is particular-

ly fascinating in the late afternoon, richening and darkening in sympathy with the reddening sun.

Two tests (the *Autotest* in our 10 April issue and the double test with the Lancia Fulvia Coupe Rallye 1.3S in *Autocar* of 7 August) and the accompanying performance figures tell most of the story about the car's performance. Contrary to appearances, Willum is not the original *Autotest* car, but was used only for the photos. At 6,000 miles and in rather better weather than the Road Test car enjoyed, he proved to be a little faster in acceleration but had approximately the same MIRA banking mean maximum speed, 101 mph. Given his head on another occasion for long enough over a straight course, Willum did 105 mph mean, with a best speed one way of 106 mph. The last check we made, at 10,000 miles, gave identical figures. The engine has always stayed crisp-sounding and eager throughout, never seeming to deteriorate, and perpetually very smooth indeed.

He will cruise at up to 90 mph, with only the wind noise really indicating how fast you are going; the engine isn't quiet, but neither does it sound hard-worked until right up at its top end. He is at his best—a very good best—over

country roads, provided that you don't drop below about 3,000 rpm. If you do, you must wait, or change down. Thanks to the very pleasing gear-change, that is no chore, but a delight. Towards the end of the test, there was a slight suspicion of stickiness going into 5th, but it was not serious.

Willum is not a little car, he weighs the same as some 2-litre GTs and tries to perform nearly as well. The result is a similar thirst, if driven to his maximum—down to around 23.7 mpg. On a gentler drive in company with a well-driven and respectable elderly lady Peugeot across from the West of Ireland to Dublin, he managed 28.8 mpg. The overall figure of 24.4 is identical to that of the Road Test car and reflects a regretted amount of town driving, though not as much as it might have been, since whenever possible, Willum travelled.

He went to Russelsheim, lingering amidst German General Motors like a sophisticated Italian gigolo amongst a party of American matrons on tour, whilst Stuart Bladon and I ran off with a Road Test Opel GT, then he romped back a little breathlessly with the very first right-hand-drive BMW 2800, thankful that 2800s don't have to be run-in at more than 100 mph. He went to Wales several times and loved it. Welsh roads are Alfa roads. Willum's nearly-neutral handling, his quick steering, excellently even gear ratios and light, powerful and superbly balanced brakes made joyous work of every open bend. I know few other cars with such safe braking; one could get away with an astonishing amount of retardation during a fast corner without either end breaking away. "Sure-footed" is I think, no. 493 in the road-testers Book of Well-Worn Clichés, but it is assuredly *votre mot juste actuelle* here. Though he seemed to dare you to try harder he never frightened you. A lot of the credit must go to the fat 165-14 in. Pirelli Cinturatos which if kept inflated at 27F/30R (motorway pressures) stuck just as well as when at normal pressures and ceased to squeal.

Part of this is also due to the steering. I stick to my belief that where cornering is concerned "feel" is as much in the senses of balance in one's head as in one's hands, and that live steering is not essential. But I do agree that it is very much better and much more pleasant to have good "feel" if possible, and it is in this respect that the Alfa is almost unapproached. Though it needs average effort to work—and rather more than average for parking—there is very little friction in the Alfa's re-circulating ball (or worm and roller) steering; certainly much less than in most rack and pinion systems. The lack of much friction and therefore damping *pro rata* is combined with just-enough castor and not too much off-set. The result is that that delightfully made two-spoke steering wheel tells you exactly how much grip there is immediately without any irritating fight over bumps (as on earlier models); it spins back through your hands as you wish when self-centering no matter how gently you're turning. Anyone sensitive reacts to this perfect behaviour and tends to find himself steering with the finger tips rather than the hands. Running straight on a motorway—the Alfa does that very well too, even in a side-wind—there is nearly ½in. of slop at the wheel-rim, but as it is progressive you don't notice it at all.

Ride has always been a little "nobbly", but not too firm, and well-damped. We all agree that it seemed to improve slightly latterly. Willum went west, almost as far west as he could go, to the beautiful wilds of Connemara, in County Galway, and there he met the road that is full of surprises, the Irish bog road. Such roads cannot help being most wonderfully bumpy, as they are not too well-founded. The result is a *chaussée* which is more *tourmentée* than *deformée*; the most flexible French cars are the only ones that seem anywhere near at home on this. In spite of some remarkable ups and downs, Willum managed quite well, moving a lot but bottoming only occasionally and then surprisingly gracefully. He appears to have unusually good bump

Above: Willum sliding wide at MIRA, one front wheel nearly off the track. Cornered hard, the Alfa understeers progressively but not too much with power on, let its tail out on lift-off (as here) and doesn't roll inordinately Left: The highly presentable engine room. Accessibility is much better than it looks here. Forward-mounted battery never seems to need topping-up Below: A neat interior. The water and fuel gauges look tidy, angled towards the driver from under the heater, but are blocked by the gearlever when in top

rubbers and also well-made rattle-free body-work; there were no nasty bangs.

Where fittings and comfort are concerned the small Alfa is on the whole well-appointed. Everyone who has made a long journey in the car has commented on how comfortable the passenger seat is. The "sofa-type" rear seat (as the handbook calls it) is habitable by one adult if one in front adjusts his seat forward appreciably. Regarding space, the boot with its very neat little door-jamb remote lock on the nearside is remarkably roomy, easily big enough for two people's holiday luggage. I badly missed anywhere to put small things in front where they wouldn't get lost. There is the small locker on the left but it is too remote for casual use by the driver. A central open tray as on BMWs would be a great boon. The locker also suffers from a release you have to push as you pull it open, not a clever idea.

Being one of the first rhd '69 models, Willum came with rubber mats, which I like, especially when they bear big Alfa Romeo insignias; cars for the British market normally have carpets like the GTV. The mat on the nearside tended to come loose at the top. They are definitely practical. The door releases outside are unnatural in action; you post your fingers

in a letter-box-like slot and must then push the tongue upwards, instead of pulling it out which is what everyone tries to do at first. Window winders are unusually light and easy to turn, which is nice to find nowadays; like other Italian cars they are of opposite sense to what is usual elsewhere. Seats slide easily; the eight-position eccentric-adjustment for rake of the seat back is not ideal, as all weight must be moved off it, not just a little. That lovely plain steering wheel has easily found horn keys, like the black notes of a piano, in each spoke. I would like the boss to work the horn as well, since I still clout that first in an emergency. It would also be easier when you suddenly have occasion to beep in the middle of twirling the wheel. The horn itself has a very fine note in keeping with the car's character, though perhaps not quite as Continental as some expect.

The instruments are straightforward and neat, which also describes the pleasing interior styling. The trip mileometer has a delightfully positive and easily worked re-set. The same does not go for the excellently comprehensive fuse box, very awkward indeed to deal with if a fuse goes because of its difficult mounting. One other really maddening item is the absence

of any provision for holding the doors open. Having to hold a door open with your boot, which marks the trim, on a car of this price is very irritating. The bonnet stay is not self-setting, and is too easily released by wind. Ventilation we have criticised before; it is not up to current British standards. The wind-screen wiper linkage tends to creak, especially on a drying screen. The handbrake is exceptionally good and easy to use.

Starting never presented any problems once one had remembered that a hot Alfa engine needs quite a few turns before it will "catch". Maintenance is not too difficult, thanks to a fairly informative handbook. I had no trouble changing the oil filter element or in getting at other routine items for servicing.

There are always things to quibble about on any car. In spite of them, Willum was a wholly delightful companion over every mile. His very great qualities bring out the best in any driver, since you feel you owe the best to this superb machine. He gave all of us who were lucky enough to drive him great satisfaction and very great fun. I admit to growing fond of most cars I've had to drive for any long-ish time; saying goodbye to this one was very sad indeed. **MS**

Willum in company. Above: After the Seaman Trophy at Oulton Park (Kenneth Neve's 1914 TT Humber and Rolls-Royce tractor behind)

Above: Willum, Modom and canistered waters of the Liffey outside a famous watering place, Nee's Bar, near Ballynahinch, Connemara

Below: In the emptying car park after the August Shelsley Walsh meeting

PERFORMANCE CHECK

Maximum speeds

Gear	mph		kph		rpm	
	R/T	Staff	R/T	Staff	R/T	Staff
Top (mean)	102	105	164	169	5,600	5,750
(best)	104	106	168	171	5,700	5,800
4th		97		156		6,200
3rd		71		114		6,200
2nd		49		79		6,200
1st		29		47		6,200

Standing ¼-mile, R/T: 19.1 sec 72 mph
Staff: 19.2 sec 73 mph
Standing kilometre, R/T: 35.7 sec 90 mph
Staff: 35.6 sec 90 mph

Acceleration, R/T:	4.3	6.6	9.3	13.2	18.8	25.3	36.3	—
Staff:	3.9	6.2	8.9	13.1	17.7	24.7	35.8	—

Time in seconds	0							
True speed mph	30	40	50	60	70	80	90	100
Indicated speed MPH, R/T:	31	42	53	63	74	85	95	106
Indicated speed MPH, Staff:	32	42	52	62	75	86	98	109

Speed range, Gear Ratios and Time in Seconds

Mph	Top		4th		3rd		2nd		1st	
	R/T	Staff	R/T	Staff	R/T	Staff	R/T	Staff	R/T	Staff
	(3.92)		(4.56)		(6.17)		(9.06)		(15.05)	
10-30	—	—	—	—	—	9.0	5.3	5.3	—	—
20-40	15.6	15.0	11.9	11.3	6.9	7.4	4.4	5.0	—	—
30-50	14.4	14.3	10.7	10.7	7.4	7.5	—	—	—	—
40-60	15.1	13.4	12.2	10.8	8.0	8.0	—	—	—	—
50-70	18.1	17.0	14.8	12.5	9.5	9.1	—	—	—	—
60-80	25.6	22.8	16.9	14.6	—	—	—	—	—	—
70-90	—	29.0	20.7	19.0	—	—	—	—	—	—

Fuel Consumption
Overall mpg, R/T: 24.4 mpg (11.6 litres/100km)
Staff: 24.4 mpg (11.6 litres/100km)

NOTE: "R/T" denotes performance figures for similar model tested in *AUTOCAR* of 10 April 1969

COST AND LIFE OF EXPENDABLE ITEMS

Item	Life in Miles	Cost per 10,000 Miles
		£ s. d.
One gallon of 4-star fuel, average cost today 6s 4d	24.4	129 10 0
One pint of top-up oil, average cost today 3s 6d	2,000	17 6
Front disc brake pads (set of 4)	18,000	2 12 0
Rear disc brake pads (set of 4)	15,000	3 3 0
Tyres (front pair)	23,000	7 10 0
Tyres (rear pair)	20,000	8 15 0
Service (main interval and actual costs incurred)	3,750	22 12 0
Total		174 19 6
Approx. standing charges per year		
Depreciation		500 0 0
* Insurance		35 9 0
Tax		25 0 0
Total		735 8 6

Approx. cost per mile—1s 5½d
Insurance is a Cornhill quotation based on business and private use, 65 per cent n.c.b., residence in "Metropolitan Surrey" and a £25 excess.

ALFA'S JUNIOR GT

THE SMALL Alfa Romeo Coupe is rather like a single raspberry — it hasn't the punch of the full punnet such as the 1750 GTV — but it has an enjoyable, individual character.

That it has only 103 bhp from 1290 cc is no handicap provided the driver doesn't want to lay great strips of rubber on the road.

In fact, when the traffic light derby begins, the only thing the 1300 GT Alfa driver can do is proceed smartly, pleasantly and off-handedly in the wake of the tyre burning local V8 machines.

Of course, when the wiggly bit comes up, the Alfa 1300 GT swoops round the bends without putting a foot wrong — or slackening pace.

It is not so much the performance as the way it is achieved. There are five speeds in the gear box, four disc brakes, a properly tied down suspension, reassuring handling and steering response from the radial ply tyres — and of course the chic Alfa coupe lines.

The 1300 GT — it is really the old Giulietta back under a different flag — is really most pleasant to drive. And for the owner who still enjoys driving, the car responds to sympathetic treatment. Further, it requires a little skill to use its abilities to the full.

Unless the right gear is used at the right

time, performance is downright mediocre. But scrambling up and down the five synchromeshed ratios is enjoyable with the great, thick pole of a gear lever.

The twin camshaft motor comes to life with the deep throated note characteristic of the Alfa exhaust. The instruments in front of the driver — a speedo and tachometer — flicker and the oil pressure gauge let into the tacho promptly registers a 55 psi plus pressure.

Water temperature and fuel gauges are well buried under the dashboard and ahead of the gear lever. A conscious look downward and peer around the driver's left hand is needed to check them.

The driving position is comfortable, there is plenty of room in front (legroom in the back is meagre) on the well shaped bucket seats and with the belt on, things you need often are in reach.

Pressing the gear lever to the left against the spring pressure and into first and the car is away. Since Alfa began building their gear boxes to the ZF design, the tiresome nonsense connected with warming up the vitals is now past.

SPECIFICATIONS

CAR FROM:
MW Motors, Elizabeth Street, Melbourne.

PRICE AS TESTED:
$4450.

OPTIONS FITTED:
None.

ENGINE:
Type: 4 cyl., DOHC, two twin choke carburettors.
Bore and Stroke: 74 x 75 mm.
Capacity: 1290 cc.
Compression ratio: 9.0:1.
Power (gross): 103 bhp at 6000 rpm
Torque: 101 ft./lbs. at 3200 rpm.

TRANSMISSION:
Five speed manual, all synchro.
Ratios:
1st, 3.20:1
2nd, 1.99:1
3rd, 1.36:1
4th, 1.00:1
5th, 0.86:1
Final drive 4.55:1

CHASSIS:
Wheelbase ....92½ inches
Length ....160½ inches
Track F................................. 52 inches
Track R................................. 50 inches
Width .... 62 inches
Height .... 52 inches
Clearance (minimum).......... 3½ inches
Test Weight ....2180 lbs.
Fuel capacity ....10½ gallons

SUSPENSION:
Front: Wishbone, stabiliser bar, coil springs.
Rear: Live axle, training arms, coil springs.

BRAKES:
Power assisted, divided systems.
Front: disc.
Rear: disc.

STEERING:
Type: recirculating ball.
Turning circle: 35 ft.

WHEELS/TYRES:
Pirelli tyres, 155 x 15 in., ventilated steel wheels.

PERFORMANCE

PERFORMANCE:
Zero to
30 mph............................ 4.3
40 mph............................ 6.5
50 mph............................ 9.1
60 mph............................ 12.5
70 mph............................ 16.1
80 mph............................ NA
90 mph............................ NA
100 mph............................ NA
Standing quarter mile: 19.1 seconds.
Fuel consumption on test 25.8 mpg on Super fuel.
Fuel consumption (expected): 24-26 mpg.
Cruising range: 230 miles.
Speedometer error:
Indicated 30 40 50 60 70 80 90 100
Actual   28 37 46 56 65 — — —

MAXIMUM SPEEDS IN GEARS:
1st.. 26 mph
2nd.. 45 mph
3rd.. 65 mph
4th.. 96 mph
5th.. 106 mph

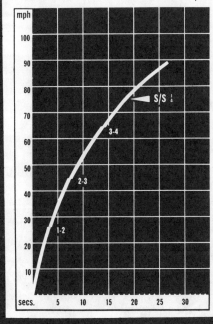

COMMENTS

ENGINE:
Response ....Good
Vibration ....Good
Noise ....Low/Moderate

DRIVE TRAIN:
Shift linkage ....Good
Synchro action.................................Good

STEERING:
Effort ....Light
Road feel ....Very Good
Kickback ....Low

SUSPENSION:
Ride comfort ....Good
Roll resistance ....Good
Pitch Control ....Good

HANDLING:
Directional control ....Very Good
Predictability..........................Very Good

BRAKES:
Pedal pressure ....Light
Response ....Very Good
Fade resistance ....Very Good
Directional stability...............Very Good

CONTROLS:
Wheel position..................................Fair
Pedal position ....Good
Gearshift position ....Good

INTERIOR:
Noise level ....Moderate
Front seat comfort ....Very Good
Front leg room ....Good
Front head room ....Good
Rear seat comfort ....Fair
Rear leg room...................................Poor
Rear head room...............................Poor
Instrument legibility................Very Good

VISION:
Forward ....Very Good
Front quarter ....Good
Rear quarter ....Good
Rear ....Very Good

CONSTRUCTIONAL QUALITY:
Paint ....Good
Stainless Steel ....Good
Trim ....Good

GENERAL:
Headlights — highbeam ....Good
Headlights — lowbeam................Good
Wiper coverage ....Fair
Wipers at speed...............................Good
Maintenance accessibility ....Fair.

ALFA'S JUNIOR GT

By turning a blind eye to the 6200 rpm red line, the car will run to 26, 45, 65, 96 and 106 mph. But this requires a very brave look at more than 7000 r.p.m.

In top gear, the gearing is spot-on. Maximum speed comes up fairly smartly together with the 6300 rpm reading. Two miles of 6300 rpm failed to produce any improvement so that seems to be it. Maximum power comes at 6000 rpm.

At high speed, there is annoying wind whistling from the door quarter vent seals and there is the sensation that things are moving along in a fairly uptight way. At 100 mph, there is a more relaxed feel but the gauges still looked good at the higher speed.

Sidewinds are no great problem and sweeping bends are taken easily and neatly. The 1300 has a small steering wheel and this makes light of the twisting hilly roads.

Despite 103 bhp from the 1290 cc, there is still not enough power to steer it out of bends with the accelerator. This is where the small coupe begins to require a light, delicate touch since it relies heavily on its excellent roadholding and balance for its handling. There is a little understeer but so small that the car seems to handle neutrally in most situations.

Bumps are taken well on bends — but there is a slightly unnerving sensation that the rubber links to the rear live axle are "walking" about.

One thing about the tachometer — the red line comes when the needle stands straight up. That's easily seen when reaching maximum revs. in mid corner and being faced with either a slackening of speed or a gearshift.

With the roadholding, a gearshift can be attempted without being then faced with a sickening slide.

Stopping is one factor which is never a worry. Four discs, power assisted are the same size as for the 1750. There is no way short of using a 100 deg. F. boiling point fluid that these will give trouble.

Wheel and tyre size also corresponds with those of the faster cars although the tyres' speed rating is lower.

Boot space is not the coupe's strong point. And back seat accommodation is strictly occasional. Further, there is little space for odds and ends inside.

But the 1300 GT coupe is every bit an Alfa from its twin-Webered, twin cam engine to the heart shaped grille centre.

Its diminutive power — even Alfa see fit to quote the 103 bhp in SAE instead of their usual net or D.I.N. figures — takes some getting used to after the bigger bore stuff, but the acquaintance once made is catching.

GIANT TEST

Alfa Romeo 1750 GTV v Lancia Flavia 2000 coupé

MOTORING JOURNALISTS OFTEN remark that cars tend to reflect the national characteristics of a country's inhabitants. Of no country is this more true than Italy, whose cars cheerfully reflect the happy-go-lucky nature of the occupants of that sunny land. Italian cars are almost always built to a formula which places performance, handling and all the dynamic qualities ahead of such mundane matters as driving position or use of interior space or—horror of horrors—safety.

Whenever one thinks of fast or beautiful cars it is not long before Alfa Romeo, Lancia, Maserati, Ferrari, Lamborghini *et al* spring to mind, for Italy is the home of fast, beautiful cars. Of the companies selling cars on a reasonably large scale, Alfa Romeo and Lancia have the sporting end of the market pretty well sewn up, Alfa with their 1300 and 1750 variants in both open and coupé form plus the long awaited production 2.6litre V8 and the Zagato Junior 1300 while Lancia have their little Fulvia coupé in 1.3 and 1.6 litre form and the bigger Flavia in 1.8 and 2litre versions.

The two cars we tested in Italy recently, the Alfa Romeo 1750 GTV and the Lancia Flavia 2000 coupé, are both edging towards the end of their careers, the Alfa having been in production for seven years and the Flavia for nearly nine years. The GTV has continued with minor modifications each year since its introduction except for the increase from 1600 to 1779cc in early 1968, and at the Geneva Show in 1969 the Flavia received a fairly substantial power increase of 30percent when the engine capacity was raised from 1800cc to 1991cc, although superficially the latest 2000 coupé bears a passing resemblance to the original 1800 coupé it has in fact been extensively revised especially at the front end and inside. The 1970 modifications for the GTV consist mostly of cosmetic surgery, new seats with integral headrests, revised door trimming and a wood rimmed steering wheel being the main changes. Mechanically, the pedals have been switched to the pendant type instead of floor hinging (except on rhd cars unfortunately) and a dual braking system is fitted.

STYLE AND ENGINEERING
The Alfa and Lancia are worlds apart both in their styling and engineering. The Alfa layout follows the conventional route of four-cylinder front-mounted engine driving via a propeller shaft to a beam axle, whereas the Flavia has a flat four all-aluminium engine driving the front wheels, with a dead axle at the rear. However, the Alfa's convention is tinged with a good deal of sophistication because the all aluminium four is an efficient twin overhead camshaft unit which gives a healthy 132bhp (SAE) and drives through a five-speed gearbox which is acknowledged to be one of the best in current production. Suspension, too, is about as sophisticated as one can get with a conventional layout, the rear axle being well tied down, with lower trailing arms and an upper 'A' bracket, springing being by co-axial telescopic coil spring/damper units. Front suspension is by double wishbones and coil springs, with separate telescopic dampers. Anti-roll bars are fitted front and rear.

The Lancia, like the Alfa, has a unit construction body/chassis unit with the complete engine/drive train package mounted ahead of the front cockpit bulkhead on a removable subframe, rather like the Mini. Unfortunately the car does not make as much use of its front wheel drive layout as most of the modern breed of fwd cars because the engine is well ahead of the front wheels, so that the bonnet is much the same length as in a conventional car. The advantage with the layout is that the complete engine/transmission unit and front suspension can be removed quickly for maintenance. Rubber mountings at the four main points absorb engine and transmission shocks. The pushrod ohv flat four in its latest 2litre form gives a virtually identical power output to the Alfa 1750, 131bhp (SAE) but it is fair to say that the Lancia engine is less highly tuned than the Alfa's, as it has only a single Solex twin choke downdraught carburettor against the Alfa's twin 40DCOE Webers and operates on a compression ratio of 9 to 1 against the Alfa's 9.5 to 1. Surprisingly, the Alfa claims a much better torque figure of 137.4lb ft at 2900rpm against the Lancia's 132.36 lb ft at 4200rpm. Although the original engine layout as designed by the late Professor Antonio Fessia has been retained in the 2litre a great deal of redesign has been incorporated; the capacity increase has not merely been obtained with a boring-out job, for the stroke has been lengthened too, going up from 74mm to 80mm while the bore is up from 88 to 89mm, thus bringing the engine much nearer square. Strangely enough, the Alfa has similar dimensions except that the bore is 80mm and the stroke 88.5mm. Although the Alfa's capacity is in fact 1779cc it is known as the 1750 presumably because it's easier to say 1750 than 1779!

The Lancia drives through an all-synchromesh four-speed gearbox which is mounted ahead of the cockpit, the drive to the front wheels being taken via constant velocity jointed shafts. The Lancia's independent front suspension is by double wishbones and a large transverse leaf spring running through the front box member, together with telescopic dampers and an anti-roll bar. At the rear the dead axle is carried on longitudinal leaf springs and is located by a Panhard rod.

Both cars use disc brakes on all four wheels assisted by a vacuum servo. The Lancia uses 15in wheels and the Alfa 14in, both with 5½J rims. For steering the Alfa uses a recirculating ball layout and the

Lancia a worm and roller. The Lancia is also available with the ZF power assisted steering as an option which, among other things, reduces the number of turns lock to lock from 4.5 to 3.5.

Bodily, both Alfa and Lancia turned to famous coachbuilders for their designs, the former to Bertone, the latter to Pininfarina. Aesthetically Alfa Romeo probably got the better of the deal, for the GT, designed by Giugiaro before he left Bertone, is probably one of the prettiest yet practical designs ever to be built by a major manufacturer. The Flavia would probably be termed as handsome rather than pretty, for it lacks the sheer beauty of the Alfa; on the credit side the body shape is more practical. In profile the 2000 coupé is rather reminiscent of certain Pininfarina body designs on Ferrari chassis.

USE OF SPACE

The Flavia is a larger car than the 1750. Its wheelbase is about 5in longer, its overall length is 1ft 6in longer, it is 1in wider and an inch higher. Therefore it is not surprising that there is more room inside the Lancia, although both cars must be classed as very occasional four-seaters. In the Alfa, with the front seats on their rearmost stops the backrests touch the cushion of the rear bench seat which gives some idea of the amount of room in the rear, although if the driver happened to be a particularly stunted specimen and sat close to the wheel the distance between the front seat backrest and the rear seat cushion grows to a comfortable 11in. On the Lancia there is 4in of legroom at the back with the front seat on its rearmost stop, so the Lancia can be occupied for reasonably long distances by four adults. Front legroom is much the same, but the balance again falls in favour of the Lancia, while headroom is virtually identical. Access to the rear seats through the two doors is about the same on both cars with, once again, a slight bias in favour of the Lancia.

Where the Lancia scores comfortably is on luggage space. That extra 1ft 6in has been used to good effect to provide a boot which would do justice to much larger cars, although the spare wheel takes up more space than it should. In spite of that the boot is still capable of swallowing all the luggage that four people might need for a longish holiday. The high sill is something of a nuisance for lifting in heavy objects. The Alfa's boot is considerably smaller, has a smallish lid and a similarly high sill. However, a reasonable amount of well stowed luggage can be squeezed in although two large suitcases and one or two squashy bags are about its limit. It is fascinating to note the odd little touches of quality which one gets in cars of this type; the Lancia's spare wheel is fitted with a plastic cover to prevent mud getting on to the luggage, a sensible rubber mat is fitted on the boot floor, the jack and tools are tightly strapped into place and an interior boot light is illuminated when the lid is lifted; the lid

itself lifts automatically on spring struts as soon as the key is turned in the lock. Tiny items but ones which are going to be appreciated by the owner in the long run. The Alfa's spare wheel is horizontally placed under the boot carpet and a reasonable toolkit, by present-day standards, is supplied.

COMFORT AND SAFETY

The seats of the two cars reflect their overall characters better than any other aspect. The new front seats for 1970 on the Alfa are contoured to fit the occupant's form closely, the side bolsters on backrest and cushion are angled to hold the driver in place under hard cornering, while the integral headrests can be raised to any height; the backrests recline fully and there is a large range of adjustment. The whole accent is on performance although the seats are extremely comfortable if a little on the hard side. The Flavia's front seats are designed more for comfort than holding the occupants in place under violent lateral G; both cushions and backrests are thick and softly padded, the seats are wider than those of the Alfa and are certainly more comfortable even though the driver tends to slide about when cornering hard. The rear seats of both cars are trimmed in such a way as to indicate that they are intended for occupation by two people but no doubt a third could squeeze on to the central section in direst emergency.

The driving position of both cars tends towards the Italian vogue for arms stretch-knees bend layouts but the Flavia can be modified to give a position more amenable to Anglo-Saxons, whereas the Alfa is less inclined to assist in this direction. Pedals and gear levers of both cars fall readily to foot and hand.

The two cars are set up rather differently in the suspension departments. The Alfa is more at home being hurled round twisting country lanes whereas the Lancia prefers to belt along autostrade at or near its maximum. The ride of the Alfa is definitely on the firm side compared with the Lancia which absorbs bumps better and is infinitely quieter. At 110mph on the autostrada the Flavia is incredibly quiet, only a whisper of noise round the screen pillars giving any indication of the speed. At the same speed the Alfa's engine is giving audible indication of its twin ohc and wind noise is much greater.

The latest trends in ventilation have not caught up with the Alfa Romeo yet, which still relies on the normal heater system to pass cool air into the interior. The Lancia has two eyeball vents at each end of the facia, one a warm air outlet through the heater and the other a completely separate fresh air system with vents in the rear threequarter panels of the car to take out stale air. Although the cars were tested in below freezing weather, thus giving little opportunity to test the fresh air systems, it seems probable that the Lancia will be superior in this respect. Both cars have opening rear three quarter windows to ▶

	ALFA ROMEO 1750 GTV	LANCIA FLAV 2000 COUPÉ
PRICES	At £2300 the GTV is a good deal cheaper than the Flavia. It is nippier, handles better but is noisier and offers less room for passengers and their luggage. One of the world's best looking production cars styled by the incomparable Giugiaro	Top of the Lancia lin the 2000 coupé sell £2907 in Britain. Ex such as ZF power steering bring it up t £3000. It offers the usual Lancia quality better than average performance and go luggage accommoda
ACCELERATION from standstill in seconds		
FUEL	24 mpg overall ★★★★★ 30mpg driven carefully 230–290miles range 10gallons capacity	22 mpg ov ★★★★ 28mpg driven carefu 240–300 miles rang 12gallons capacity
SPEEDS IN GEARS		
HANDLING	Handling on Michelin XAS tyres about as good as possible with a live rear axle. Some understeer when approaching the limit accompanied by tyre squeal. A very safe car with light, quick steering and fade-free brakes. Inspires the driver with endless confidence	Roadholding on Mic XAS tyres good on f curves but 'chuckab limited on slow curv by slow steering rat Some understeer no able but front wheel drive characteristics are not prominent. A very quiet car at maximum speed
LUGGAGE CAPACITY cubic feet		

BRAKES RESPONSE in normal use. Deceleration (percent g) vs pedal load (lb) A = Alfa Romeo B = Lancia

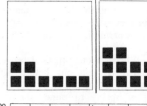

FADE peak deceleration achieved in 10 crash stops from 60mph at one minute intervals A = Alfa Romeo B = Lancia

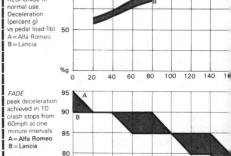

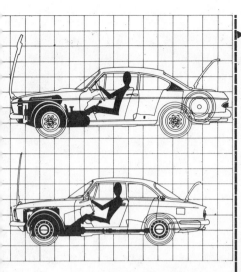

assist through ventilation.

PERFORMANCE, HANDLING, BRAKES

The Alfa undeniably has the upper hand when it comes to acceleration, handling and braking; one does not have to look far to discover why, for the Lancia weighs a good 400lb more than the Alfa at the kerb, which is quite a handicap when both cars have similar power outputs. With four passengers and 88lb of luggage the Lancia turns the scale at over 1.5tons, putting it at a distinct disadvantage to the Alfa which barely tops the ton. Even so the Lancia is

not desperately slower than the Alfa, their respective 0–60mph times being 9.5sec for the Alfa and 11.4sec for the Lancia; further up the scale the Lancia drops away more, its 0–90mph figure being a good five seconds slower. The Alfa is better served by its superb five-speed gearbox than the Lancia with its four-speeder because the extra gear enables the Alfa to have a ratio suitable for any contingency, whereas the Lancia does tend towards typical Italian ratios, with a lowish first gear, the other three gears being grouped closer together. As far as top speed is concerned there is very little in it; the Alfa will touch 120mph under favour-

Instruments: 1 Speedo **2** Fuel **3** Water temp **4** Oil pressure **6** Tach **8** Ignition **9** Main beam **Warnings: 10** Oil pressure **11** Indicators **13** Sidelights **14** Handbrake **15** Fuel low level **Controls: 16** Choke **17** Ign/start **18** Indicators **19** Lights **20** Dip **21** Flash **22** Horn **23** Panel lights **25** Wipers **26** Washers **27** Heater **28** Face level vent **Special items: A** Heater fan **B** Cigarette lighter **C** Bonnet lock **D** Hand throttle **E** Choke warning **F** Clock **G** Ash tray

New seats in the Alfa (top right) are shaped to support back and to hold occupant in place: Flavia seats (centre left) are wider, plusher and less figure hugging than the Alfa's. The familiar Alfa twin cam (bottom left) gives 132bhp in GTV form while the Flavia flat four (bottom right), almost hidden beneath its accessories, gives 131bhp

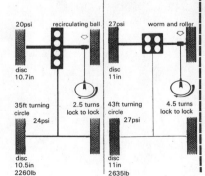

	ALFA ROMEO 1750 GTV	LANCIA FLAVIA 2000 COUPÉ
DIMENSIONS	inches	inches
Wheelbase	92.5	97.62
Front track	50.0	51.96
Rear track	51.5	50.38
Length	156.5	178.75
Width	62.25	63.22
Height	51.75	52.36
Ground clearance	5.5	5.0
Front headroom	33	34
Front legroom	35/44	37/40
Rear headroom	32	33
Rear legroom	18/29	22/27
ENGINE		
Material	aluminium	aluminium
Bearings	5	3
Cooling	water	water
Valve gear	twin ohc	pushrod ohv
Carburettors	twin Weber 40DCOE32	one Solex C34 EIES
Capacity cc	1779	1991
Bore mm	80	89
Stroke mm	88.5	80
Compression to 1	9.5	9.0
Gross power bhp	132 (SAE)	131 (SAE)
rpm	5500	5400
Gross torque lb ft	137.4	132.36
rpm	2900	4200
TRANSMISSION		
Control	direct floor	remote floor
Synchromesh	1-2-3-4-5	1-2-3-4
Ratios to 1	3.3	3.315
2	1.99	1.960
3	1.35	1.359
4	1.0	1.0
5	0.79	—
Final drive ratio	4.10:1	3.545:1
Tyre size	165-14in	165-15in
Rim size	5½J	5½J
SUSPENSION		
Front	double wishbones, coil springs, telescopic dampers, anti-roll bar	double wishbones, transverse leaf spring, telescopic dampers, anti-roll bar
Rear	live axle, trailing arms, 'A' bracket, coil springs, telescopic dampers	dead axle, leaf springs, telescopic dampers, panhard rod
LUBRICANT		
Engine oil type SAE	20W/40	10W/40
Sump capacity pints	12	15
Change miles	3750	4500
Other lube points	3	6
Lube intervals	3750	4500
STEER	20psi recirculating ball	27psi worm and roller
BRAKES	disc 10.7in	disc 11in
STEERING	35ft turning circle 24psi	43ft turning circle 27psi
	2.5 turns lock to lock	4.5 turns lock to lock
BRAKES	disc 10.5in	disc 11in
WEIGHT	2260lb	2635lb

able conditions but it is a 115mph car under normal conditions, exactly the same speed as the Lancia reaches at its 5600rpm red line in top gear.

The Alfa has always been noted for its handling and we were not disappointed with the GTV; it can be tossed around extremely rapidly, showing increasing understeer to indicate that the limit is coming up, and always being a delight to drive. It is taut, quick to react and instills in the driver tremendous confidence. Although the recirculating ball steering is not as light as rack and pinion it is only heavy at parking speeds and with only 2.5 turns lock to lock it is fantastically quick.

The Flavia, being much heavier than the Alfa, is not so manageable on twisting roads, largely because its steering requires 4.5 turns lock to lock, the sheer logistics of getting the wheel back and forth quickly enough defeating attempts at high speed motoring. On faster curves it is more at home, cornering in a very stable way and rolling remarkably little. Surprisingly it does not betray its front wheel drive as much as some smaller fwd cars; understeer there is but not enough to cause any difficulty, while the car does not show any peculiar habits if the throttle foot is lifted in mid-corner. The average motorist need never know he is in a front wheel drive car.

The steering of the Lancia is very heavy at low speeds, parking in confined spaces being quite difficult for a male driver let alone a member of the fair sex; this task is rendered more difficult by the restricted lock. However, once on the move the steering begins to lighten and little more effort is needed on the Lancia's worm and roller than on the Alfa's steering. The optional ZF power steering would, of course, obviate much of the criticism.

The brakes of both cars are power assisted, giving smooth, progressive repeated stops with no sign of fade or grab under our test conditions. The pedal travel on the Lancia did lengthen after half a dozen stops from 60mph but braking efficiency was barely affected.

CONCLUSION

Although these two cars are similar in many respects they have obviously been designed with different purposes in view. The Alfa is at its best being hurled round winding roads and streaking up mountain passes, the Lancia comes into its own when storming along the autostrada at 110mph in almost complete silence. The Flavia has more room both for passengers and for luggage but is heavier on fuel. Both cars are well made and beautifully finished, with the Lancia having a slight edge in the quality stakes, although the well used test car slightly blotted its copybook by having a soggy carpet because of a water leak.

Perhaps the final decider for British buyers will be based on image and price. For the small quantity production Lancia the price in Britain is a rather elevated £2900 against the Alfa's £2300. Even so it will be a difficult decision to make. ●

photography: Karen Heddle

Fifteen thousand on.....

Alfa Romeo 1750 GT Veloce long term test

Autocar has carried out long term tests on a number of Alfa Romeos in the past few years — making for each staff member involved and in each case a pleasure out of a duty. "Indigo grey" 1750 GT Veloce YYR 126H came into our care a year ago with 197 miles done; 11 months, three generally very pleased drivers and 15,737 miles later it was reluctantly returned to its importers.

Ray Hutton, who had the most recent experience of the car, driving it for the last 5,000 miles, opens the report. Michael Scarlett, who ran it from take-over until David Thomas' tenure from 7,000 miles, adds a postcript.

B Y any standard the GTV is a quick, if not brutally fast car. It is interesting that the figures recorded for our staff car at 15,500 miles are significantly quicker than those of the car supplied for test in our issue of 26 September 1968. Since that car (the first 1,779 c.c. coupé) a number of detail changes have been made to the specification but none which would be expected to create a dramatic performance increase; we think therefore that the original test car was slightly below par. Our 1970 model, which is still current, differed from the earlier car in having dual-circuit brakes, with a brake power regulator to the rear, and twin servos which necessitated a new and smaller carburettor air cleaner, an alternator, quartz-halogen headlamps (adjustable for load height) and re-positioned sidelamps, new shape seats and a heated rear window as standard equipment. Like other Italian manufacturers, Alfa buy-in components from several suppliers, in an attempt to stay immune from their industrial problems. Thus Alfas can be fitted with Weber, Solex or Del Orto carburettors, all of which reach their exacting standards for performance, though one might expect there to be some small differences in the power curves between the three types. Our staff car, like the original road test model, was fitted with twin Weber 40 DCOEs.

I could have cried when Geoff Howard walked into my office one spring morning and said that the GTV had to go. It wasn't altogether unexpected; we don't keep any of our long-term test cars indefinitely, much as we would sometimes like to, but quite apart from scotching my plans to complete the assessment with a combined business and holiday round trip to the Targa Florio and the Monaco Grand Prix, I had grown to love the Alfa dearly in my all-too-brief three months "possession". I dismissed my immediate thoughts of absconding with it for ever and rapidly arranged a few delightful days touring in Britain with an equally delightful companion before it was finally relinquished.

Motoring writers, myself included, are often unduly cynical about the cars that they drive — I suppose it is a side-effect of sampling so many different types, only a few of which can ever really appeal to any one person. It is not often that one appreciates a car so much that it seems worth positively striving to own one, even if it is outside the realistic price bracket — for me, the Alfa Romeo 1750GTV is that sort of car. It is not the ultimate (what is?), but it is a car that I have enjoyed more than any other I have used regularly.

David Thomas' spell with the car had been spoilt somewhat by an unexplained misfire at around 4,000 rpm. At first he had thought that it was due to a contact breaker or an out-of-adjustment carburettor that could easily be corrected in the routine serivce which was due (servicing intervals are 3,750 miles – 6000 km). Unfortunately it wasn't. It was taken back to Alfa Romeo's service depot in Edgware and they thought that the sparking plugs were the

cause. The four were replaced but the car still was not completely right. Otherwise David had enjoyed the car, though he expressed a preference for the 1750 *Berlina* on which he had previously carried out a long-term assessment, on the grounds of its quieter and better ride and driving position.

The mileometer was at 10,535 when the car was handed over to me. It has just been returned from a further check by Alfa Romeo GB's service department in another attempt to find the elusive cause of its misfire. This time incorrect seating of the choke valve was blamed, giving rise to over-richness. This was corrected and at the same time the valve clearances and the timing were adjusted, as were the contact points, and the front brakes were bled. Sad to relate, the misfiring had not been cured, though it was scarcely perceptible at town speeds, so 500 miles later it was returned to the service department again. Another check revealed a faulty plug insulator; a new set of Golden Lodge plugs was fitted and thereafter we had no more misfiring trouble.

I suppose the real reason that journeys in the Alfa are so satisfying is that it is tremendously rewarding to drive. The steering, another item that can come from more than one source of supply (ours was Burman recirculating ball), is positive nicely geared and with just the right amount of castor – though on the heavy side at parking speeds. The gear ratios are well spaced and the gearchange precise and deliberate – just right for the sort of fast downchanges that you thought only Fangio could manage so smoothly. The lever is spring-loaded towards the centre plane (like all Alfa gearboxes, 1st to 4th are in the 'conventional' positions, 5th is up to the right above reverse). As fifth is an overdrive, in towns one uses the gearbox as a four speeder, though fourth is not really happy below 30 mph. On fast winding roads, letting the twin-cam sing up towards its 5,700 maximum before changing into third, fourth or fifth, it is a delight. I enjoyed it too much to give much thought to economy, but in fact thoughtful use of fifth gear can make the difference between consumptions of 22 and 24 mpg.

Balance the Keynote

The car's roadholding is not of an exceptionally high order, but its handling is such that one can drive close to its limits without drama — slight understeer can be turned into oversteer in the dry, which is easily controlled thanks to the taut responsiveness of the steering. Balance is the keynote here. On an unexpectedly snowy Christmas Day I had to travel some 40 miles across country roads, thick with snow but polished by the infrequent passage of others. You can learn a lot about a car's balance, the smoothness of its controls and the soundness of its assembly, on a quiet drive all alone in the snow. The Alfa's traction could hardly be described as good but a smooth throttle linkage, snatch free transmission and sensitive steering made this gentle journey strangely enjoyable. In less extreme conditions, such as normally wet roads, straight-line wheelspin on accelerating from a standstill was extraordinarily easy to induce — in fact difficult to avoid. Our car was fitted with Pirelli Cinturatos, but we would suggest that the Michelin XAS fitted to our original 1750GTV test car, or perhaps Dunlop SP Sports, might be a better bet for this particular model.

The GTV's ride is normally adequate, if firm, and the damping highly effective, never reaching the bump stops even on hump-backs taken at speed. Curiously, it is short frequency bumps at low speed that catch it out, producing a sharp jolting accompanied by a good deal of steering kick-back. But the only aspect of the car's behaviour that shows a real disadvantage of the live axle arrangement over the independent rear suspension of most of its rivals, is the bad axle tramp that follows a high-speed take off from rest. The all-disc twin servo brakes are nicely progressive and very powerful; towards the end of the test they developed a tendency to pull slightly to one side. The handbrake, operating through drums machined into the rear disc centres, is also highly effective, though the lever ratchet is rather vague.

Starting the car was never a problem once one had mastered the technique. Unlike most Weber installations we found that this one responded best to a short burst of choke following a couple of pumps on the throttle. Immediately the engine had fired the choke could be returned home and the idle-speed increased for a minute or so with the hand throttle. After that it would tick-over evenly and quietly at 750 rpm and pull away cleanly. There used to be a recommendation in the handbook that the engine be run for five minutes before setting off — I confess that we rarely complied with this, though getting the gearbox oil warm obviously makes sense as it is very difficult to engage any gear but first when stone cold.

Cold starting procedure reminds me of winter mornings, defrosting and car heating in general, and this is one area where the Alfa is deficient, though the standard Triplex heated rear window is a godsend — no one should be without one. The heating system itself is powerful enough but of the all-or-nothing variety, despite the gradations of its controls. The windscreen demisters that double as interior ventilators are not really very satisfactory in the latter capacity; what is needed is an independent flow-through ventilation system. The quarter lights and rear side windows do

Opposite: YYR 126H basks in far western afternoon sun near Killary Harbour, in Connemara; though a fair distance from its driver's home, the Alfa made long journeys to such places the greatest of pleasures. Above: Tail up on a Westmorland bridge looking up towards Wrynose Pass during a rest from running-in; thanks to high overall gearing in top and a generous allowed cruising speed, a round trip starting in Surrey and touching parts of southern Scotland, the Lake District and the Peak District was made comfortably in a day

PERFORMANCE CHECK

Gear	mph		kph		rpm	
	R/T	Staff	R/T	Staff	R/T	Staff
Top (mean)	116	117	187	188	5,300	5,350
(best)	118	118	190	190	5,390	5,400
4th	104	98	168	158	6,000	5,700
3rd	77	73	124	118	6,000	5,700
2nd	52	51	84	82	6,000	5,700
1st	31	31	50	50	6,000	5,700

Standing ¼-mile, R/T: 18.0 sec 79 mph   **Standing kilometre, R/T:** 33.0 sec 98 mph
Staff: 17.5 sec 79 mph   **Staff:** 32.2 sec 98 mph

Acceleration, R/T:

R/T:	3.7	5.9	7.9	11.2	14.6	19.0	25.9	36.9
Staff:	3.1	5.0	7.1	10.1	13.3	18.2	23.6	34.4
Time in seconds 0—								
True speed mph	30	40	50	60	70	80	90	100
Indicated speed MPH, **R/T:**	32	43	53	64	74	85	96	106
Indicated speed MPH, **Staff:**	32	42	52	62	72	82	93	104

Speed range, Gear Ratios and Time in seconds

Mph	Top		4th		3rd		2nd		1st	
	R/T	Staff	R/T	Staff	R/T	Staff	R/T	Staff	R/T	Staff
	(3.24)		(4.10)		(4.65)		(8.16)		(13.52)	
10–30	—	—	—	—	7.2	—	4.5	3.4	2.8	2.3
20–40	—	—	9.2	—	5.6	5.5	3.7	3.7	—	—
30–50	12.8	12.4	7.9	7.7	5.7	5.5	4.0	3.7	—	—
40–60	11.9	11.9	8.0	7.5	5.8	5.5	—	—	—	—
50–70	12.9	11.6	9.1	8.1	6.4	6.1	—	—	—	—
60–80	15.6	13.1	10.1	8.9	—	—	—	—	—	—
70–90	19.4	14.6	12.1	10.1	—	—	—	—	—	—
80–100	22.1	20.4	16.4	—	—	—	—	—	—	—

Fuel Consumption
Overall mpg, R/T: 23.9 mpg (11.8 litres/100 km)
Staff: 23.3 mpg (12.1 litres/100 km)

NOTE: "R/T" denotes performance figures for the Alfa Romeo 1750 GTV tested in *AUTOCAR* of 26 September 1968.

Fifteen thousand on Alfa GTV . . .

open, but then the noise level at high speed is such that one cannot hear the little Courier Minimate radio we had fitted. Once a worn rubber sealing strip had been replaced, radio listening at 100 mph with all the windows closed was possible, even enjoyable.

Most of the other interior fittings work well. The traditional Italian matched speedometer and rev counter are positioned at just the right level and have their scales arranged so that the 'working' area is sensibly displayed at the top; a minor criticism here is that the green panel light cancels out the red 'prohibited' area on the rev counter at night. The dials on the centre console, which like the facia strip is finished with wood veneer, are angled towards the driver and while the far water temperature gauge is OK, the position of the rather vague fuel gauge is exactly wrong, being behind the natural place for one's hand on the wheel. The wipers (two speed) are not all that good, although they can cope with heavy rain at 100 mph. Being of the 'clap hands' type they do not need alteration for right-hand drive but that only means that both sides of the screen have a serious blind corner. The blades could usefully be $1\frac{1}{2}$ inches longer. Windscreen washing is electric, actuated by a floor mounted switch. which with greater pressure operates the wipers as well. This is a good system, but not a perfect one, as unfortunately it does not allow the wipers a few extra strokes to remove the drips after the washer jet has stopped. A couple of other irritations are the sharp lid on the console-mounted ashtray which is uncomfortably close to the gearlever and, more serious, the twist/push-in/up-and-down-to-dip lighting stalk on the steering column is within $\frac{1}{2}$ inch of the gearlever when in fifth, which can make flicking from dip to high beam, or indeed changing down on a fast main road run, awkward.

The new seats are terrific. I'm told that they are one of only three types that are approved by an eminent orthopaedic doctor; certainly they provide good support for the thighs and the small of the back, while the high backs to which the headrests lower flush, nicely enclose the shoulders. They recline to about 30 degrees by means of a large knob at the sides, while the headrests (which extend far enough to be head-*rests*, rather than just safety restraints, though the driver's one never worked) are moved up and down by thumb screws. The range of rearward adjustment is somewhat limited, though one can compensate for this to some extent by reclining the backs. This suited me, but anyone taller and bulkier might have to drive bow-legged to avoid the contact of knees and steering wheel. I personally used the seat right back to the stop beyond the last positive catch and found the driving position was almost perfect. The super thick-rimmed polished wood steering wheel is small and just nicely angled, while the long awkward-looking console-mounted gearlever falls immediately to hand. The only thing that spoils it are the pedals, which have thankfully been revised on the very latest model. The pendant throttle in ours was all right, but the floor-pivoted brake and clutch had to be pushed near the top to get any positive pressure – which with my size sevens meant taking my heels some inches clear of the floor and required an unnatural ankle movement. Since the clutch has a longish travel and is on the heavy side anyway, this can be tiresome in traffic.

There are two quite comfortable small seats at the rear but the GTV can be considered as no

The beautifully neat little twin-cam engine is always a pleasure to look at and never showed any oil leaks. The bulky twin servos – one of the more noticeable differences on the latest models – do not get in the way seriously. Space in the boot – here shown with the sensible rubber moulding rolled back – is just right for two people's touring luggage. A pleasing arrangement is that of the spring-loaded boot lid which opens itself when the lock release in the left hand door-jamb is pulled

more than an emergency four-seater for adults, as though there is adequate headroom (the headlining is cut away for the purpose) there is nowhere for legs with the front seats back in a comfortable position. Far better to leave your not-so-close friends at home and use the back for luggage. The boot, opened via a locking handle in the nearside door pillar (handy if, like the Italians you drive from that side, not so good for us) is shallow, though it goes back a fair way and can contain a large suitcase and several other sizeable bags. The boot sides are single skinned, and with the spare wheel mounted beneath the floor there is nothing to prevent a heavy object denting the outside bodywork from the inside – as unfortunately happened when carrying our test gear fifth wheel. Otherwise the paintwork weathered constant outside garaging quite well, though its grey colour would not have been my choice – it's the sort of colour that always looks dirty even when it is clean. The brightwork, despite regular cleaning, survived less well, with rust appearing round the bumper rivets, side window finishing strips and the doors.

What type of driver is likely to buy and enjoy the 1750 GTV? Well certainly not a lazy one. It is a car that needs to be thoughtfully driven. If *you* are not working well, tired after a long day or irritable, it can be really horrid. On the other hand, driven with care and enthusiasm, it repays you handsomely. I suppose one should also add not a poor one, for at a price of £2,450 it is not exactly cheap.

I had always thought of rugged blood-and-thunder sports cars as for me – not something with the almost feminine grace of this neat Bertone coupé. My friends think I've gone soft – but then they haven't spent three months with a GTV.

Ray Hutton □

AS you will see on reading this article, colleague Ray Hutton deals very fully with the few faults and many virtues of YYR 126H. I was lucky enough to have custody of the car for the first 7,000-odd miles, one of the happiest 7,000 miles of my motoring experience. There are few points I can add to the Sports Editor's story other than ones mainly of personal feeling.

Above: Space in the back looks limited, but by very cleverly dishing the seats deeply, Alfa ensure that two average-sized adults can be carried – with knees bent – surprisingly comfortably. The obviously carefully designed seats suit some drivers better than others; the "rack" with its double row of teeth which forms the stem of the head restraint is made of a laminated wood material. Handle for raising it is on door side. Most of what one needs to know is clearly visible through the handsome wood-rimmed steering wheel, but gauges on the centre console can be obscured by the gearlever when in 5th

The first feeling was of gratitude for the fact that you are allowed to run-in 1750 Alfa engines at up to 71 mph in top which, provided one applied normal running-in practice conscientiously, still meant that a long day trip from my Surrey home to Cumberland and the Lake and Peak Districts via a bit of southern Scotland was a good way to start up acquaintance. Initial breaking-in was thus easily knocked over between Friday (197 miles on the clock) and Monday (1,244 miles).

I was never so happy about the new seats as Ray Hutton is. They may be frightfully orthopaedic, but I found them a little on the hard side, particularly around the small of the back, where there is a little too *much* support. It was nice to find that one could retract the headrests out of the way, although the winding arrangement was always rather heavy and awkward. But after the previous Veloce-bodied Alfa I had run on long-term test – the 1300GT – it was delightful to find so many of the minor annoyances eliminated.

Door keeps had been incorporated; it is funny how maddening a door that won't stay open can be. The improvement was most welcome. I found that the new twin-servo'd braking system had not the perfect front-rear balance of the 1300 GT (too much on the back), but the reduction in pedal effort was all to the car's credit in most circumstances; experience with other examples now convinces me that this was peculiar to "our" car. And of course the superb all quartz-halogen four-headlamp system was marvellous.

During my time with the car it went to many places – Wales to play with all-terrain vehicles, several racing circuits to cover Formula 5000 races, the West Country for a delightful summer weekend at Dartmouth with a long return eastward via Snetterton in Norfolk, and, most memorable of all, to Dublin and Connemara for a week's holiday. There through the kindness of a friend, I was able briefly to sample an MGB immediately after driving the Alfa. I had always thought the Alfa's only serious failing was its ride – not nearly good enough for the modern Grand Touring car that it otherwise is; it was still a little of a surprise to find that the MGB's ride was most noticeably better, and not at the expense of handling either.

But overall I felt and still feel as my colleague does. The car did nothing untoward during my tenancy, and gave me nothing but the very greatest satisfaction. It is a car in which a sensitive driver, perhaps a little jaded by too much dreary traffic driving, rediscovers the pure pleasure of motoring. And unlike a host of other cars which are pleasant to drive, the Bertone body is always, from all sides, a delight to look at. No car is perfect, but despite any faults, that GT Veloce approaches nearer to practical ideals than many others. I could most cheerfully live with it. **Michael Scarlett** □

COST AND LIFE OF EXPENDABLE ITEMS

Item	Life in Miles	Cost per 10,000 Miles (£)
One gallon of 5-star fuel, average cost today 36p	23·3	154·50
One pint of top-up oil, average cost today 17p	1,500	1·13
Front disc brake pads (set of 4)	35,000	3·59
Rear disc brake pads (set of 4)	35,000	2·89
Tyres (front pair)	20,000	10·22
Tyres (rear pair)	17,500	11·70
Service (main interval and actual costs incurred)	5,000	27·20
Total		**211·23**
Approx standing charges per year		
Depreciation		700·00
Insurance		49·85
Tax		25·00
Total		**986·18**
Approx cost per mile = 9·86p		

LARRY GRIFFIN PHOTOS

ALFA ROMEO 2000 GTV

Bigger engine and detail improvements for an old friend

OVER THE YEARS Alfa Romeos have been a favorite of R&T. Obviously designed for sporting drivers, they also have stood out for their civilized nature; Alfas already had supple springing, radial tires, windup windows and easy-folding roadster tops when most other sports cars rode hard, had crude side curtains and guaranteed two rain-soaked people if a storm ever broke out suddenly when the top was folded. But Alfa Romeo of Milano, a government-owned Italian company, is not what you'd call a dynamic company. It moves very slowly, sometimes taking many years to get a new model into production after showing it at an automobile show; the prestige V-8 Montreal coupe, just now becoming available in Europe after being shown in 1967, and the current Spider which was put into production in 1966 after being shown in 1961, are examples of the company's leisurely way of doing things as is the fact that Alfa has missed two model years in the U.S. market since 1967.

Likewise, the 2000 GTV *(Gran Turismo Veloce)* is an updated version of a very old model. The Bertone-designed coupe was first sold in 1964 as the Giulia Sprint GT with a 1570-cc engine, got an engine stretch to 1779 cc and the 1750 name in 1969, and now comes to what must be the final stretch of an engine that began at 1290 cc, becoming the 2000 with 1962 cc. There's not a single identifying badge outside to identify it as such; the wheels and grille are restyled, and those who look inside

will find 2000 in chrome on the dash, but in general only those who know Alfas will notice the difference.

The added displacement for the all-aluminum twincam engine was achieved by increasing the bore from 80 to 84 mm. U.S. models use the Alfa-Spica fuel injection that has distinguished U.S. from home-market 1750s and helped Alfa to meet our emission regulations while retaining full power output, and the 9.0:1 compression ratio of the European version has been kept despite calibration changes that enable the unit to run on 91-octane fuel. The 2000 engine develops 129 bhp net at 5800 rpm, about 15 bhp more than the 1750's, and similarly its maximum torque is up by about 16 lb-ft. Other changes for the GTV include a revised instrument panel and improved ventilation, redesigned upholstery and the availability of a limited-slip differential. Selling only the 2000 line in the U.S., Alfa offers a roadster (Spider) and sedan (Berlina) also.

We chose the 2000 GTV for our full road test, having tested the 1750 Spider and Berlina when they were new and not having done a full test on the GTV since 1967. But the bigger engine is the main part of the story. It sounds very much the same as always—not a particularly quiet engine, but a virile-sounding one with a rather raucous exhaust note. A familiar rattly resonance in the exhaust system at low speed and wide throttle opening is still there, but in general the sounds are music to an enthusiast's ear. The big difference is in low- and middle-

range torque, not ultimate performance. Step on the accelerator of the 2000 at a given speed in a given gear, but especially at the low end of the rev range, and you'll get a more eager response than in the 1750. This makes it an easier car to drive and certainly a more responsive one—effectively a quicker car in most traffic situations. But for all-out performance, such as our standing-start acceleration tests, there's not much difference between a 2000 and a 1750; our 0-60 mph and standing quarter-mile times for the 2000 were 9.6 and 17.6 sec, vs 9.9 and 17.3 for the 1750 Spider which weighs almost exactly the same. These differences are within normal variations for a single model. That's because the 2000 engine has a lower rev limit— 5800 vs 6300 rpm—than the 1750. It was all too obvious that performance times could have been improved by going farther in each gear, but we always observe the manufacturer's maximum engine speed unless there's good reason to do otherwise.

At cruising speeds of U.S. variety there are no bothersome resonances; 5th gear gives mechanically relaxed running on freeways. We're also happy to report that there are no driveability problems. The engine starts and runs well when cold, though a manual throttle must be juggled to maintain a working idle speed during warmup, and there is none of the unsatisfactory low-speed throttle response so common in today's engines even though the spark is highly retarded in that range.

Gearing for U.S. 2000s is the same as for their 1750 predeces-sors; though 5th gear is technically an overdrive, applied to the 4.56:1 final drive it is in reality a normal top gear giving 3600 rpm at 70 mph. The 5-speed gearbox is as good as ever, with light and precise action and powerful synchromesh, but continues to suffer a minor fault that could be solved by minor redesign: the shift from neutral to 1st gear is not synchronized because the synchro doesn't work in that direction. So to avoid

COMPARISON DATA

	Alfa Romeo 2000 GTV	Lotus Elan +2S	Volvo 1800E
List price	$5299	$6597	$5060
Curb weight, lb	2325	1975	2540
0-60 mph, sec	9.6	9.8	11.3
Standing ¼ mi, sec	17.6	17.6	18.2
Stopping distance from 80 mph, ft	287	239	299
Brake fade, 6 stops from 60 mph, %	nil	20	50
Cornering capability, g	0.715	0.757	0.660
Interior noise @ 70 mph, dBA	78	79	77
Fuel economy, mpg	23.8	20.8	22.5

ALFA ROMEO 2000 GTV

grinding gears on this shift the driver needs to first make at least a little jab toward one of the other gears—2nd is the most convenient—to stop the gears turning.

The Alfa's cornering power is good but not top-notch as sports cars go; of course, getting more cornering power is about as simple as switching to larger tires, and provided there's enough clearance for them under the sheet metal (we didn't check) larger tires—say 175-14—would be a good thing for the GTV as they would not only improve its cornering power but correct some of its great speedometer error.

In other matters of road behavior the 2000 is a mixture of first-class and mediocre. The steering, an Alfa strong point over the years, is still great—precise and light, giving a most intimate feeling of contact with the road through responsive radial tires. In on-the-road handling maneuvers the car's response is close to neutral and gives one a great sense of control, and despite the live rear axle bumps in the road don't upset the car's aplomb very much. However, Alfa's seemingly dogged devotion to their live axle arrangement (even the snooty Montreal has it) extracts its penalties. There's limited space for the axle to move up and down in a low car like this, so suspension movement has to be curtailed in a way not needed with independent suspension. This shows up in the GTV's ride, which is unduly bouncy for a GT car of its class despite the nice way its tires and bushings soak up small irregularities like lane-divider dots, and a really large bump in the road is going to upset the GTV's roadholding before it will a more softly sprung car.

All Alfas sold in the U.S. have 4-wheel, vacuum-assisted disc brakes, and for years they have been the kind of brakes a fast driver can trust. They remain unchanged in the GTV and are still good brakes, but evolving standards of performance find them not as outstanding as they seemed a few years ago. They do pull the GTV down from highway speeds in short distances,

but in our opinion the vacuum assist is far too eager to help. Only 13 lb pedal force is needed to achieve a 0.5g stop—we consider 30-35 lb to be ideal—and as a result it's all too easy to lock up the front wheels in a hard stop. Thus the GTV wants to slide straight ahead, and to have any steering control during a stop the driver must keep enough cool to pump the pedal.

Outside, as we mentioned, there's little to distinguish the 2000 GTV from any of its predecessors back to 1964, and the Bertone lines are still handsome. Inside, the instrument panel is nicely redesigned with two minor gauges that used to be down in the center console moved into the main cluster, and new fresh-air vents at either end of it deliver fresh air in good quantity to rectify a long-standing fault of the series. The speedometer, however, is illogically marked.

Other long-standing faults of the GTV's people accommodations are not corrected. The driver position, for instance, is something not a single staff member finds comfortable, and the trouble stems from the relation of seat, steering wheel and pedals as we have often pointed out. The glaring fault—at least from the American point of view, since Italians apparently like it—is the extremely high accelerator pedal which makes double-clutch downshifts awkward and leaves the poor accelerator foot quite unsupported and uncomfortable on long runs at steady speed. The front seats themselves, with handsome new upholstery, were right for most people who drove the car, but one staff member found the protruding lumbar support area excessive and all had difficulty adjusting the seatbacks as the lap belt passes right across the adjustment knob. Speaking of belts, there are a couple of curiosities. One is that with the federally required belt warning system Alfa has done a nasty job of wiring, bringing the right-seat wire right through the rear floor carpet into plain view. The other is that there are no belts for the occasional rear seats, a fact which explains the 2-passenger capacity given in the owner's manual for what is actually a 2+2 car. We think the children also deserve belts—at least lap belts.

The GTV's controls fall behind the best current practice. There are two stalks on the left side of the steering column, one for directionals and the other for main lighting, and it's easy to grab the wrong one. The wiper control is a toggle switch 'way down on the center console; heating-defrosting controls are a long reach for a belted driver; and there's still that cranked-back gearshift lever that we've never liked. The driver, already feeling somewhat buried with the window sills so high, finds the top of the rear window so low that long-distance vision to the rear is restricted. And wind noise around the front-door ventwings, always a GTV fault, remains one.

And so it goes. The GTV is a good 1964 design, overdue for a change. Don't get us wrong; the 2000 GTV is still a good car and a capable performer, and with all those years of production behind it it should be a reliable machine. And, as the Comparison Data box shows, directly competing 2+2 GTs are not formidable enough to embarrass it. Its price puts it well below the expense of a Porsche 911T or Lotus +2S, the Datsun 240Z isn't a 2+2, etc. However, there are new and better things coming from Alfa in the future and the reader should take a look at page 71.

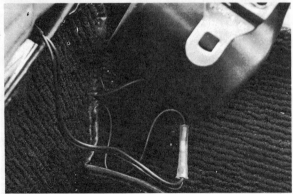

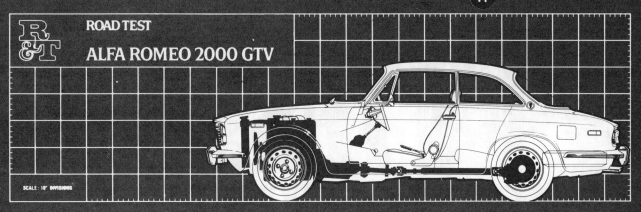

ROAD TEST
ALFA ROMEO 2000 GTV

SCALE: 10" DIVISIONS

PRICE

List price, East/Gulf Coast .. $5249
List price, West Coast......... $5299
Price as tested,
West Coast $5464
Price as tested includes standard
equipment (4-wheel disc brakes,
fuel injection, 5-speed transmission), limited-slip diff ($115),
dealer prep ($50)

IMPORTER

Alfa-Romeo, Inc.
250 Sylvan Ave.,
Englewood Cliffs, New Jersey 08732

ENGINE

Type .... dohc inline 4
Bore x stroke, mm ..... 84.0 x 88.5
Equivalent in........... 3.31 x 3.48
Displacement, cc/cu in.. 1962/120
Compression ratio 9.0:1
Bhp @ rpm, net .... 129 @ 5800
Equivalent mph 112
Torque @ rpm; lb-ft. 132 @ 3500
Equivalent mph 68
Fuel Injection........ Alfa-Spica mech.
Fuel requirement .... regular, 91-oct
Emissions, gram/mile:
Hydrocarbons 2.00
Carbon Monoxide 16.2
Nitrogen Oxides 1.53

DRIVE TRAIN

Transmission .... 5-speed manual
Gear ratios: (0.79) 3.60:1
4th (1.00) 4.56:1
3rd (1.35) 6.16:1
2nd (1.99).............. 9.07:1
1st (3.30) 15.05:1
Final drive ratio.................. 4.56:1

CHASSIS & BODY

Layout ....front engine/rear drive
Body/frame .... unit steel
Brake system ....10.7-in disc front,
10.5-in. disc rear;
vacuum assisted
Swept area, sq in 397
Wheels ....steel disc 14 x 5½
Tires ..... Pirelli Cinturato 165HR-14
Steering type.....recirculating ball
Turns, lock-to-lock 3.8
Turning circle, ft................. 34.8
Front suspension: unequal-length
A-arms, coil springs, tube shocks,
anti-roll bar
Rear suspension: live axle on trailing
arms & upper transverse-trailing
link; coil springs, tube shocks,
anti-roll bar

ACCOMMODATION

Seating capacity, persons ...... 2+2
Seat width, front/rear 19.0/19.0
Head room, front/rear .. 36.0/34.0
Seat back adjustment, degrees .. 50

INSTRUMENTATION

Instruments: 140-mph speedometer,
8000-rpm tachometer, 99,999
odometer, 999.9 trip odometer,
oil pressure, coolant temperature,
fuel level
Warning lights: brake system, alternator, oil level, fuel pressure,
throttle, heater blower, lights on,
high beam, directionals, seat belts

MAINTENANCE

Service intervals, mi:
Oil change......................... 3000
Filter change 3000
Chassis lube 3000
Minor tuneup 6000
Major tuneup 12,000
Warranty, mo/mi........6/unlimited

GENERAL

Curb weight, lb 2325
Test weight 2660
Weight distribution (with driver),
front/rear, % 56/44
Wheelbase, in 92.5
Track, front/rear 52.1/50.1
Length 161.4
Width 62.2
Height 51.8
Ground clearance.................... 5.0
Overhang, front/rear 29.4/39.5
Usable trunk space, cu ft 8.7
Fuel capacity, U.S. gal 14.0

CALCULATED DATA

Lb/bhp (test weight) 20.6
Mph/1000 rpm (5th gear) 19.0
Engine revs/mi (60 mph)..... 3550
Piston travel, ft/mi 2060
R&T steering index 1.32
Brake swept area, sq in/ton .. 299

RELIABILITY

From R&T Owner Surveys the average
number of trouble areas for all models surveyed is 11. As owners of
earlier-model Alfa Romeos reported
11 trouble areas, we expect the
reliability of the Alfa Romeo 2000
GTV to be average.

ACCELERATION

Time to distance, sec:
0-100 ft..........................4.5
0-500 ft..........................9.8
0-1320 ft (¼ mi) 17.6
Speed at end of ¼-mi, mph...80.5
Time to speed, sec:
0-30 mph 3.3
0-40 mph 4.7
0-50 mph 6.8
0-60 mph 9.6
0-70 mph 13.1
0-80 mph 17.3
0-90 mph 23.3

SPEEDS IN GEARS

5th gear (5800 rpm) 110
4th (5800)........................ 89
3rd (5800)........................ 66
2nd (5800) 45
1st (5800) 27

SPEEDOMETER ERROR

30 mph indicated is actually .. 27.0
50 mph 46.0
60 mph 55.0
70 mph 65.0
80 mph 74.0
Odometer, 10.0 mi 9.5

BRAKES

Minimum stopping distances, ft:
From 60 mph 150
From 80 mph 287
Control in panic stop .... good
Pedal effort for 0.5g stop, lb .. 13
Fade: percent increase in pedal effort
to maintain 0.5g deceleration in
6 stops from 60 mph .... nil
Parking: hold 30% grade? .... yes
Overall brake rating .... good

HANDLING

Speed on 100-ft radius, mph .. 32.7
Lateral acceleration, g 0.715

FUEL ECONOMY

Normal driving, mpg.............. 23.8
Cruising range, mi (1-gal res.) .. 309

INTERIOR NOISE

All noise readings in dBA:
Idle in neutral...................... 56
Maximum, 1st gear.............. 85
Constant 30 mph (4th gear) ... 68
50 mph (5th gear) 71
70 mph 78
90 mph 86

ACCELERATION

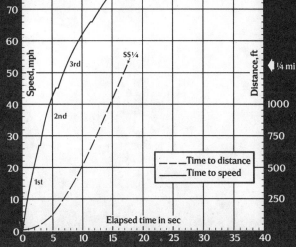

Legend:
- - - Time to distance
——— Time to speed

Elapsed time in sec

AUTO TEST
ALFA ROMEO 2000 GTV

Above and below: The GTV shape remains the same, with no more than a few detail changes to distinguish the 2000. The front grille has been restyled, and there is a single "2000" badge

Same style, more punch

AT-A-GLANCE: Larger engine gives classic coupé much better performance, at some cost in fuel consumption. Steering and handling as nice as ever; very comfortable car for medium-sized drivers, but revised interior not a great improvement.

In a world which usually dictates that the more stylish an object, the more frequently it needs changing, the Alfa GTV has been a refreshing exception. It has been much changed through the years, but mostly under the skin. The most recent advance—the boring-out of the engine to give a capacity of well-nigh two litres—was rather slow coming to Britain owing to difficulties at the Milan factory, but supplies are now flowing.

The 2000 engine replaces the 1750 in all three of the top-line Alfa models: Berlina, GTV and Spider. The 1750 is no longer available for the time being, although it will reappear in this country in due course as the power unit of the new Alfetta saloon. The 2000 differs only in its bore, increased by 4mm to 84mm, giving a swept volume of 1,962 c.c. and lifting the power output to 131 bhp (DIN).

Although our test car had covered only 3,000 miles at the time of our test—rather soon for an Alfa to be giving of its best—it showed convincing improvements over

the 1750GTV which we tested in 1968. Comparisons are apt because Alfa have chosen not to change the gearing for the larger engine: final drive remains at 4.1 to 1 and the tyre size is still 165-14 in., giving an overall gearing of 21.9 mph per 1,000 rpm in the overdrive fifth gear.

This choice of gearing turns out to be a good one, with the car achieving its maximum speed almost exactly at the 5,500 rpm power peak. The Alfa is happy to keep going at its 120 mph as long as the fuel lasts, although 100 mph is more relaxed.

The red line is set at 5,700 rpm, a very modest figure for a race-bred twin-cam engine, but Alfa engineers regard this as a continuous maximum, and countenance 6,000 rpm for quick overtaking: our maxima in the intermediate gears therefore take this as the limit. In normal use, the gears prove admirably spaced, except for very fast drivers who may find something of a gap between second and third on minor roads.

Right: The similarity continues under the bonnet; the 2000 engine is no more than the familiar 1750 twin-cam unit with the bore enlarged to 84 mm. Note the twin vacuum servo for the split-circuit brake system. Most items are easily accessible

ALFA ROMEO 2000GTV (1,962 c.c.)

ACCELERATION

SPEED MPH TRUE INDICATED	TIME IN SECS
30	3.1
32	
40	4.7
41	
50	6.7
51	
60	9.2
60	
70	12.1
70	
80	16.2
80	
90	20.9
90	
100	27.7
100	
110	42.1
110	
120	—
120	

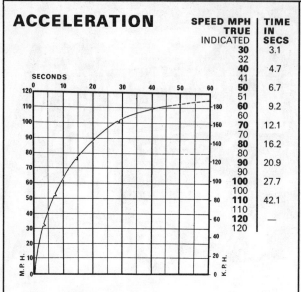

GEAR RATIOS AND TIME IN SEC

mph	Top (3.24)	4th (4.10)	3rd (4.65)
10–30	—	—	6.6
20–40	—	8.6	5.5
30–50	12.1	6.6	4.7
40–60	9.6	6.3	4.8
50–70	9.8	7.2	5.4
60–80	11.6	7.8	—
70–90	14.3	9.2	—
80–100	17.9	12.7	—

Standing ¼-mile
16.4 sec 81 mph

Standing Kilometre
30.2 sec 101 mph
Test distance
1,025 miles
Mileage recorder
accurate

PERFORMANCE

MAXIMUM SPEEDS

Gear	mph	kph	rpm
Top (mean)	120	193	5,480
(best)	122	196	5,570
4th	104	168	6,000
3rd	77	124	6,000
2nd	52	84	6,000
1st	31	50	6,000

BRAKES

FADE
(from 70 mph in neutral)
Pedal load for 0.5g stops in lb

1	35–20	6	30–20
2	35–20	7	30–25
3	30–20	8	30–25
4	30–20	9	30–25
5	30–20	10	30

RESPONSE
(from 30 mph in neutral)

Load	g	Distance
20 lb	0.30	100 ft
40 lb	0.60	50 ft
60 lb	0.75	40 ft
80 lb	0.95	32 ft
100 lb	1.00	30.1 ft
Handbrake	0.35	86 ft
Max. Gradient 1 in 3		

CLUTCH
Pedal 42 lb and 5 in. travel

COMPARISONS

MAXIMUM SPEED MPH

Datsun 240Z	(£2,311)	12
Lotus Plus 2S 130	(£2,573)	12
Alfa Romeo 2000GTV (£2,433)		**12**
BMW 2002Tii	(£2,349)	11
Fiat 124 Coupé 1600	(£1,739)	10

0–60 MPH, SEC

Lotus Plus 2S 130	7
Datsun 240Z	8
BMW 2002 Tii	8
Alfa Romeo 2000GTV	**9**
Fiat 124 Coupé 1600	10

STANDING ¼-MILE, SEC

Lotus Plus 2S 130	15
Datsun 240Z	15
Alfa Romeo 2000GTV	**16**
BMW 2002 Tii	16
Fiat 124 Coupé 1600	17

OVERALL MPG

BMW 2002 Tii	25
Fiat 124 Coupé 1600	23
Lotus Plus 2S 130	23
Datsun 240Z	21
Alfa Romeo 2000GTV	**21**

GEARING
(with 165-14 in. tyres)

Top	21.9 mph per 1,000 rp
4th	17.3 mph per 1,000 rp
3rd	12.8 mph per 1,000 rp
2nd	8.7 mph per 1,000 rp
1st	5.2 mph per 1,000 rp

CONSUMPTION

FUEL
(At constant speed—mpg)

30 mph	37
40 mph	35
50 mph	32
60 mph	29
70 mph	26
80 mph	24
90 mph	21
100 mph	19

Typical mpg
23 (12.3 litres/100 kr
Calculated (DIN) mpg
24.4 (11.6 litres/100 kr
Overall mpg . 21.1 (13.4 litres/100 kr
Grade of fuel
Premium, 4-star (min. 98 RN

OIL
Consumption (SAE 20W/50)
2,000 miles/p

TEST CONDITIONS:
Weather: Showers Wind: 10–20 mph.
Temperature: 13 deg. C. (56 deg. F).
Barometer: 29.5 in. hg. Humidity: 60
cent.
Surfaces: dry concrete and asphalt.

WEIGHT:
Kerb Weight 20.6 cwt (2,301
1,044 kg) (with oil, water and half
fuel tank).
Distribution, per cent F, 56.3; R, 43.7
Laden as tested: 24.9 cwt (2,781
1,262 kg).

TURNING CIRCLES:
Between kerbs L, 39 ft 0 in.; R, 35 ft 11
Between walls L, 40 ft 6 in.; R, 37 ft 5
Steering wheel turns, lock to lock 3.6
Figures taken at 3,000 miles by our ow
staff at the Motor Industry Resear
Association proving ground at Nuneate

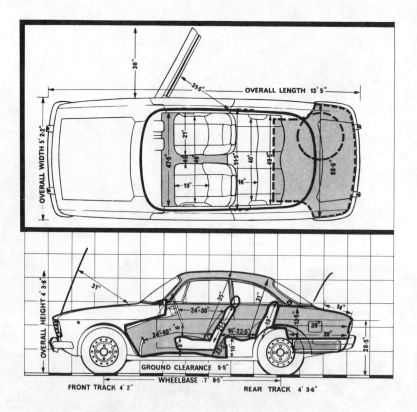

OVERALL LENGTH 13' 5"
OVERALL WIDTH 5' 2²"
OVERALL HEIGHT 4' 3-6"
GROUND CLEARANCE 5-5"
WHEELBASE 7' 8-5"
FRONT TRACK 4' 2"
REAR TRACK 4' 3-6"

STANDARD GARAGE 16 ft × 8 ft 6 in.

PECIFICATION

RONT ENGINE,
EAR-WHEEL DRIVE

NGINE

ylinders	4, in line
ain bearings	5
ooling system	Water; pump, fan and thermostat
ore	84.0 mm (3.31 in.)
roke	88.5 mm (3.48 in.)
isplacement	1,962 c.c. (120.0 cu. in.)
alve gear	Twin overhead camshaft, direct-acting, chain-driven
ompression ratio	9.5-to-1 Min. octane rating: 98 RM
arburettors	2 Solex C40 DDH5
uel pump	Fispa mechanical
il filter	Full flow, replaceable element
ax. power	131 bhp (DIN) at 5,500 rpm
ax. torque	134 lb.ft (DIN) at 3,000 rpm

RANSMISSION

utch	Diaphragm-spring, hydraulic operation
earbox	5-speed, all-synchromesh
ear ratios	Top 0.79
	Fourth 1.00
	Third 1.35
	Second 1.99
	First 3.30
	Reverse 3.01
nal drive	Hypoid bevel, ratio 4.1-to-1, 25 per cent limited-slip

HASSIS and BODY

onstruction	Integral, with steel body

USPENSION

ont	Independent: double wishbones, coil springs, telescopic dampers, anti-roll bar
ear	Live axle, trailing arms, A-bracket, coil springs, telescopic dampers, anti-roll bar

TEERING

pe	Cam and peg or recirculating-ball
heel dia.	15.0 in.

RAKES

ake and type	ATE, disc front and rear, split circuit
rvo	Dual Bonaldi vacuum
mensions	F 10.7 in. dia.
	R 10.5 in. dia.
wept area	F 238.4 sq. in., R 158.4 sq. in.
	Total 396.8 sq. in. (319 sq. in./ton laden)

HEELS

pe	Ventilated pressed steel disc, 4-stud fixing, 5.5 in. wide rim
res—make	Michelin
—type	XAS radial ply tubed
—size	165-14 in.

QUIPMENT

attery	12 Volt 50 Ah.
ternator	Bosch 35 amp a.c.
eadlamps	Carello tungsten-halogen, 220/110 watt (total)
eversing lamp	Standard
ectric fuses	10
reen wipers	2-speed
reen washer	Standard, electric
erior heater	Standard, water valve type
ated backlight	Standard (UK specification)
fety belts	Standard
erior trim	Cloth seats, pvc headlining
oor covering	Carpet
ck	Screw pillar
cking points	Two each side, under sills
ndscreen	Laminated
derbody	
protection	Bitumastic overall

AINTENANCE

el tank	11.6 Imp. gallons (53 litres)
oling system	16.8 pints (including heater)
gine sump	11.9 pints (6.7 litres) SAE 20W/50 Change oil every 3,750 miles. Change filter element every 3,750 miles
arbox	3.2 pints SAE 90EP. Change oil every 12,000 miles
nal drive	2.5 pints SAE 90EP. Change oil every 12,000 miles
ease	1 point every 7,500 miles
re pressures	F 22; R 26 psi (all conditions)
ax. payload	706 lb (320 kg)

RFORMANCE DATA

o gear mph per 1,000 rpm	21.9
ean piston speed at max. power	3,187 ft/min.
p per ton laden	105 (DIN)

AUTOTEST
ALFA ROMEO
2000GTV...

While the maximum speed may be academic in poor 70-limited Britain, the improved acceleration will be worth a good deal to the enthusiastic driver. The 2000 leaves the 1750 well behind all the way from a standing start, with 30 mph coming up in 3.1 instead of 3.7 sec. The start is helped a good deal by the limited-slip differential which is part of the British specification, but even so an over-enthusiastic start can result in too much wheelspin and too little forward movement.

The 2000 gains all the way down the line, with 60 mph coming up in a respectable 9.2 sec compared with the 11.2 of the 1750. The 100 mph mark comes up in well under the half-minute (compare 36.9 sec for the 1750), and it is possible to achieve a sensible time to 110 mph even though the rate of acceleration falls off once the car is in fifth gear. Over a second and a half is carved off the quarter-mile time, and nearly three seconds from the kilometre.

Further comparison shows that there are gains in every gear at every speed; the 2000 engine endows the GTV with greater flexibility as well as better performance. In the Alfa, though, flexibility is a relative term. The car will potter along gently in high gear on a very light throttle with no trouble, but if the driver asks it to pull away strongly from less than 1,500 rpm a violent judder sets in and the only solution is to change down; we could only record figures from 20 mph in fourth gear and 30 mph in fifth.

One area in which the 2000 suffers when compared with the 1750 is in fuel consumption. The 1750 was quite remarkably economical at low, steady speeds, bettering 60 mpg at 30 mph; by contrast, the 2000 does not even achieve 40 mpg at that speed. In practice, however, no Alfa is subjected to much in the way of economy driving and the 2000 managed 21.1 mpg overall compared with 23.9 mpg for its predecessor.

Alfa somehow manage to endow all their cars with superb steering despite rejecting rack-and-pinion (at least, until the Alfetta) and using worm and roller or recirculating-ball systems as production alternatives, just as they use Solex or Dellorto carburettors without discrimination. The fact remains that Alfa steering is always precise and responsive, and the 2000GTV is no exception.

To a very large extent, this is due to clever chassis engineering. The GTV carries a good deal of its weight over the front end—nearly 57 per cent—and the steering has to be fairly low-geared if it is not to be impossibly heavy. It is a tribute to the skill with which it is done that many Alfa drivers would probably dismiss an allegation of low-geared steering as nonsense; yet there is no getting away from the GTV's 3.6 turns of the wheel between extremes of a far from distinguished 37 ft turning circle.

Alfa get over the problem by keeping the GTV's handling very close to neutral, with a fair degree of castor to provide sufficient natural self-centring. On the open road, the results are excellent and the Alfa is one of the most "swervable" cars there is, but it is much harder work to drive slowly around town.

The 2000GTV's handling is brought even closer to racing- rather than rally-car characteristics by the fitting of a limited-slip differential. The car goes exactly where it is put in any corner, and applying more or less power hardly changes the line at all, although up to a point the GTV feels more stable the more power is applied. Beyond this point, all Alfas used to lift and spin the inside rear wheel—though much later in the GTVs than in the saloons. With the limited-slip differential coming into play traction is much improved, and far more power can be used much earlier. This permits a higher cornering speed but

CONTINUED ON PAGE 81

New instrument cluster inserts minor dials and warning lights between speedometer and rev counter. Choke and hand throttle controls are blended into the lower edge of the facia to the right of the steering column. The floor-hinged pedals are not easy to use without practice

ALFA ROMEO **ALFA GTV**

TOP LEFT: Small boot takes surprising amount of luggage — carpet is removed in this shot to show floor layout. TOP: Boot flap/lock is in passenger's door pillar. LEFT: Huge boosters crowd under-bonnet area. BELOW LEFT: Gauges are poorly designed. BELOW: Pedals are badly set-up.

2000

IF THE NAME Alfa Romeo GTV on a road test suggests you are about to indulge in a delightful series of lyrical phrases that transform the magical motoring moments achieved in an Italian thoroughbred into poetic prose before your very eyes — be disappointed!

My memories of more than 1000 Alfa roaming miles are not filled with the heart-rending sound of throbbing exhausts making music in my ears, as I swiftly shift slots to avert certain disaster on a slippery series of ess-bends. I have no recall of carving my way across the top of a sun-touched ridge in the crisp dawn air, making ever-so-gentle corrections on the small wood-rimmed circle beneath my fingertips. And I don't look longingly back at the thought of quad headlights stabbing a yellow path to glory in a winding traverse into the black hell of a steep canyon road.

I'll tell you what I do remember though . . .

I remember fighting understeer on turn after turn, struggling at the slippery tiller, sweating from the brow, trying desperately to equal point-to-point times I'd set easily the previous week over the same course in a Holden V8.

I remember taking more grip on the wheel than was necessary to get around a fast sweeper, just to stay fixed in the seat, and I will never forget the dread feeling of a full front-end "lose" at low speed in a tight corner unexpectedly washed by a water splash.

I remember being desperately tired, fighting for sleep with the passenger's seat laid back while a very capable pilot tried to make the ride smooth enough — and failed.

I remember the constant pitch of the suspension on a bumpy bitumen road, and the seat springs phasing-into the suspension for a full harmonic effect. And I can't forget my back aching two hours later when I climbed gladly from the driver's seat.

My lasting impression of the Alfa Romeo GTV is of a totally uncompromising car built to suit the narrow demands of one country's motorists by an arrogant design team with a total disregard for the motoring demands of the rest of the world.

If you like to pull-on your stringbacks and slip down to the footpath restaurant and park where you can look at the chicks and see your car at the same time, you'll love the Alfa.

If you can stand thrashing away at a long winding section of road in a car with average cornering capabilities, but below-average comfort standards, you will love the Alfa.

And if you just like the name Alfa, you will love the Alfa 2000 GTV.

The Alfa Romeo 2000 GTV is a very good 1964 grand touring car — produced in 1972. In the old days, it surprised the world with (for then) revolutionary handling, with good ride, sensitive steering isolated from road shock and a remarkably clean, crisp, body style.

Today it is the same — as it was in

ALFA GTV 2000

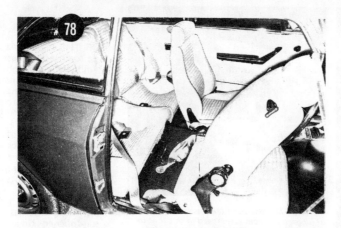

1964. Certainly it has more power than its 1600cc great grand-pappy and it has a few more refinements and creature comforts. But only a few more.

Most of the bad points of that original car remain, and even some of the good points have gone bad.

Take the gearbox. The five-shifter was the delight of the sporting afficianado when it was dropped on the motoring world of 1964 — purely because they didn't know or have any better then.

Today most people do. It is a golden rule amongst Alfa Romeo owners that the car should be warmed for several minutes after starting before the first ratio is selected. When the temperature gauge registers, you should gently push into the second gear gate before selecting first.

And every gear you select thereafter should be interspersed with a gentle pause at the neutral gate. To add to the problems the gears are stirred with a badly cranked gearlever that does nothing to promote fast or smooth shifts.

Multiplying the problem is the fact that the box only really enjoys moving down the ratio range when ample engine revs are applied. This is made difficult by the footpedal arrangement which is aligned for heel-toe downshifts but with awkward pedal operation. In fact the accelerator pedal is placed so high that only an Italian could be comfortable on long trips (I was in agony after 150 miles).

The frustrations spread into other areas of driving. The two footpedals have longish throw, which means lifting the feet through a longer arc than is desirable for speed, safety or efficiency. Braking on the big four wheel disc brakes is assisted by two huge power boosters crowded in odd fashion into a corner of the already cramped under-bonnet area — and braking is just too sensitive.

The car proved it could pull-up with incredible regularity in excess of 0.9g at less than 50psi pedal effort and absolutely no fade was experienced.

But gentle pedal effort induced such forceful braking, that it was very easy to lock the front brakes — obviously not a desirable situation on a wet road.

Progressive braking is something you have to master on an Alfa with practice, and no-one can guarantee to brake progressively in an emergency. At one stage, I recorded less than 15lb pedal effort for a 0.5g stop which is incredibly light — and far too sensitive.

While the feet are trying to control the mobility of the beast, the arms are wrestling away with the genuine woodrim wheel above. Why Alfa has retained the woodrim is completely

ROAD TEST DATA – SPECIFICATIONS

Manufacturer: ALFA ROMEO, Via Gattamelata, 45-20149 Milano.
Make/Model: . . . . Alfa Romeo 2000 GT Veloce
Body type: 2-door
Pricing: as tested: $6790
                basic: $6660
                options/prices: . . . . LSD $130
Test car supplied by: Alfa Romeo Australia Pty. Ltd., 14 Dickson Street, Artarmon, NSW
Mileage start/finish: 4045/5087

ENGINE
Cylinders: . . . . 4 in line
Bore x stroke: . . . . 3.3in. x 3.5in. (84mm x 88.5mm)
Capacity: . . . . 1962cc (119.7cu. in.)
Compression: . . . . 9.0 to 1
Aspiration: . . . . Two horizontal twin-choke
Fuel pump: . . . . Mechanical
Fuel recommended: . . . . .100 Octane
Valve gear: . . . . Double Overhead Camshafts
Max. power (gross): . . . . 150 (SAE) bhp @ 5500rpm
Max. torque: . . . . 152.6 (SAE) lb.ft (21.1kg.m) @ 3500rpm

TRANSMISSION
Type/locations: . . . . Five speed, floor console
Clutch type: . . . . sdp diaphragm

Gear	Direct Ratio	Overall Ratio	MPH/1000	(KPH)
1st	3.30	13.54	5.28	(8.49)
2nd	1.99	8.15	8.75	(14.08)
3rd	1.35	5.55	12.90	(20.76)
4th	1.00	4.10	17.41	(28.02)
5th	0.79	3.24	22.04	(35.47)

Final drive: 4.1

CHASSIS AND BODY
Type: . . . . Unitary
Kerb weight: 2288lb (1040kg)

SUSPENSION
Front: Independent by inclined transverse A-arms; coil springs; anti-roll bar.
Rear: . . . . . Live-axle, trailing arms, coil springs; anti-roll bar
Shock absorbers: . . . . Telescopic double-action
Wheels: . . . . 14 x 5½J
Tyres: . . . . .Kleber Radials, 165HR14
Pressures: . . . . 32lb front/28lb rear

STEERING
Type: . . . . Recirculating ball
Ratio: . . . . —
Turns lock to lock: 2.75
Wheel diameter: 15in. (38cm)
Turning circle, between kerbs: 39ft 0in. (11.8m)
                    between walls: 40ft 6in. (12.5m)

BRAKES
Type: . . . . . . Discs all round, dual system, vacuum operated servo
Dimensions: . . . . fr: 10.7in. (27.5cm); rear 10.5in. (26.8cm)
Swept area: . . . . 396.8sq in. (2549.4sq cm)

DIMENSIONS
Wheelbase: 92.7in. (235cm)
Track, front: 52.1in. (132.4cm)
          rear: 50.1in. (127.4cm)
Overall length: 13ft 5.4in. (410cm)
          width: 5ft 2.2in. (158cm)
          height: 4ft 3.8in. (131.5cm)
Ground clearance: 7in. (17.78cm)
Overhang, front: 34in. (86.4cm)
          rear: 40in. (101.6cm)

EQUIPMENT
Battery: . . . . 12V/60 A.H
Alternator: . . . . .420 W
Headlamps: . . . . 55 W
Jacking points: . . . . 4 sidepoints

CAPACITIES
Fuel tank: . . . . 11.6 gallons (53 litres)
Engine sump: . . . . 11.90 pints (6.75 litres)
Final drive: . . . . 2.5 pints (1.40 litres)
Gearbox: . . . . 3.2 pints (1.68 litres)
Water system: . . . . .2.1 gallons (9.7 litres)

PERFORMANCE

Test conditions for performance figures: Weather: . . . . Fine
Wind: . . . . 2-12 knots
Humidity: . . . . 34 percent
Max. Temp. . . . . 58 degrees
Surfaces: . . . . Dry hotmix
Top speed, average: 114mph (183kph)
          best run: 118mph (190kph)
Standing Quarter Mile, average: . . . . .16.6 secs
Standing Quarter Mile, best run: . . . . .16.4 secs
Speed at end of Standing Quarter: 81mph (130kph)

0-30mph: 2.9
0-40mph: 4.5
0-50mph: 7.1
0-60mph: 10.1
0-70mph: 13.0
0-80mph: 16.6
0-90mph: 18.2
0-100mph: 28.3

Speeds in gears:

Gear	Max. mph	(Kph)	rpm
1st	33	(52.8)	6000
2nd	55	(88)	6000
3rd	80	(128)	6000

beyond me. I can't help but doubt its safety in a crash, but then, most Alfa poseurs protest they would rather go down with the ship than be maimed and scarred for life.

But it is clumsy and slippery — and not nearly as effective to twiddle in the tight bits as a genuine leather-bound alloy wheel. This contention is borne out by public opinion among Alfa owners — leather-bound, small diameter wheels are easily the best selling option.

However, the wheel does have its good points — like the deep recessing that provides a more comfortable driving position for long-legged drivers trying to get a satisfactory distance from the pedals without losing touch with the tiller.

And it has three neat little horn tabs that you can't miss with the thumbs when you want to scare off one of Australia's sightless road users.

However the Alfa cockpit engineers managed to foul-up other aspects of driving equipment in the wheel area. Not the least of these is the stalk system which for some annoying reason is grouped together on one side.

Presumably some bright Italian decided when engineering the original left-hand-drive GTV, that by putting two stalks on the left side of the column, the driver's right hand would

be released for gearchanging.

In practice, such an event rarely occurs, although the way I've seen some Italians drive they could possibly be flashing their lights while groping for the handbrake to perform a 180 degree spin.

In any case, two hands logically means two controls, one on each side of the column.

At the same time as they're giving consideration to re-engineering this problem, Alfa should think about including the wiper/washer functions in one of the stalks. This would do away with the current clumsy set-up of a foot-pedal washer stuffed up under the dashboard and separated from a two-phase wiper switch down on the centre console (where it just happens to be the most reachable control on the car — thank God they didn't put it up on the dashboard which would put it way out of reach).

However Alfa didn't even bother to swap the wiper switch with the heater fan switch to place it more conveniently for the right-hand-drive driver. The wiper switch operates a curious set of over-lapping wiper arms which are presumably designed to give a similar wipe-pattern for both left-hand-drive and right-hand-drive models, but the overall effect is to leave a big blind spot for both

versions.

Since Alfa has done nothing to correct this voluntarily over the years, world-wide legislation is about to force them — standards that will apply in Australia from early next year for instance, will make it compulsory for the right hand blade to sweep parallel with, and up to, the right hand pillar.

There are other glaring examples of left-hand-drive engineering. The heater slides are located on the awkward side, the boot-opening catch is on the passenger's side door pillar, the gearlever is canted over the wrong way, the bonnet catch is on the passenger's side and so on.

The driver doesn't even get good treatment with the instrumentation. Alfa has long been criticised for hiding the auxilliary dials away in canted binnacles on the centre dash panel.

This year they made the bold move of switching them to the dash area viewed through the wheel, in a cunning little quad arrangement that bears more than a slight resemblance to the Quadrifoglio Alfa emblem — even the lower "dials" are split into four-leaf clover warning lights.

The ultimate effect is to make the important dials — speedo and tacho — less readable, since they are pushed so far outward that the hands partly cover them and the rim of the wheel

4th	107	(171.2)	6000
5th	114	(182.4)	5000

Acceleration holding gears:

	2nd	3rd	4th	5th
20-40	3.2	5.0	8.1	—
30-50	3.4	5.0	7.5	12.2
40-60	—	5.4	6.7	12.2
50-70	—	5.5	7.3	10.0
60-80	—	6.0	7.5	10.3

Fuel consumption:
Average for test: 21.5mpg (7.6kpl)
Best recorded: 24.8mpg (8.8kpl)
City average: 26mpg (9.3kpl)
Country cruising: 23.8mpg (8.5kpl)

Braking: Five crash stops from 60mph

Stop	G	Pedal	Time
1	.96	50 psi	3.7 secs
2	.95	45 psi	3.5 secs
3	.94	50 psi	3.6 secs
4	.98	40 psi	3.2 secs
5	.93	50 psi	3.6 secs
30-0 mph:			1.6 secs
60-0 mph:			3.2 secs

Calculated Data:
Bhp/ton: ....128 bhp/ton
Piston speed at max rpm: ....3208 ft. min/972 m.min)

Speedo Corrections:

30	40	50	60	70	80	90	100
29	39	50	60	71	80	89	99

WARRANTY, INSURANCE, MAINTENANCE, RUNNING COSTS

Registration: $121.00

Insurance:
Quoted rates are for drivers over 25 with 60 percent no-claim bonus

and where the car is under hire purchase. This is the minimum premium level — decreasing rates of experience and lower age groups may have varying excesses and possible premium loadings.

Non tariff company: $187.42
Tariff companies: $195.45
NRMA ....Will not insure Alfa Romeo

Warranty:
Six months — unconditional mileage. Covers all parts and labor charges for defective materials, components or workmanship. Also covers components from outside suppliers such as batteries, tyres etc.

Service:
A Service: ....Free
B Service: ....Free
A & B Services cover first 3750 miles (6000km) and include lubrication and maintenance service. Materials (oils, greases) are chargeable.

1-7 Services ....Chargeable
These are alternating lubrication and maintenance services covering the period 3750 miles (6000km) to 30,000 miles (48,000km). These are fully chargeable including labor, materials and replacement parts. Costs for labor are:—
Lubrication service (approximately 2 hours) $14.00
Maintenance service (approximately 5 hours) $35.00
Oil change every 3750 miles. No chassis lubrication is needed.

Spare Parts — Recommended Cost Breakdown:
Front disc pads: $27.72
Rear disc pads: $22.97
Clutch plate: $43.34
Pressure plate: $65.56
Shock absorbers (each) $25.52
Headlamp assembly: $37.18
Taillamp assembly: $17.60

Workshop Manuals: None available

Color Range (Upholstery colors in brackets).
White (Black, Maroon, Tan), Light Moss Green (Tan), Quarry Beige (Black), Pine Green (Tan), Dutch Blue (Tan), Le Mans Blue (Tan), Alfa Red (Black), Maroon (Light Pigskin), Yellow Piper (Black) Metallic Light Grey (Black), Metallic Light Beige (Black), Metallic Olive Green (Tan), Metallic Blue Perewinkle (Tan) — metallic colors $135 extra.

Measured garage width:
Measured car width, plus one fully open door . . .8ft 3in (251.46cm)

MODERN MOTOR ROAD TEST
FIFTH WHEEL

ALFA GTV 2000

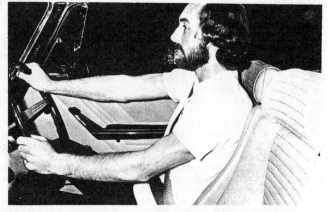

describes an arc across their outer edges when viewed from the normal driving position.

The readibility is further canned by the illegible dial markings — white lettering on a grey background, with a too-subtle red warning strip on the tacho. The old-series tacho which was angled so the tacho read vertically on the red line (a racing technique) was far more successful.

Inexplicably each 10 mph speedometer section is divided into thirds, which makes rapid appraisal of speed very difficult. An almost completely accurate speedometer compensates.

The tachometer also incorporates the oil pressure gauge. This appears to be a good idea, but in practice the gauge is harder to read than a separate gauge. The fuel and water temperature gauges in the centre are far more readable.

As the driver is trying to adjust to the minor frustrations in the controls/steering wheel/footpedal areas, he must also learn to adjust to deficiencies in the seating.

Alfa Romeo have apparently caught the dreaded Japanese disease in this area — namely, "it doesn't matter what it feels like, so long as it looks good."

And the Alfa seats look good.

Most people who take a glance inside immediately proclaim the car has the best looking seats they've ever seen. That could be the ultimate measure of success — if you don't measure the quality of the product beyond the showroom floor.

While they look great, the Alfa seats are thin and over-rigid in their springing. They are shallow, and the impression of big rolls of lateral padding are false since the seats do not isolate the occupants from the heavy side-loadings imposed by notable body roll movement in cornering.

The lumbar support is too pronounced and too firm — and without exception all our test drivers found themselves slouching forward to avoid excessive back pressure.

The headrests look great, and would probably provide the necessary protection in a rear-impact, but they can't be adjusted for comfortable sleeping. The screw-up adjusters are virtually unreachable from the seated position.

The rear seats are even worse, with deep sunken individually tailored buckets and poorly padded squabs. However their seat belts fit really well

— the front belts suffer from the common fate of coupe-style installations and the mounting points mean the front seat occupants rarely get a satisfactory belt location.

The poor location of the armrests does little to increase driver comfort, and the hands and arms invariably tire from hanging constantly from the relatively high wheel.

The Alfa is generally spartan in the interior and displays only average finish. There are some redesigned switches, a new steering lock and a different glovebox arrangement (awkward lock system) but little else is seriously changed from the original and (probably) the best of 1964. Windows roll-up with an effortless five turns and there are knurl knobs to wind out the quarter-panes.

This is one of the areas where the Alfa really excells. Its ventilation and heating system is first class. The quarter panes combine with rear windows that jack-open on their trailing edges and supplement a new through-flow system with eyeball vents on the dashboard.

The combination is great — even in the hottest Australian summer the Alfa can be cooled, and I can think of no other sports machine that achieves this so well. Conversely, the car starts, runs and heats quickly in the ultimate cold conditions — and I was able to test it with a run to the snow country.

The Alfa's other forte is in visibility — and in 1964 it must have been regarded as something of a phenomenon. Despite relatively high waistline, the visibility all round is superb, and the tight body package makes for remarkable manoeuvreability in tight situations. Reverse parking is a snack.

The Italians, apparently more intent in getting there than seeing where they've been, failed to take advantage of the excellent rear screen area with a puny interior mirror. However the rear quarter pillars are so slim they couldn't hide a midget on a pushbike.

The cockpit is quite well sound-proofed and reasonably free of most motoring noises — particularly road and mechanical noises. However the test car would have been even more enjoyable if it had been fitted with softer tyres than the relatively harsh Klebers. There is some wind noise intrusion that is introduced at the front corner of the quarter panes and increases with speed. It is by far the loudest noise to be heard.

By far the most pleasurable motoring I experienced in quite a long test was extracting good performance figures with the fifth wheel attached.

The car works well when it's worked hard, and the engine loves to rev out. It's only when you screw it up tight that the rattly exhaust note changes to an enjoyable roar. And it has much more torque — notable when clocking the upper gear figures. This of course makes the car an immensely more satisfying town car than the 1750 if you are lazy with gears.

There's some satisfaction in matching revs with gearshifts, hurrying through the gate, but pausing long enough to avoid the graunch you'll surely get if you belt it through regardless. The engine is true to its redline, and refuses to pull faster beyond it, as I found by comparing the relative performance figures.

Getting it off the line is a work of art, as the car breaks quickly into wheelspin and screams away far more than necessary beyond that initial break of traction that usually provides the best standing start figures. In the wet, the car is hopeless to shift off the line — particularly from an uphill traffic light.

This points up the car's deficiency in tyres — riding on 165 x 14 radials on 5½in. rims it is clearly undertyred by modern standards — and by nature of its own improved power output.

But Alfa engineers must have been in a quandry when they elected to stay with the smaller rubber — bigger wheels and fatter tyres would undoubtedly have increased the handling capabilities, but at the expense of ride softness, noise transmission and steering weight and feel. Which only goes to prove the Alfa's undergear is out of date.

The Alfa 2000 GTV test car was delivered to me for test with the usual loving attention that you come to expect from Alfa Romeo. It was the most exceptional color I've had in a test car all year — a bright lush, expensive green — and the most disappointingly difficult color to capture on film.

I tried desperately hard to become involved in the car and discover the Alfa mystique that captivates most owners.

But I failed.

Looking at the car in a cold, hard, analytical light, I have to come to the conclusion that the fault lies in the age of the product.

I have little doubt that cars like the Alfa Montreal, and the new generation of sedans including the Alfetta and the Alfasud, really impart the intangible motoring mystique that was once applied to the origins of this *genre*.

And I believe the GTV's replacement — when it comes — will be as modern tomorrow as this car must have been in 1964.

Until then, I have no answer for the owner of the 1967 Alfa 1600 GTV who asked me candidly on the street corner — "give me one good reason why I should lose at least $2000 and trade up to a 2000." ∎

AUTOTEST ALFA ROMEO 2000GTV...

CONTINUED FROM PAGE 75

also brings the car up against a limit when it runs out of roadholding and slithers sideways on all four wheels. In the dry this limit is very high (though lowered noticeably by camber changes or generally uneven surfaces) but in the wet it is much lower.

As in all GTVs, the 2000 has big disc brakes all round, and these now have split hydraulic circuits, each with its own servo. As always, they are superbly responsive and normal check braking requires very little pedal effort. It is now more difficult to lock the wheels, taking 100 lb to achieve a 1g stop with the front wheels just locked; the 1750GTV locked everything with a 65 lb shove. Hard drivers will certainly prefer the present arrangement.

The brakes seemed to thrive on hard work. As they warmed up in the course of our fade test they became more consistent; when cold, they are speed-sensitive, requiring more effort at higher speeds. Fully warmed up, the effort required is the same at any speed, and the overall effort is reduced.

The handbrake proved very efficient, giving a 0.35g stop on the level and holding the car either way on the 1-in-3 test hill. A restart was possible on this slope without much difficulty, thanks to the low first gear.

Considering its short wheelbase and high roll stiffness, the GTV rides very well. It makes the most of its limited suspension travel, ironing out small bumps and moderately rough surfaces, but once it reaches its limit everything becomes much less comfortable. It was noticeable that on the MIRA banking, where the car was subjected to perhaps 1.5g vertically at maximum speed, the ride was rock-hard and very harsh. It seems clear that the GTV is set up to give the best ride with two occupants, and indeed the maximum payload is rather limited.

In practice this limit does not matter very much, because there is no room for a back seat passenger behind any but a very small driver. Most of the time, there is no leg room to speak of.

The two front seat occupants are very well looked after, with excellently shaped seats. These provide good support where it is needed; sideways, under the thighs and in the small of the back. They are an object lesson in many ways, and are even more comfortable now that they are faced in high-quality cloth.

The stalk-type pedals are poor in the way they move, but good in the way the shape of the accelerator makes it easy to heel-and-toe. The gearchange is typical Alfa, not particularly light but extremely precise, with strong spring loading towards the third/fourth gear plane. Synchromesh is unbeatable except first thing in the morning, but the clutch pedal does need to be fully depressed—and the clutch is not light by modern standards.

From the driver's point of view, the streamlined GTV shape is not as easy to judge as some, but the car could hardly be called a handful in traffic or when parking. It is pleasantly unfashionable in having slender rear pillars instead of heavy quarter panels, and there are no serious blind spots. The situation is less happy in the rain, when the small "clap-hands" wipers clear too little of the screen. The headlamps are excellent, well up to the car's performance on main beam, and the outer (dipping) units are externally adjustable for height.

The GTV has good through-flow ventilation, and a heated rear window is standard as an extra aid to keeping the interior free from misting-up. The heater is less satisfactory, having the typical all-or-nothing response of a water-valve system, and the re-arrangement of the minor controls has left the heater controls further away from the driver and not easy to reach.

It is not easy to be objective about noise in the Alfa. Some of it, like the exhaust note, is unashamed and sets out to be pleasant rather than inaudible. For the rest, road noise is well suppressed but wind noise rises slowly with speed. Mechanical roar forms the main part of high-speed noise, but even at 100 mph it is far from intolerable, though the radio has to be turned up to be clearly heard, and conversation has to be carried on with raised voices.

Our drivers were not greatly impressed by the new instrument and centre console arrangement. The instrument binnacle looks cheap and the instruments themselves are slightly curious, with the minor dials interposed between the speedometer and rev counter—and the 10 mph increments of the speedometer dial split unhelpfully into three rather than five. The two warning lamp clusters (eight lamps in all) varied considerably in brightness.

With the 2000 engine, the GTV moves into the performance class many customers expect of it; it is now a genuinely quick car with relaxed 100–110 mph cruising capability. Alfa's efforts of recent years to improve detail and overall finish show to advantage; the car is a really attractive package for those prepared to spend that much extra for the pretty GTV body rather than the angular saloon. As always, the real attraction of the car is its feeling of precision and responsiveness; the extra power seems to have added to this without detracting from anything. □

Above: Front seats are exceptionally comfortable, although the seat/wheel/pedals relationship is not quite right for a tall driver

Above right: The boot is relatively small and has a restricted opening and high sill. The spare wheel lives in a well beneath the floor

Right: Although the back seats have too little leg room to cater for full-sized occupants on a long journey, they are well shaped and finished in the same comfortable cloth as the front seats

MANUFACTURER

Alfa Romeo SpA, Via Gattemelata 45, Milan, Italy

UK CONCESSIONAIRES

Alfa Romeo (GB) Ltd., Edgware Road, London NW2

PRICES

Basic	£2,012.00
Purchase Tax	£420.73
Total (in G.B.)	£2,432.73

EXTRAS (inc. P.T.)

Heated rear window*	£19.33
Limited slip differential*	£38.67
Air conditioning	£319.00
Alloy wheels	£96.67
Electric windows	£58.00

* Fitted to test car

PRICE AS TESTED . . . £2,490.73

BRIEF TEST

Alfa Romeo 2000 GTV

FOR : GOOD VISIBILITY ; WELL FINISHED ; GOOD HEATING AND VENTILATION ; EXCELLENT PERFORMANCE ; SUPERB GEARBOX

AGAINST : SMALL BOOT ; CRAMPED REAR SEAT ; HEAVY STEERING ; TOO MUCH UNDERSTEER ; POOR PEDAL ARRANGEMENT

Middle-aged maturity is as much responsible for the many endearing qualities of Alfa Romeo's Bertone-bodied coupes as antiquity is for their faults and imperfections. A classic case of evolutionary development rather than bold innovation, the 2000 GTV is a car that no discerning driver could fail to like, even though he might find several things about it to criticise.

Outwardly, it is scarcely distinguishable from the Giulia that sired it or, for that matter, from its present junior, the 1600GT. That it is only now beginning to look slightly dated by the unfashionably high waist is ample testimony to the purity of the original design. Despite the shallow side windows, the unimpeded all-round view you get from the driver's seat puts to shame many heavy-pillared modern coupes in which style for style's sake has been allowed to overrule more important matters — like seeing out. However, pretty though it remains, the GTV's shape is now perhaps too familiar to attract much attention and as an exercise in packaging it fares rather badly by current standards, the small boot and cramped rear quarters severely restricting the car's role as family transport.

While nothing can be done to make the cockpit more roomy, much has been accomplished over the years to make it more habitable and attractive. The 2000 GTV's opulent furnishings, its contoured cloth-covered seats, and its efficient heating and ventilation are just some of the tangible results of evolutionary refinement that has transformed the Alfa coupe over the years from a rather stark and fragile fun car into the compact executive's express it is today. That such refinement has been achieved while amplifying, not sacrificing, those qualities that make it so enjoyable to drive is surely the root of the GTV's success. It's

certainly why we still rate it among our favourites.

What makes the car even more attractive now, of course, is its bigger engine, increased from 1779 cc to 1962 cc a little more than 18 months ago. And what a superb engine this venerable light-alloy twin-cam hemi-head is. Although an increase in stroke has meant imposing a modest rev limit of 5700 rpm, its performance would do justice to an engine of three litres, let alone to one that displaces less than two. Fed now by twin Dellorto (or Solex) carbs, which don't seem to provide quite such easy chokeless cold starts as the earlier Webers, the engine delivers 150 (gross) bhp—an increase of 18 (gross) bhp on the 1750. There's also a useful improvement in torque, up now to 134 lb. ft. ·

The engine pulls with tremendous vigour from about 2000 rpm —at lower revs it felt rather flat. Even though now unfashionably under square, with a stroke that's longer than the bore is wide, the engine feels and sounds utterly smooth at (and even beyond) the recommended rev limit. The characteristic deep throaty thrum, a lot of it from the exhaust, was never a strain on our ears—largely because there are no disturbing boom periods or mechanical thrash, though you could hardly call it quiet when accelerating hard. Nor is wind noise particularly low at speed.

Since it's with torque rather than power that the 2000 scores over the 1750, it is the improvement in mid-range acceleration in the upper three ratios that you notice most. For instance, 30-50 in fourth is down from 8.1 to an impressive 6.8 sec., 70-90 in fifth from 17.0 to 12.7 sec. There are also modest gains from rest through the gears: the 0-100 time, for instance, has been cut from 29.7 to 27.2 sec. It may be that our test car was slightly short of top-end power because

the maximum speed of 115.3 mph round MIRA's banked circuit (equivalent to perhaps 118 mph on a flat road), though impressive, was no better than that we recorded for the 1750 GTV four years ago. Something nearer 120 mph was expected.

Even so, given the right road the Alfa will lope along at a relaxed 110 mph, an easy 5000 rpm in fifth. Such is the engine's excellent torque that it can sustain very high cruising speeds up long gradients without a downchange into direct top—good itself for 100 mph.

Not that shifting gear is a chore. If anything betters the Alfa's engine it is its superb five-speed gearbox, about which we have drooled often enough before. The travel of the stout, smooth-topped lever is quite long but it slices through the five-bar gate with a slippery action that the synchromesh, even though it cannot be beaten during snatched changes, does nothing to baulk. The ratios, too, are well chosen and the gear trains reasonably quiet.

Not surprisingly, the bigger engine proved to be more thirsty than the 1750, especially if you make the most of its strong performance—and what Alfa owner wouldn't ? Our overall consumption of 20.8 mpg is probably fairly typical—on the heavy side perhaps, for such a small car (especially one that needs best fuel) but by no means unreasonable for one so fast. It does, however, make the 11.6 gallon fuel tank seem rather mean on a long journey.

Alfa Romeo were controlling things at the back with radius arms and a stout A-bracket long before other manufacturers followed suit to make the live rear axle respectable wear again just when it seemed to be going out of fashion. The all-coil suspension gives a firm ride—rathei jittery over secondary surfaces but seldom harsh or crashy—indicating that some resilience has been sacrificed in the interests of handling. In that it feels very taut and fairly responsive, the 2000 GTV does handle well, though in terms of physical effort it's no featherweight to conduct. We didn't like what seemed to us unnecessarily strong castor action that made the steering of our test car very heavy on sharp turns. On the other hand, by tugging so firmly against your grip, such castor imparts a vivid feel of the road through the steering. We were also surprised to find that the test sample understeered quite strongly when pressed through sharp corners, to some extent marring the balance of a car that we'd previously noted for its almost neutral handling. Since excessive castor would tend to exaggerate understeer, it may be that the steering geometry of our test car was not quite as it should have been.

With a limited slip differential fitted as standard, there's no trouble getting the power on to the road in mid-corner—a real

Cornering power is high—with strong understeer on our test car, though the limited-slip differential makes it easy to get plenty of power down.
Accommodation in the rear seats (right) is pretty cramped: more suitable for children than for adults. We liked the big instruments (left), were less keen on the stalks, and objected strongly to the awkward action and poor layout of the pedals

PERFORMANCE

Weather Warm and dry, wind 7 mph
Temperature 54-58°F
Barometer 29.6 in. Hg
Surface Dry tarmacadam

Maximum speed

	mhp	kph
Banker circuit	115.3	185.7
Best ¼ mile	118.3	190.5

Terminal speeds:
at ¼ mile	82.3	132.1
at kilometre	102.5	
at mile	112.5	181.0

Speed in gears (at 5700 rpm)
1st	30	48
2nd	50	80
3rd	73	117
4th	99	159

Acceleration from rest

mph	sec	kph	sec
0-30	2.7	0-20	—
0-40	4.5	0-40	2.1
0-50	6.4	0-60	3.9
0-60	8.9	0-80	6.2
0-70	11.7	0-100	9.4
0-80	15.7	0-120	13.6
0-90	20.3	0-140	18.9
0-100	27.2	0-160	26.9
Stand'g ¼	16.6	Stand'g km	30.8

Acceleration in top

mph	sec	kph	sec
20-40	...	40-60	—
30-50	10.9	60-80	5.2
40-60	9.8	80-100	6.4
50-70	9.7	100-120	7.0
60-80	10.7	120-140	8.6
70-90	12.7	140-160	10.8
80-100	16.4	160-180	—

Acceleration in 4th

mph	sec	kph	sec
20-40	7.4	40-60	3.9
30-50	6.8	60-80	3.9
40-60	6.3	80-100	4.0
50-70	6.7	100-120	4.5
60-80	7.3	120-140	5.5
70-90	8.4	140-160	8.0
80-100	11.6		

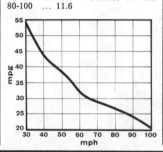

Fuel consumption

Touring*	26.9 mpg	
	10.5 litres/100 km	
Overall	20.8 mpg	
	13.6 litres/100 km	
Fuel grade	98 octane (RM)	
(Premium)	4 star rating	
Tank capacity	11.6 galls	
	53 litres	
Max range	312 miles	
	503 km	
Test distance	894 miles	
	1435 km	

*Consumption midway between 30 mph and maximum less 5 per cent for acceleration.

Speedometer (mph)

Speedo	30	40	50	60	70	80	90	100
True	30	40	50	60	70	80	90	100

Distance recorder 0.5 per cent fast

Weight

	cwt	kg
Unladen weight*	20.2	1028
Weight as tested	23.9	1214

*with fuel for approx 50 miles

Performance tests carried out by Motor's staff at the Motor Industry Research Association proving ground, Lindsey.

Test Data: World copyright reserved; no unauthorised reproduction in whole or in part.

GENERAL SPECIFICATION

ENGINE
Cylinders	4 in line
Capacity	1962 cc (120 cu in)
Bore/stroke	84.0 x 88.5 mm (3.31 x 3.48 in)
Cooling	Water
Block	Aluminium
Head	Aluminium
Valves	dohc

Valve timing
inlet opens	41 btdc
inlet closes	60 abdc
ex opens	54 bbdc
ex closes	35 atdc
Compression	9.1:1
Carburetter	Twin Dellorto or Solex
Main bearings	5
Fuel pump	Mechanical
Max power	131 bhp (DIN) at 550 rpm
Max torque	134 lb ft (DIN) at 3000 rpm

TRANSMISSION
Type	Manual, five-speed, floor change

Clutch
sdp diaphragm
Internal ratios and mph/1000 rpm
Top	0.79/22.0
4th	1.00/17.3
3rd	1.35/12.8
2nd	1.99/8.7
1st	3.30/5.3
Rev	3.01/
Final drive	4.10:1 hypid

BODY/CHASSIS
Construction	Unitary
Protection	Electrophoretic dip

SUSPENSION
Front	Independent, coil springs, wishbones and anti-roll bar
Rear	Live axle, coil springs, radius arms, A-bracket and anti-roll bar

STEERING
Type	Recirculating ball
Assistance	No

Toe-in	1.5 mm
Camber	0° 20' ± 30'
Castor	1-2°
Rear toe-in	None

BRAKES
Type	Discs all round
Servo	Yes
Circuit	Divided—front and rear
Rear valve	Yes
Adjustment	Self adjusting

WHEELS
Type	Steel
Tyres	165 HR14 Michelin XAS
Pressures	Front: 21 psi Rear: 26 psi

ELECTRICAL
Battery	12v 60 ah
Polarity	Negative earth
Generator	Alternator
Fuses	10
Headlights	4 x 55w halogen

COMPARISONS

	Capacity cc	Price £	Max mph	0-60 sec.	30-50* sec.	Overall mpg	Touring mpg	Length ft in	Width ft in	Weight cwt	Boot cu ft
Alfa Romeo 2000 GTV	1962	2636	115.3	8.9	10.9	20.8	26.9	13 4.5	5 2.3	20.2	6.8†
Audi 100 Coupe S	1871	2575	112.7	10.8	10.9	23.1	30.4	14 7.8	5 8.8	21.3	12.7
BMW 2002 Tii	1990	2499	113.5	8.2	7.8	24.0	—	13 10.5	5 1.5	20.2	10.8
Ford Capri 3000 GXL	2994	1831	119.5	8.6	7.7	19.4	24.7	14 1.0	5 5.0	21.1	7.8†
Lotus +2 130	1558	2720	121.0	7.7	8.5	21.0	26.1	14 0.5	5 3.5	17.2	4.2†
Reliant Scimitar GTE	2994	2398	113.2	10.2	7.9	19.2	27.9	14 2.3	5 5.0	22.7	—
Rover 3500 S	3528	2207	119.0	9.3	8.1	19.3	23.6	15 0.5	5 7.3	26.1	9.3
Triumph Stag	2997	2570	116.5	9.7	7.6	20.9	25.5	14 6.8	5 3.5	25.9	3.6

* In top
† Measured with boxes, not suitcases

Make: Alfa Romeo
Model: 2000 GTV
Makers: Alfa Romeo SpA, Via Gattamelata 45, Milano, Italy.
Concessionaires: Alfa Romeo (Great Britain) Ltd, Edgware Road, London, NW2 6LX.
Price: £2192.00 including limited slip differential and heated rear window plus £458.23 purchase tax equals £2650.23.

boon when, say, accelerating from a side street across a wet and greasy main road. The Michelin XAS radials tolerated pretty high lateral loads before losing their grip in a reasonably progressive way, so the Alfa could be cornered very rapidly indeed without getting out of line. When you tot up all the assets—the vigorous performance assisted by five perfect gear ratios, the high cornering powers allied to the handy size—it's easy to understand why the 2000 GTV makes such short (and entertaining) work of cross-country journeys. There's nothing lacking in the immensely reassuring all-disc brake department, either, though some drivers found the twin-servo assistance over sensitive at low speeds, making "feathered" release and heel and toe changes rather difficult.

Which brings us to our biggest gripe—the pedals. For some time, left-hand-drive Alfas have had modern hanging pendant pedals but those in the right-hand-drive samples are a legacy of the bad old days when a floor-hinged brake and clutch were in vogue. They sprout from beneath at an awkward height and they protrude too far, enforcing a splayed legs stance that most of us found awkward, especially our long-limbed drivers who caught their thighs on the steering wheel. They're also badly aligned, making a quick switch from the hanging throttle to rampant brake rather awkward.

To be fair, you get used to what initially feels an uncomfortable driving position, aided no doubt by the excellent contoured seats which are bolstered round the edges to hold you firmly in place, and covered in non-slip cloth for added location. A large knurled knob allows very fine adjustment of the backrest so you can settle exactly where you want behind the nice thick wood-rimmed steering wheel, even if your legs are not always where you want them.

The switchgear is passable. There are two column stalks on the left, one for the indicators, the other for the headlights, dip and flasher. A single stalk could cover the lot, leaving the other (on the right perhaps) for the wipers and washers. As it is Alfa prefer a wash/wipe button on the floor and a separate, and not very handy, toggle for the two-speed wipers. Not the best of arrangements. You also have to stretch for the heater controls on the far side of the middle divide, but they do give fine adjustment over the powerful heater, as do the centre twist grips over the efficient ventilators, one each end of the wood veneer facia. We also liked the big-dial instruments and the colourful clusters of tell-tale and warning lights.

The Alfa bears its years remarkably well. It has its faults but for us the virtues overshadow them. It also has style and character, coveted qualities these days when there are far too many anonymous motor cars around.

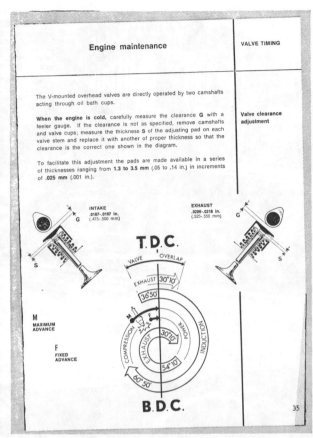

This page, torn from the instruction book for the Alfa Romeo GTV, emphasises the racing pedigree of the twin-cam engine's valve gear.

CONTINUED FROM PAGE 47

This console carries water thermometer (normally reading approx. 190° F.) and vague fuel gauge, the latter blanked by the steering wheel. the heater controls, lidded ash-tray, and three flick switches for two-speed wipers, facia lighting and two-speed blower. Further back, the central hand-brake is well located. There is a foot-operated wipers-cum-washers knob. The oil gauge, showing a reassuring 75 lb./sq. in. at speed, is a small segment of the tachometer, and the speedometer incorporates total and decimal-trip mileometers. These are high-grade Italian Jaeger instruments with Alfa Romeo badges; eight such badges can be counted inside the car. Not only the small dials on the console but the main dials are angled to the driver's eyes and the former stand proud of the wood-simulated mounting.

Further refinements include a cushion in the boot for additional driver support, a tool-kit with sensible contents even to a Phillips screwdriver, a handbook which quotes torque wrench loadings even for the plugs, Alfa Romeo anti-freeze, two keys with different shaped handles, and so on. The equipment includes a reversing lamp and alternator and the metallic medium grey colour of the test car was much admired. The doors have lift-up external handles, easy to grip and incorporating the locks but a trifle stiff. At night the headlamps cut-off on dip is lethal for fast driving, and the illumination of the plated under-facia choke and hand-throttle levers a cause of irritation.

The lightweight bonnet opens from the back, to reveal exciting and traditional machinery (lit at night) and the boot lid cannot be released until a substantial plated lever on the n/s door pillar has been operated. In contrast, the fuel filler flap on the n/s of the body does not lock and the cap is not secured. Typical Alfa Romeo pedals, lockable steering column, pendant choke and hand-throttle levers and not altogether satisfactory l.h. stalk controls for turn-indicators and the dual Carello lamps, are featured, and there is a small lockable cubby-hole and scuttle map-containers. The horn pushes are in the steering-wheel spokes.

The body is rather dated by having no extractors, apart from neatly openable rear quarter-lights, but swivelling vents on the screen-cill enable various permutations of cold-air entry to be obtained at the expense of much wind noise, and the front quarter-lights are controlled by turn-buttons, but hiss irritatingly when tight shut. The body is rather cramped, with low roof and not much elbow room. But it is beautifully made. It may "proudly carry" the *Quadrifoglio* crest, although this actually looks ugly on the body sides, being over-large.

As I have tried to convey, driving this, or any modern Alfa Romeo and most of the older ones, is a motoring experience to be remembered and enjoyed. The 1750 GTV gave me some memorable miles, without putting a wheel wrong. In some pretty all-embracing motoring it did 26.8 m.p.g. of premium petrol and the full/empty range proved to be 286 miles. The racing pedigree engine consumed no oil after 900 miles. The test car was shod with Michelin XAs tyres, 165 × 14, and although the treads looked as the very comprehensive Alfa instruction book shows them to wear if underinflated (the car had done 7,000 miles, so one supposes these were its original set) they gave impeccable road-clinging, but squealed slightly at times, even when not very heavily stressed.

To add any more to this account would be to repeat the enthusiasm expressed for previous Alfa Romeos. I can only say that if the price, £2,300, of the GTV is high in this country, (it is 50% lower in Italy), the performance, finish, allure and subtle handling qualities of the car justify it in the eyes (and hands) of those who extract pleasure from such things.

With the new Alfa Romeo London Service Centre and showroom in the Edgware Road near Staples Corner, convenient for access from the North Circular Road, operating under the control of Dr. Tassan, and 100 dealers in this country, the one-time servicing and spares anxieties which bedevilled this famous make should have vanished forever. And it is a make that is irresistible, so it is not surprising that British sales rose by 42% last year and are aimed at over 2,000 cars this year. On overall sales Alfa Romeo have been forging right ahead (97,054 last year). Soon they will have the new small Alfa (rumoured to be a high-grade transverse-engined f.w.d. model, embodying the traditional handling qualities, which should be cause for another shy Issigonis smile!) to add to the preset seven-model 1300/ 1750 range. A Rover is more restful, a Lancia gives similar motoring with perhaps even more refinement, and a car costing over £2,000 might be expected to have leather upholstery and a properly vented body with face-level fresh-air inlets. But Alfa characteristics excuse such omissions, and these cars remain—irresistible!—W. B.

Familiar frontal view—today's Alfa Romeos retain the familiar grille and badge which they have carried proudly for so many years.

midshipman
ALFA

with the familiar 1600 cc engine dropped into it.

The 1.6 is also something of an "economy" model as well as being a gap-stopper. If you will pardon the frightful simile, compared with the 2000 GTV it is rather like a Belmont against a Kingswood. Interior fittings have been kept quite spartan — for instance, there is no console, and the fuel and temperature gauges are merely tacked on under the dashboard instead of being worked into it. Trim is also at a lower level than in the GTV, and the seats aren't so lavishly styled. Nor do you get that superb woodrim wheel.

Body-wise, the 1.6 and GTV are similar except for the grille and the 1.6's single headlights.

Of course, the main difference is under the bonnet where the 1570 cc mill rather than the 1962 cc one lurks.

As we've grown to expect, the engine fires quickly and easily. Not surprisingly, you soon realise how first the 1750 and then the 2-litre engine were developed from this engine, feeling the strong bloodline, yet noting the difference between the three. Even by Alfa standards this engine is beautifully smooth and clean. It doesn't have the slight peakiness of the 1750 when it hits 4500 rpm, and it doesn't have the more gutsy feel of the 2-litre.

Like the others, it is red-lined at 5700 rpm but gives its ultimate performance when taken out to 6500 before changing.

Here, you get standing quarter times of 17.6 seconds and 0.100 mph in 32.7, which is pretty damned good for a 1600.

While this engine is a little honey, we still rate the 1750 as our favorite of the three (four if you count the 1300) because it has just that little more sparkle high in the rev range.

In its handling and braking the 1.6 is entirely similar to the 1750 and 2-litre, of course. This car wore Italian CEAT tyres which suited it much better than the Klebers on the GTV but not quite as well as

THIS IS GOING to be a very brief test because we've written a great deal about Alfa Romeos lately and we fear that yet another essay on them might just have you thinking we're a little biased towards them.

And since that could never be true, we will not go to great lengths to tell you what a sweet motorcar Alfa Australia's latest acquisition is.

The car in question is the "new" GT 1.6 — which you might correctly say is hardly new at all since it was in this form that the present GT/GTV body was introduced way back in the early sixties.

What has happened is that with the demise of the 1750 GTV Alfa customers began asking for a model in between the baby 1300 GT Junior and the 2000 GTV. In particular, they asked for the respected and popular 1600 engine.

So along comes what is basically the GT junior

PERFORMANCE

Engine . . . . DOHC in-line four, 1570 cc
Power . . . . 125 bhp at 6000 rpm
Torque . . . . .116 lb/ft at 2800 rpm
Speedo error: (mph):

Indicated	30	40	50	60	70	80	90
Actual	28	38	48	57	66	75	85

Gear maximums:
First .26 mph (5700 rpm)
Second 45 (5700)
Third 67 (5700)
Fourth 91 (5700)
Fifth 112 (5700)
Acceleration:
0-40 mph . . . . 5.1 secs
0-50 mph . . . . 7.5 secs
0-60 mph . . . . 10.3 secs
0-70 mph . . . . 14.2 secs
0-80 mph . . . . 18.9 secs
0-90 mph . . . . 24.6 secs
0-100 mph . . . . 32.7 secs

	2nd	3rd	4th	5th
20-40 mph	3.4 secs	5.7 secs	8.1 secs	
33-50 mph	3.7 secs	5.7 secs	8.5 secs	12.2 secs
40-60 mph		5.8 secs	8.0 secs	11.1 secs
50-70 mph		6.0 secs	8.0 secs	11.0 secs

Standing quarter mile . . . . 17.6 secs
Braking:
30 mph-0 . . . . .25 ft
60 mph-0 . . . . 120 ft

midshipman ALFA

Pirellis mated up to the 1750 we ran some months back. Alfa Romeo itself agrees that the cars are better on Pirellis than any other tyre.

We won't go into another epic about Alfa motoring. Suffice to say we went out for a Saturday run in pouring rain, did a round trip of 400-odd miles over varying terrain and thoroughly loved every minute of it. The car's behavior was impeccable, particularly on 60 miles of dirt that had turned into clay with the rain. We thought we'd slowed to a crawl on it, only to glance at the speedo and still see better than 60 mph.

Since we ran softer pressures than we'd been able to use in the GTV, the 1.6's ride was a little better.

Faults? Yes, there are quite a few but none we found you don't learn to live with quite quickly unless you are very tall. Then, the lack of seat travel makes driving the GT very awkward; almost impossible.

Next — the windscreen wipers and washers. The short wiper blades don't sweep enough of the screen and the washers have to be pumped with the left foot. They should have an electric pump.

The location of the minor instruments looks quite cheap and makes them hard to read, too.

Like most Contintal cars, the headlights cut-off is too severe on low beam. On high they're okay, but not up to the standard of the GTV's four-beam jobs.

On our car, the push-button/telltale switch for the optional electric rear window demister kept popping out of the dash. Occasionally, there was a whirring from the speedo cable at very low speeds.

The thing that aggravated us most were the door handles. You have to get your hand under them and pull them up, and if they're a little stiff as this car's were it can take quite a tug.

Without the slippery diff (mandatory on the GTV) the old problem of lifting inside rear wheels returns under very vigorous cornering.

However, as we said, the 1.6 offers so much in sporty car/GT motoring, performance, handling, braking, safety and that all-important character that is all these things added together.

So, if you can't rake up the $6790 for a GTV but can just make the 1.6's $5785, rest assured that the little car is a delightful compromise.

—MEL NICHOLS

Ever wondered what it's like to go along on a road test? We invited a young Sydney journalist to accompany us in the Alfa 1.6. Here is the report he filed—

IT'S AN interesting twist sitting in the passenger's seat of a road test car and watching the driver at work.

Sort of a road test of the road tester.

Personally, I was really pleased to be along for the ride because I'd never been in an Alfa before.

I'd met SCW Editor Mel Nichols, who was doing the test, at Hornsby (as arranged) on a soaking Saturday morning. The Alfa's headlights winked as he spotted my car sitting at the side of the road. The Alfa was silver-grey and I remember thinking at the time that its color matched that of the leaden sky. Not a very good day for a road test, I thought.

I jumped in and we were off up the Pacific Highway, going north from Sydney. Nichols had already set Dungog as our first destination and I wondered as we shot up the expressway if he was going to be restricted to main roads because of the weather. I was to find out soon enough!

During the first few miles my interest had centred on the car's interior. I was interested to see if the Alfa would measure up to its reputation.

My first impression was the firmness of my seat, it was almost hard. But it proved to be very comfortable over the 400 miles of our trip.

Considering the fairly steep price of the car I was surprised to find rubber floor mats and a very noisy blower fan on the demister.

But, back to the driving . . . There we were, snaking down a sodden, streaming road on the way to Singleton when we flew over a crest and the bitumen turned to dirt. Or rather mud.

What was 90 mph became 60 as Nichols dabbed the Alfa's brakes. As soon as we hit the dirt Nichols began making minute steering corrections, keeping the silver-grey bonnet in front of us on a straight line.

Through the Alfa's floorpan you could feel the suspension working pitter-patter, the car dancing slightly on occasion, but perfectly controllable. Incredibly — to me anyway — the speedo continued to hover on the 60 mph mark.

The Alfa's stability was almost unaffected by the uneven road surface, patches of slush and loose rocks.

Maintaining the same speed in some cars I've driven would have had us making an in-depth survey of the roadside shrubbery.

The car was being driven smoothly and well. Very well. Driver inputs-delicate use of the throttle, fingertip manipulation of the wheel were answered instantly and with equal precision by the car.

Came the first really tight bend. And my first surprise.

Nichols changes down just ONE gear — fourth to third. From my seat it looks like a second gear bend, very tight, very slushy. Our speed is hardly checked by the downchange and Nichols gives the brakes a firm push, both hands back on the wheel, the gearstick forgotten for the moment.

The Alfa's nose hunches down under braking and tucks tight into the apex of the corner, the driver's right foot hovering over the throttle.

We hit the apex and he's pushing gently on the accelerator. The tail slides out a foot. Nichols twists on an eighth turn of opposite lock and slide stops.

More pressure on the throttle. Slide. Quarter turn of opposite lock. More throttle as we exit. Slide. Half turn of opposite lock and Nichols takes the car to the very outside edge of the road. His foot stabs the clutch and we're back in fourth and away.

At all times the car is being balanced on the throttle, using power and the steering wheel instead of brakes and gearstick to get through.

It's not new. But you tend to be a bit startled when the driver's foot is pressing the throttle at a time when YOU'D still be on the brakes. At other times the brakes are *on* — gently mind you — *right in the middle of a bend* to bring the nose in tight. At high speed this requires real judgment. As Nichols said, it takes a lot of practice.

And it was like that, very clean and smooth as well as fast, for much of the way — particularly on the dirt section which Nichols claims he had taken by mistake. From the grin on his face I'd just bet it was a bloody mistake!

There was one straight stretch on that bit of road which we didn't realise was really deep slush until we hit it. The Alfa's tail immediately went out.

He just swung the wheel, catching the slide beautifully, and then worked the car back onto a straight course again.

As for the Alfa's reputation for handling, I can only say that this car's ability to stick to the road in bad conditions was staggering. This was backed up by the tremendous stopping power of the four-wheel discs.

Another thing was the apparent lack of body roll. Even through very, very tight bends the car stayed incredibly flat.

The sacrifice for the brilliant roadholding is the Alfa's ride, which is firm to say the least. But you can always feel the car through the seat of your pants. I'd rather have that than wallow.

I thoroughly enjoyed watching SCW expertly put the car through its paces, sometimes with Nichols making a running commentary, but most often just concentrating intently, snapping the gearstick up and down, keeping the revs up in the power band.

It may sound far-fetched to say that cruising along a winding road at 80 mph and more with the rain beating down felt entirely safe. But there it is. The stability of the car and the driver's judgment made it a relaxing, but lively, trip for the passenger.

There's not much more I could say except that the car is totally responsive to driver and these SCW guys really can drive (or else it was a great act, pretending everything was under control all the time!).　　　*

ALFA ROMEO 1750 CONTINUED FROM PAGE 51

CONTINUED FROM PAGE 51

identical through the quarter-mile. The Duetto, with its better weight distribution, turned a 17.3 seconds at 79.7 miles per hour, while the GTV recorded 17.4 seconds at 79.0 mph on its best run. Thus, despite its more easy going nature, the 1750s are significantly quicker, but not much faster, than the non-smog-controlled 1600 Duetto Spider the late Ken Miles tested for *C/D* in 1967, which turned 17.7 at 78 mph. Nowadays the only Porsche selling for anywhere near the price of either Alfa is the 4-cylinder 912, which, when we tested it in March with Mark Donohue's assistance, turned in a best time of 18.2 seconds at 77 mph.

Another comparison with the current Porsche is more direct. Alfa's 5-speed transmission uses Porsche-patent synchronizers so, on occasion, there is that nerve-shattering clash of gear teeth when the car is shifted from neutral to first. Unique in another respect, Alfa continues to employ that long wand of a gearshift lever and its peculiar up and down motion. Mechanical advantage it's got, along with relatively long throws and, until you become used to the fact that there is no lock-out between second and fifth, you can expect to slide it into that "overdrive" gear range by mistake every once in a while. The shift lever also seems to have an eerie mind of its own, every motion of the driveline exaggerated by the lever's length and, particularly over bumpy roads, you'd swear that some poltergeist wants to help you shift.

Strictly speaking, both the GTV and Duetto are 2-seater vehicles (the GTV's vestigial rear seats should be thought of as a well upholstered luggage rack). The seating position and relationship of the controls is best in the GTV but the Duetto boasts better seats (impressive looking, the GTV's buckets are too wide to provide the proper lateral grip for anyone under 200

lbs.). The passenger compartment of the Duetto is vertically thin, so your legs must stretch out more in order to provide proper thigh clearance at the steering wheel. When this is done you need ape arms to reach the gearshift.

Although different in design, both the GTV's and the Duetto's dashboards give proper display to the most important instruments. On both cars an enormous white on black tach and speedometer are placed directly in front of the driver and are very easy to read, with the most crucial portion of each dial (4000-8000 rpm on the tach, and 60 to 120 mph on the speedometer) located in the 8 to 12 o'clock range. (Whether you want to believe the speedometer is your own business.)

Visibility in the GTV, however, is far better than in the Duetto where rear quarter vision is completely blocked when the wind-proof, leak-proof top is wrestled into place. Neither car can boast of excellent rear visibility because of the very small interior rear view mirrors (barely covering one-and-a-half lanes of traffic at cruising speeds on multiple lane highways).

Whoever designed the interior of the Duetto did everyone a favor by selecting rubber upholstery mats in place of carpets. It looks fine, better in fact than the wood and black carpet interior of the GTV, and is impervious to rain—face it, you're going to get caught with the top down sometime in any open car.

In both cars there are a number of trick creature comfort items that have one thing in common, they are intended to make things easier for the *driver*. Consequently all are aimed at the driver's line of vision or are positioned so that he can get at them without diverting his attention. Leader in the gimmick parade has got to be the amazing, do everything but give-you-a-boot-in-the-butt-to-get-you-started cigarette lighter, with more practical items being a

gas level warning light and headlight controls that can be either foot or fingertip operated.

Alfa has seen fit to employ larger rear disc brakes on all the 1750 models (10.5 in. vs. 9.7 in.) and in our earlier test of the Berlina they proved to be truly impressive, consistently generating stops in excess of .90g. Neither the Duetto or GTV came anywhere near those earlier figures. The problem was in brake proportioning and both our test cars relied almost entirely on the rear wheels to do the job. The culprit in both instances was probably a malfunctioning brake proportioning valve. We would be skeptical of the faith Alfa places in its brake system had we not had prior experience with the Berlina, and anyone considering purchase of a 1750 would be well advised to test for the same malfunction before taking delivery.

In the inevitable comparison with Porsche, Alfa comes off pretty well. Performance is well above the level attained by a 912 and, considering the difference in price, can be compared favorably with the 911T. Alfa's less elaborate suspension design has been developed to where it provides ride comfort of about an equal level, and when it gets down to handling it's a battle between whether you prefer understeer or oversteer and we'll steer clear of that one, thanks.

Alfa's one big trump card is its price, its major weak point is the small dealer network (120 dealers) and availability (less than 10% of Alfa's production is sold in the U.S.). For the past two years, Alfa Romeo has been overhauling its dealer network and service training programs in order to get over a well-deserved and truly atrocious customer service image in preparation for a major assault on the American market. It all adds up to conservatism, Italian-style (which is a wild contradiction in terms), and it's the best news the GT market has heard in a long time.　　●

Buying Secondhand
Alfa Romeo 1750/2000

THE FACT that Alfa Romeo have convincingly won outright the World Championship for Makes may or may not explain the still-powerful attraction of any of the 1750 or 2000 Alfa saloon and sports-car range to the secondhand buyer. For all its supposed publicity value, success in motor racing is not always reflected in the successful maker's production cars. And a superbly handling racing car does not mean that the firm which made it necessarily offer road cars with proportionally good handling, performance and character. Yet it is so with Alfa; every Alfa Romeo in the present car range has something about it that makes it stand out refreshingly from its competitors – even the Alfasud, which though underpowered, has extraordinary handling by any standards. None are by any means perfect. But all are fun to drive – a rare and precious thing in cars.

For a long time, Alfa have produced a typical range of cars – a compact saloon, a fixed-head coupé and a two seater sports-car, or spider. The 1750 engine introduced to the British market in March 1968 first appeared in a neat, Bertone-styled revision of the extraordinarily shaped Giulia saloon, which had been powered by a 1500 unit. The new engine had an enlarged bore (2mm more) and stroke (6½mm more) of 80×88·5mm which in fact put its swept volume at 1,779 c.c., the car's name being a sentimental reminder of the immortally beautiful pre-war 1750 Alfas. A new, stiffer block casting was adopted, but apart from the use of an alternator instead of a dynamo, all the other details of the engine were the same – notably the handsone twin overhead camshaft alloy head with its two Weber twinchoke carburettors and elegantly branched exhaust manifold. The gearbox, like the engine an entirely characteristic Alfa unit, was a five-speed, with a long but stiff gearlever and one of the most pleasing and sweetly moving gearchanges we know – although the synchromesh was always a little weak, and needed cossetting before the gearbox oil had started to warm up. The makers were unusual in laying more stress than is usual now (or then) on warming the car up for two minutes or so before moving off – a hand throttle

was provided for the purpose.

Another Alfa distinction was their adherence to a live back axle, which, by positive and geometrically ideal location (by A-bracket and trailing links), provided a back end with none of the usual vices of cruder live axles. Front suspension was the usual independent wishbone arrangement; coil springs were used as before, and telescopic dampers, plus a front anti-roll bar. For reasons presumably of production flexibility, steering was either Burman cam and peg type or recirculating ball – not the usual rack and pinion associated with good steering, yet providing steering of unusually high and delightful quality, with very little feel-blurring friction but no unpleasant over-liveliness. All-disc brakes were used. All of these points were of course inherited from the previous Alfa range, as were the bodies of the GT Veloce coupé and the Spider Veloce two-seater.

The saloon offered comfortable seating – more comfortable if the driver was not too tall and had short-ish legs and long arms (this applied to all Alfas as it does still to the majority of Italian cars), tolerable room in the back, and a usefully sized boot. We found the turning circles rather too wide, and the brakes at first a little fierce. Minor control layout was criticized. The four-lamp lighting system came in for high praise, but we didn't think much of the ventilation, in spite of the provision of cabin outlets.

The Sprint GTV has always been a darling of enthusiasts, to a large extent because of its perfectly proportioned Bertone

body, yet also thanks to its performance, character and handling. In most opinions, there isn't a view of the car which is poor, which always made it a delight to own. The personality of the engine and transmission – Typically Italian in the best sense – eager, responsive, obedient yet restive, made the car feel as good as it looked, and as both are the same as in the saloon, the same comments applied. Handling and road behaviour – with the notable exception of ride – were (and are) superb, and because of the lower build of the car, that much better than the saloon. Ride was firm and joggly. The brakes and the way they were balanced front and rear impressed greatly. The body was reasonably practical, with a useful boot with a self-raising lid released from inside a door pillar. Headlamps, twin each side on this model, gave a flood of light that allowed the GTV driver to progress safely at night on country roads almost as quickly as he could by day.

One tended to approach the long-tailed Spider open two-seater a little suspiciously, questioning its perhaps too-styled appearance. A decent drive in the car quickly convinced one otherwise, that it had all the good characteristics of the GTV married to the delights of a good convertible which was also practical. The long tail meant a long boot, of great value on holiday for two. The hood remains an example to other (notably British) sports-car makers of how to provide a traditional soft top that is truly simple and quick to erect or take down.

What to look for

Being cars with a sporting flavour, any secondhand Alfa should be inspected carefully for any of the unfortunate results of hard use. On the engines of all 1750 and 2000 Alfas, one should look for cylinder head oil leaks, and down the sides of the block – these are common. Another usually small oil leak which may appear to stem from the back main bearing – oil from the bellhousing – in fact is more likely to be from the front of the gearbox, and we are told that generally it isn't worth worrying about. There are two timing chains driving the camshafts; the top one is adjustable, but the bottom one is not, so that if the latter sounds as if it will need replacing, an expensive job is likely.

It is worth checking the water pump, since unlike other such units, it also includes the rev counter drive, which makes it more costly to replace, if that is necessary; such trouble is unusual however. A noisy alternator is another trouble which can mean expense.

The transmission is something which some sorts of enthusiastic driver can misuse easily. Clutches on all Alfas tend to be a weak link, or at any rate over-worked. The usual tests should be applied; checking whether the take-up of drive occurs early or late in the pedal movement as it is allowed back (if late, near the fully-released end of the pedal travel, then the clutch is going to need relining soon); if it is late, then checking for clutch slip by momentarily over-loading the clutch with an abrupt full-power start.

The gearbox has quite a good reputation. Even a brand new Alfa box will grunt if hurried from 1st to 2nd when the oil is still cold, so don't' worry too much if the synchromesh doesn't seem as good as it is on a lot of humbler cars, like a Ford Escort, or Morris Marina. Check however for whether the gearlever will stay in reverse – jumping out is not unknown. Back axle trouble is not common, but if it did need attention it could be costly, because until recently, no exchange service was available.

Steering itself is usually all right. If a clonk can be induced by turning the wheel, it is usu-

Everything that's Alfa . . . a 1750 Veloce Spider in full flight at Silverstone

Above: The handsome and very conventional 1750 Berlina, which was to become the 2000

Above: The 1750 Spider had faired-in headlamps and minimal front bumper protection

Left: Alfa Romeo cockpits are designed very much for the driver; note the bottom-hinged pedals

Right: The rear of the 2000 Berlina, with the lamps slightly recessed in the tail panel

Below: The classic lines of the 1750 GTV two-door coupé

Buying Secondhand

ally the result of the large nut holding the steering drop arm which has worked loose. It should not do this, and if it has been allowed to remain thus for a long time, the steering box will need renewing. If not, it is possible to get away with tightening it "very tight."

The front suspension will in high mileage cars sometimes squeak when the front of the car is pushed down. This stems from the suspension bushes, which have no grease nipples, and are not cheap to replace.

Noises in the rear suspension are generally not worth worrying about. They can be removed sometimes by spraying the A-bracket pivots with oil (not grease). If they are serious, and will not go away when sprayed, proper stripping and replacement of worn bushes will be needed.

Brakes tend to take a beating in many Alfa drivers' hands. In too many cases, through no fault of the car, "a lot of people go right through pads" – to the destruction of discs, which have to be renewed. So even if the brakes seem all right when you try an Alfa, take the trouble to inspect the disc surfaces to see if they bear the scars of metal-to-metal contact.

As far as the bodywork is concerned, it is well to be wary of cars that have obviously been used for a lot of towing. The proper towing hitch set up for an Alfa is a comprehensive fitting that strengthens the back of the car suitably. If it has not been used, there is the possibility of body damage aft of the back doors. One might wonder a little at an owner who had bought an Alfa, even the saloon, and used it for towing a caravan; the car is not meant for that sort of carthorse job, of course. The proper tow hitch fitting can be spotted by inspection of the rear wheelarches, whose inner panels should have been strengthened in the join with the rest of the body by extra gas-welding along the seam.

Rust can attack an Alfa Romeo as much as any other car. Weakness of the sills due to corrosion may manifest itself just as it does with a BMC 1100/1300, by a collapsing jacking point. Rust can work out from the trim round the windows, on the tops of the front wings where mud can collect – another point of corrosion weakness in common with other makes – on the lower parts of the insides of the doors (where bubbling is usually the first sign), and, superficially, wherever there has been poor finish.

There is no shortage of Alfa Romeo dealers, who should have some secondhand stock to choose from. Their spares, in our experience of long term test cars, are not difficult to find, although they are naturally not the cheapest. The quotations and advice are from Mr Kensit, service manager of Hexagon of Highgate, to whom we are indebted for help with this article. □

All current Alfa Nord cars have the beautifully clean twin ohc engine, with aluminium cylinder head

Milestones

March 1968: Alfa Romeo 1750 saloon first imported to GB; smoothed out, sleeker Bertone-styled version of Giulia Super, but with enlarged 1,779 c.c. version of classic Alfa twin-ohc engine. Spider Veloce imported at same time.
April 1968: GT 1750 Veloce coupé introduced here, as previous 1600 with twin lamp system, and like Spider, shorter wheelbase.
March 1970: Saloon and GTV given halogen headlamps with load adjustment, sidelights and flashers on body instead of bumpers, with repeaters on wings. Twin servo, twin circuit brakes. Heated rear window standard on coupé.
July 1970: Import of long-tailed Spider stop.
April 1971: Spider with new short tail introduced here.
October 1971: 2000 saloon, GTV and Spider introduced here, to replace 1750 (last imports in February 1972), Bigger bore engine, 1,962 c.c. Exposed wheel nuts. Headlamps all same size and altered grille.
March 1974: Automatic saloon introduced. Special Equipment GTV with alloy wheels, tinted glass, vinyl roof introduced.

Chassis indentification

Dates and details	Series and chassis numbers	
March 1968: 1750 saloon imports start	AR	1460001
1750 Spider imports start	AR	1470001
April 1968: GTV imports start	AR	1450001
March 1970: Saloon with halogen lamps	AR	1464001
GTV with similar mods	AR	1454001
July 1970: long-tailed Spider stops	AR	1470674
April 1971: short-tail Spider starts	AR	1835001
October 1971: 2000 saloon introduced here	—	2400301
2000 GTV starts here	—	2410001
2000 Spider Veloce starts	—	2470001
March 1974: 2000 saloon automatic	—	2490001

Approximate selling prices

	1750			2000		
Price range	Sal.	GTV	Spider	Sal.	GTV	Spider
£400–£450	1968					
£450–£550	1969		1968	1968		
£550–£700	1970	1968	1969			
£700–£900	1971	1970	1970			
£900–£1,100	1971					
£1,100–£1,200			1971			
£1,200–£1,300				1972		
£1,400–£1,600				1973	1972	1972
£1,600–£2,000				1974	1973	1973
£2,000–£2,200				1975		
£2,300–£2,400					1974	1974
£2,400–£2,700					1975	1975

Performance Data

	1750 Sal.	1750 GTV	2000 Sal.	2000 GTV
Road Tested in *Autocar*:				
Mean Maximum speed				
(mph)	116	116	114	120
Acceleration (sec)				
0–30 mph	3·2	3·7	2·8	3·1
0–40 mph	5·4	5·9	4·6	4·7
0–50 mph	7·8	7·9	6·8	6·7
0–60 mph	10·8	11·2	9·9	9·2
0–70 mph	14·3	14·6	13·7	12·1
0–80 mph	20·2	19·0	18·6	16·2
0–90 mph	26·4	25·9	25·5	20·9
0–100 mph	40·1	36·9	38·9	27·7
Standing ¼-mile (sec		18·0	17·4	16·4
Top gear (sec)				
10–30 mph		—	—	
20–40 mph	13·3			
30–50 mph	11·3	12·8	11·9	12·1
40–60 mph	12·2	11·9	10·1	9·6
50–70 mph	13·7	12·9	11·4	9·8
60–80 mph	14·3	15·6	13·9	11·6
70–90 mph	19·7	19·4	16·6	14·3
80–100 mph	29·0	22·1	22·5	17·9
Overall fuel consumption				
(mpg)	23·1	23·9	21·8	21·1
Dimensions				
Length	14 ft 5in.	13ft 5in.	As	As
Width	5ft 1·7in.	5ft 2·2in.	1750	1750
Height	4ft 8·3in.	4ft 3·8in.	Sal,	GTV
Weight (cwt)	22·1	20·0	22·2	20·6

Spares prices – ex-concessionaires

Alfa Romeo	1750 Berlina	2000 Berlina	750 GTV	2000 GTV
Engine assembly (exchange)	£593.99	£630.73	£593.99	£630.73
Gearbox (exchange)	£183.71	£183.71	£183.71	£183.71
Final drive assembly (exchange)	£140.84	£140.84	£140.84	£140.84
Half shaft	£50.14	£50.14	£50.14	£50.14
Clutch assembly	£63.47	£65.28	£63.47	£65.28
Exhaust system complete	£52.65	£52.65	£51.43	£51.43
Front disc brake pads (set of four)	£7.83	£7.83	£7.83	£7.83
Rear disc brake pads (set of four)	£7.02	£7.02	£7.02	£7.02
Front suspension spring and damper	£20.78	£20.78	£19.46	£19.46
Rear suspension spring and damper	£20.85	£20.85	£18.99	£18.99
Alternator (exchange)	£34.29	£34.29	£34.29	£34.29
Starter motor (exchange)	£35.35	£35.35	£35.35	£35.35
Front wing panel	£46.02	£46.02	£66.34	£66.34
Front door shell (complete)	£86.67	£86.67	£101.15	£101.15
Windscreen	£48.99	£48.99	£47.77	£47.77

All prices supplied by Alfa Romeo (GB) Ltd. All include VAT at the standard rate of 8 per cent.

Continuing the new series on post-war classics and those who own and love them

"I BOUGHT it for £1,800 two years ago and I've just rejected an offer for much more than that." Vernon Thompson probably *will* sell his 1974 2000 GTV this year, but only because he's got his eye on another Alfa Romeo. "As soon as I got into my first Alfa (a Spider), the handling, the feel . . . it's hard to describe. You just become part of the machine."

Having raced a 2000 GTV, and driven many other variations of the same car on the road, I know what he means. So, I imagine, does technical editor Michael Scarlett who said of his long-term 1750 GTV back in 1971: "It is a car in which a sensitive driver rediscovers the pure pleasure of motoring." And isn't that what this series is all about: pleasure?

A Latin gem of an earlier era, the delectable Giulietta Sprint, sired the Bertone-styled Sprint GT 1600, the more angular lines of which were not initially greeted with universal acclaim after the gracefully curvaceous Giulietta, though you may find few styling critics today. Built at Alfa's own Arese plant rather than at Bertone's Turin body works, the new car was based on the mechanicals and shortened floorplan of the Giulia TI, with disc brakes all round, a higher final drive, five-speed gearbox and two twin-choke carburetters (Webers, Dellortos and Solex have all be used since) to feed the classic light-alloy twin-cam four-cylinder engine that was far from new when the car was first introduced at the Frankfurt Show in September, 1963.

Beneath the skin the car has changed a great deal — mostly for the better — throughout its 14-year lifespan, but the basic lines and mechanical configuration have remained fundamentally unaltered, despite numerous model changes that would tax the memory of the

corrosion." Although by no means the most civilised cars in the series with their spartan trim, minimal sound proofing and Perspex windows they have certainly proved to be the most durable with their rust-free aluminium bodies.

Then there was the rare and rather floppy open GTC (for Cabriolet) of 1965-66 built by the now defunct Touring concern — and not to be confused with the mechanically different Pininfarina-styled Spider, or Duetto as it was initially known following a competition to christen it. The 1300 GTA Junior (1968 to 1976) was another road-cum-competition car; the GTAm (1969 to 1971) a fuel-injected steel-bodied 1,779 c.c. model for the American market, using Spica fuel injection to satisfy emission regulations.

Some highly successful racers were based on the GTA (and GTAm) lightweights, of course, the most powerful and fastest of which was the supercharged 220 bhp, 155 mph Sport GTA Group 5 1600, though it is the unblown Autodelta cars that will be best remembered for their astonishing run of victories that spanned more than a decade and included the European Touring Car Championship. Although the BMW 2002 tii I raced in 1972 was a Group 1 winner on British tracks, the speed with which the 2-litre Autodelta Alfas passed it during the Spa 24 hours that year bordered on the humiliating.

Competition success has certainly underlined and glamorised the Alfa's sporting pretensions but the car's feel and performance as a road burner is sufficient to set it apart as something with extraordinary appeal that does not yet seem to have been inherited to quite the same degree by its successor, the Alfetta GTV. Although Vernon Thompson would like to replace his 2000 GTV with an Alfetta Strada, and very nice too, he concedes that certain aspects of the new car, notably its balance and gearchange, do not match up to his older Bertone model.

So what is it that makes this Alfa so attractive to drive, that endears it to so many enthusiastic owners? Of those I spoke to, most put its handy size, handling and road manners at the top of the list, particularly those with 2000 GTVs which have a limited slip diff to eliminate the infuriating wheelspin that afflicted earlier cars when accelerating on the turn. Despite the indiscriminate use of

ALFA ALLURE

Roger Bell looks at the Alfa Romeo GTVs, cars which bring back the pure pleasure of motoring

most ardent Alfa buff. Although the model nomenclature provides a fair guide to what's what, a brief recap would not go amiss.

The first 1,570 c.c., 106 bhp Sprint GT, soon joined by the GTV (V for Veloce) with better breathing, brakes and seats, was supplemented in 1966 by the 90 bhp 1300 GT Junior (using a twin-carb version of the old Giulietta engine) and replaced in 1968 by the 116 bhp, 1,779 c.c. 1750 GTV, which many owners contend is the best model of a classic series. *Autocar* was certainly pretty enthusiastic about it in the 1968 test: "The engine is a much beefier unit, always running more smoothly and with much less fuss than the 1600." Even so, despite higher gearing, a lower rev limit meant poorer intermediate maxima, and the acceleration of *Autocar's* test car (subsequently thought to be below par) was little better than that of the earlier 1600. It showed a marked improvement in economy, though, returning 24 mpg overall and recording some astonishing steady-speed figures (over 60 mpg at 30 mph) in its high (21.9 mph/1000rpm) overdrive fifth. "Compared with the 1600" said the glowing report "the 1750 felt a whole lot livelier, with even better steering, handling and brakes, and a much nicer interior." Vernon Thompson, who is also secretary of the Home Counties (NW) Alfa Romeo Club, shares this view. "I much prefer the 1750 engine and so do lots of other club members. I think it's because it revs so much more readily . . . "

The 1750GTV was superseded in 1971 by the big-bore 1,962 c.c. 2000GTV which delivers a healthy 122 bhp, though just to confuse the issue, a 1.6 GT Junior was re-introduced to run with the 1.3 in 1972 until production ceased in 1977. There were, in addition, several other more exclusive variations on the Sprint/GTV/Junior theme, the most cherished of which is the 125 mph lightweight Sprint GTA (1965 to 1969) which, thanks to its Alleggerita construction, weighed 190 kg less than the steel-bodied car, besides having a more powerful big-valve, twin-plug 115 bhp engine and a close-ratio gearbox. A boy racer it may have been, but a deadly serious one and a formidable contender in any 1600 competition. Writing in the excellent Alfa Romeo Owner's Club monthly, dicer and Alfa expert John Dooley states: "The GTAs will always be the most desirable, both for their history and their resistance to

two types of steering gear, neither of them rack and pinion, the car's precision and responsiveness are virtues that no keen driver can fail to appreciate. The unusual coil-sprung live back axle, located by low tailing arms and a high central trunnion bushed to the final drive assembly to provide secure lateral location, has a lot to do with the car's sharp handling.

To me, though, the Alfa's greatest attraction has always been the performance and guttural delivery of its evergreen engine, and the slickness of its delectable five-speed gearbox. Don't concern yourself about the engine being as long in the tooth as it is in stroke. Old and technically unfashionable it may be, but like Jaguar's ancient XK engine, which also has two chain-driven camshafts operating inclined valves in hemispherical combustion chambers, the classic specification is matched by rewarding and endearing results. And in the end it's results that count.

The 2000 GTV was — and still is — a very fast car. *Autocar's* 1972 test car clocked 122 mph and did 0-60 mph in 9.2 seconds. The report was even more glowing than previous tests: "The 2000 leaves the 1750 well behind all the way . . . with great flexibility as well as performance. The real attraction of the car is its feeling of precision and responsiveness; the extra power seems to have added to this without detracting from anything." Here, here. Although the 2-litre engine is much more of a gutsy slogger, red-lined at a modest 5700 rpm, than the high-speed revver you might expect of a race-bred twin-cam, its solid punch in the low and mid-speed ranges makes it in my book the best of the bunch. In character, it's certainly a very different engine from the original 1600 which, according to *Autocar's* road test "ran smoothly without clatter right up to 7500 rpm." Try that with a 2000 and you are likely to put a valve through a piston if not a rod through the side. Even so, if it's performance you want, particularly torquey performance, there's a simple Alfa rule: the bigger the engine the better.

And then there's that marvellous gearbox with its positive knife-through-butter change once the syrupy EP90 lubricant has thinned out after a cold start (Alfa purists say you should run the engine for a few minutes before moving off just to let the oil penetrate every bearing and cone to alleviate notchiness. It wasn't

Vernon Thompson (right) with his 1974 2000 GTV, worth more now than he paid for it two years ago. But he admits that you must pamper the car. "After I've been out on snow or ice I hose down underneath to get rid of salt." Such dedication is needed if you run a classic that is so vulnerable to rust

The interior (top right) is classic Alfa. Deep cowled instruments and dished steering wheel give the car an uncluttered yet purposeful air. The big-bore 1,962 c.c. engine delivers 122 bhp and superseded the 1750 GTV in 1971. An engine of great flexibility as well as performance

so long ago that this Alfa box was the one by which all others were judged, so it's not surprising that so many owners express disappointment in the gearchange of the Alfetta GTV, with its long, contorted linkage to the rear-mounted transaxle. "It's got a linkage like a rubber band" says a disparaging John Goodchild who, like many GTV fanatics (including me) prefer the old car to the new, at least as a pure driving machine.

With partner Malcolm Morris, John Goodchild specialises in servicing, repairing and restoring Alfas from somewhat primitive quarters under the railway arches in Galena Road, Hammersmith. It goes without saying that they operate outside the importer's dealership umbrella, but low charges and good workmanship nevertheless attract many owners from the Alfa Romeo owner's club, of which Goodchild is himself a member. "An engine rebuild, with new pistons, liners, camshaft chain, guides, valves, reground crank and so on, costs £300-£400". For a sophisticated twin cam, that's not bad, though corrosion in the alloy casting around the wet liner seats will mean a new block and a fatter wallet. Mechanical trouble is not the main worry with these Alfas, though. "The mechanics are basically very sound and reliable – a well maintained engine is good for at least 80,000 miles" says Goodchild. "What's more, they're dead easy to work on once you know what you're doing, and spares are readily available, even for early 1300s." Vernon Thompson reinforces both points. "I commute to London every day in my car and I've had no serious problems in two years. The plugs foul in traffic sometimes, but they soon clear after a quick blast. Spares? No problem. You soon get to know from other club members where the good discounts are."

Morris and Goodchild can reel off the trouble spots by heart, not all of them confined to elderly cars either. "We must have changed 20 brake master cylinders on relatively young 2000 GTVs in the past six months. They get bombarded with muck from the offside front wheel, the protective rubber seal perishes and salty water penetrates the cylinders and corrodes them." The floor-hinged pedals, so often criticised in road tests because of their awkward angle, are also prone to seizure. "Snow and water dribble off your feet onto the pivot rod which can rust solid in no time." Fortunately, the pendant pedals of the Alfetta GTV are not so vulnerable.

Although mechanically sound, the steel-bodied Bertone coupés were regrettably not built with longevity in mind, at least not in cold, wet climates. "The odd left-hand drive cars we've had from sunny places are invariably quite good bodily." nevertheless,

terminal corrosion has already sent many cars that were imported to Britain to the breaker's yard. "Don't look at a car that's bodily unsound" warns Goodchild. "You can rebuild the mechanical bits without much trouble but once the body's gone, that's it." Body expert Malcolm Morris continues the tail of woe. "Everything goes . . . the sills, wings, doors, floorpan, boot, the lot. We've seen jacking points collapse after two years. Morris, who races an Alfa and loves his road car, doesn't pull any punches about the notorious rust problem that afflicts these Alfas, as it does so many Italian cars. "There's a lot of GTVs around that *look* good" he warns. "But they're actually full of filler. And beware of an old car that's been recently treated with an under sealant. All that does is trap the damp and accelerate the corrosion." Body spares are readily available but they're not cheap says Morris: "A boot lid costs about £75, a bonnet over £100. And to replace a door skin can mean buying a complete new door, with all its winder and latch mechansim."

It is partly because the aluminium-bodied GTAs are immune to rust that they command the highest prices, though body panels for them *are* scarce, not to say expensive. Even though they buckle easily in a knock, dents are preferable to rust. On buying a used Alfa, Goodchild takes a firm line. "Be very careful. Vet it properly otherwise you could finish up with a heap of junk". Glass-fibre panels *are* available but, needless to say, scorned by the purists. Better to get hold of a car *before* the rot sets in and then pamper it. And I mean pamper! Says Vernon Thompson: "After I've been out on snow or ice, I hose the car down underneath to get rid of the salt." Such dedication, it seems, is the price you have to pay for running a vulnerable classic.

Ironically, it is because they are so prone to rust and therefore diminishing in numbers that good GTVs are appreciating in value. "I reckon 70 per cent of them are going or gone" says Goodchild. So it's not surprising that good ones are snapped up pretty quickly. when a car with such a good pedigree, attractive looks and dynamic driving qualities starts to get scarce, it soon becomes an appreciating asset as well as a fun machine. Vernon Thompson's 1974 2000 GTV, which is in first-class condition if not quite to concours standard, could well fetch £2500 – £700 more than he paid for it two years ago. It indicates the way prices are going for pristine examples. A good Spider of the same vintage, incidentally, would be worth even more. On the other hand Alfa bangers – and there are a lot of them around, so beware – can be picked up for little more than scrap value.

PROFILE

Alfa Romeo 2000 GTV

The stylish Giulia coupés marketed between 1963 and 1977 represent many people's idea of what an Alfa Romeo is. 2000 GTVs, like this above, are becoming collector's items

BERTONE'S BEAUTY

On paper, the 2000 GTV has plenty going for it. It has a famous name, a fine competition pedigree and is a genuinely satisfying driving machine. Jon Dooley looks back at this 'end of an era' Alfa Romeo

The 2000 GTV comes from one of the oldest and most romantic names in the business. It isn't perfect, but it is bursting with character, has a competition pedigree in its own right, and has a shape that is hard to better these days. It has a body styled by one of Italy's leading houses that is still beautiful and surprisingly modern 19 years after it first appeared. It actually represents many people's idea of what an Alfa Romeo is. And it is a totally practical buy.

Strangely enough the Alfetta 2000 GTV replacement is only just becoming appreciated for the very capable car it is, for the first examples were, unfortunately, not too well set up. This gave a kicker to old model 2000 GTV demand right from the end of its new availability.

But perhaps most of all, the 2000 GTV represents the last expression of those carefree days before emissions and blanket speed limits. Drive one today and the experience of uncluttered engine breathing brings back all the nostalgic memories of sunshine, mini or midi skirts, wonderful inflation and property

booms that made life so much fun! Nostalgia it's true, but what a practical tonic this can be.

It is surely appropriate that the word Veloce translates as something altogether more subtle than the crudity of the English word fast. It embodies the effortless nuances of rapid, the accurate direction of swift and most of all the total capability of A to B travel in short shrift summed up in that modern motoring word, quick. And while we are on the dictionary stuff, it's pronounced vay-loh-chay, with pure vowell sounds, please.

Tremendous little road cars

The first Alfa Veloces were lightweight Giulietta Sprint Veloces, hot perspex windowed, twin Webered Bertone-bodied coupés, launched just in time for the 1956 Mille Miglia. A genuine 90bhp and over 112mph, coupled with famed Giulietta nimbleness, made them tremendous little road cars for the enthusiast and competitive contenders in racing or rallying.

Those first Veloces were aimed specifically at the two lane give and take roads that covered most of Europe at that time. Regular use of the gears was expected and running up to 7000rpm plus, was all part of the recipe. The succeeding 20 years saw the growth of motorway networks and gradual overcrowding of the traditional roadways, so that the need for virtuoso driving performance on journeys was replaced by the need for instant pick-up from any speed and for high speed cruising ability.

The introduction and development of the Giulia range from 1962 was Alfa's response to that change, a response that was to increase hugely their market share and bring alloy twin cam engines within the purchasing power of the man in the street. The 2000 range represented the culmination of that development in circumstances that can truly be described as the end of an era.

The 2000 GTV on which we are concentrating, traces not only its name but also its mechanical ancestry back to the Giulietta. Launched in 1954 in

Rear three quarter view emphasises the compact overall shape and cleanliness of line. Bumper overriders and rear tail lights incorporating reversing lights make this a 2000 GTV

Sprint coupé form initially, the Giulietta presented, for the first time, the formula of an alloy twin cam engine within a shell mounted on coil springs all round with wishbone front suspension and a well located lightweight live axle at the rear. Sound, if not revolutionary, design backed by accurate execution ensured outstanding performance for a 1290cc car, capable of just under 100mph even in relatively humble TI four-door saloon form.

Those first Giulietta engines relied heavily on sand castings, but by 1959 the factory had tooled up to die-cast a new block with sufficient meat to permit future enlargements. Giuliettas from that time on carried the type number 101 and had the benefit of a new gearbox with Porsche synchromesh, introduced in 1958, with various body and chassis improvements.

First of a new generation

In June 1962 the first Giulias were ready. The Sprints and Spiders were, however, nothing more than 1570cc-engined Giuliettas, although with five speed gearboxes, and therefore continued to be 101 types. The new saloon, the TI, was quite different – though following a similar formula – and was the first of the new generation Tipo 105. Engine and gearbox were nothing new – size apart – and continued to be built at the old Portello factory for a while. The chassis on the other hand was assembled, like the boxy new body, at a completely fresh factory complex erected at Arese on the outskirts of North West Milan and reflected modern technology and thinking. Modern maintenance free bushings cut greasing to a minimum and front end spring rates and roll bar stiffness were significantly increased over the Giulietta's, to take advantage of improving tyre technology. Massive lower front wishbones were bolted to an equally massive front cross member that ran under the engine and supported it. The upper front wishbone assembly became a triangle formed by a straightforward tie arm and an adjustable castor control arm. At the rear, the live axle was well located by a pair of trailing arms and a 'T' shaped arm attached to the top of the diff casing, ensuring excellent behaviour apart from the effects of a rather high roll centre.

Brakes at that stage were glamorous and very powerful finned drums, with three leading shoes 2.75ins wide at the front. For cost reasons these were superseded by a Dunlop disc system from the end of 1963 which unfortunately was not totally satisfactory in service and was itself superseded by the altogether better Ate disc system from 1967. All had five speed gearboxes, a welcome feature that was to become an Alfa Romeo trademark over the coming years.

By the end of 1963 more progress had been made at Arese and the next contributor to the star of our piece was shown to the world, at Frankfurt. The Giulia Sprint GT, unlike any previous Alfa coupé, was to be built in house. It was still a Bertone design – *disegno di Bertone* the badge says – and was one of the early works from the pen of a youthful Giugiaro. As a shape, it resembled his first Bertone contribution – the Gordon GT/Alfa 2000 soon to be 2600 Sprint – but was on a smaller scale. It had a character all its own contributed by aggressive flare lines running from front to back atop and to the side of the wings. As a design to live with, it was much more practical than the beautiful Giulietta Sprint and offered quite a practical +2 rear seat, not just for the *bambini* but even for *giovanotti*. It must be said that at the time enthusiasts thought it would never be a successful classic like the Giulietta Sprint! Some 14 years later enthusiasts were trying to track down the last remaining new 2000 GTVs and 1.6 GT Juniors, displaced by the next doubtful bit of Alfa progress, the equally commercially successful Alfetta GT.

Within those years Alfa continued evolving, developing and selling a whole range of variants. Concentrating on the Giugiaro coupé, and ignoring all the saloons (probably more outstanding in their market place than any of the coupés) and the two-seater Spiders, you are still confronted by lists of models as Alfa play musical chairs with engine sizes in shell variants.

In February 1965 a competition version of the GT was launched, the GTA. A for *alleggerita* meant lightened and as this was a car designed to win, that meant 4.5cwt saved. All the outer panelling was in thin alloy sheet, pressed out on the steel dies and pop riveted to the frame. Even the spare wheel well was alloy!

In March 1965, the world's press was taken to a misty Monza and hurtled round the road circuit, four up, in a new open Cabriolet version of the Sprint GT, the GTC. Like the GTA, the GTC is now a rare model and a collector's item. It also, sadly, represented one of the final flings of the coachbuilder Touring, who were descending into the Italian equivalent of receivership and ultimately absorption by Alfa. Touring's contribution was to add substantial strengthening of the standard floor pan and front and rear bulkhead areas, so that structural rigidity was conserved in spite of the lack of a roof. They largely succeeded, but only 1000 were produced before commercial and logistical problems called a halt.

Exactly a year later a Veloce reappeared, the Giulia Sprint GT Veloce. Following various experiments Alfa had actually discovered that reducing inlet port diameters improved power, torque and fuel economy. Whether because of this or the various other small improvements, the 1600 GTV, as it became known, was a particularly pleasant model, especially when fitted with Ate brakes. It was certainly more easily capable of 0-100mph inside 30secs than its non-Veloce forbear.

In the second half of 1966 another reason for the 1600 Veloce appeared in the shape of the 1300 GT Junior, a cut-price version fitted with the ex-Giulietta 1290cc engine, now updated with smaller ports, two twin choke carbs, improved camshafts from the 1600 and so on. Early road test figures indicated that the Junior could run the non-Veloce Sprint GT close on performance to about 90mph.

From a marketing standpoint the Junior was very significant in Italy, because of the Italian road tax system which attacks cars heavily according to engine size. These 1300s were especially sweet running and, although a little heavy for the torque available, could reward the keen driver with exceptional journey times, rather in the mould of those original Giulietta Veloces, in return for plenty of revs and use of the gearbox.

1750 versions launched

In complete contrast was the next development in January 1968. Following the path of offering slightly better performance for considerably less driver effort, Alfa replaced the 1600 with the 1779cc 1750, as always in saloon, coupé and open two-seater forms. The coupé, named the 1750 GTV, now featured a four headlamp frontal arrangement within a particularly tasteful matt black grille and, whereas previously the leading edge of the bonnet had been raised relative to the top front panel, the 1750 bonnet became flush fitting. Inside the facia had improved with the addition of instrument binnacles for the large round rev counter and speedometer, and lesser instruments were repositioned on a new centre console. Seating was improved with some orthopaedically fitting, but corrugated looking front seats that were extremely comfortable. The new power unit was created by taking liners out to the maximum of 80mm bore and fitting a larger 88.5mm stroke crankshaft. The result was a rated 9bhp increase in power at 500 fewer rpm and a massive improvement in peak torque. The necessary higher gearing made flat out acceleration barely better than a well tuned 1600, but the gain in refinement and ease of travel at less than full tilt was more than worthwhile.

Helping refinement was the adoption, for the first time, of a hydraulically operated diaphragm clutch to replace the cable operated predecessors. This was extended to the rest of the range, the GT Junior, the Spider Junior and the Giulia saloons, from January 1969, as were wider 14in diameter wheels and rear anti-roll bar first seen on the 1750.

From early 1971, a 1600 coupé returned to the range when the 1300 Junior was revamped to accept 1750 panelling and dash, while being renamed the GT Junior 1.3 and having a 1.6 option.

During the summer came the culmination of this line of development when Alfa showed their full 2-litre, still within the same basic block layout. However, the overboring on the 1750 had proved a little marginal for head gasket sealing, so that the necessary 84mm bore for the 2-litre was achieved by juggling the liner centres a little to provide some more meat. The crankshaft was similar to the later 1750s with tuftrided journals and high accuracy matched bearing shells. The same high ratio axle gave almost 22mph per thousand revs and almost invariably came with an optional ZF limited slip diff installed. In the UK the lsd was standardised on all 2-litres from about February 1972 and helped to overcome a developing major criticism of the series as power increased, the tendency to spin an inside rear wheel on tight turns. The ability to maintain traction at all times also did a lot to keep the handling balanced.

Thanks to a different cylinder head with bigger valves, the 2-litre pushed out another 14bhp compared to the 1750 with a significant increase in torque as well. Performance again showed only a marginal gain versus the watch but felt a lot better to the driver.

Some restyling had to take place for the new model. A revised front grille had a mixed reception after the far more successful 1750 layout. And the instrumentation, though perfectly effective and attractive, lacked the purist appeal of the 1750s. The rear wheelarches were lifted slightly, apparently to give greater clearance for wider tyres which were never actually fitted by the factory. Larger rear lamp units incorporated reversing lights and yet another seating revision occurred, with cloth trim proving a popular option.

The final fling of this particular dynasty was the production of GT Junior 1.3s and 1.6s, using the revised 2000 shell, from 1974 onward, although in the UK as part of the tidying up of the last remaining 2000 GTV stock an SE version was offered with vinyl roof, alloy wheels, rear fog warning lights and radio cassette standardised. The SE version, although well equipped, was a rather tarty affair.

High standing floor pedals

Stepping into a right hand drive GTV, one of the first things you notice are the high standing pedals (which are pendant with lhd), which can be a problem to the unagile with small feet. Those, like me, with size 12s find them ideal! The accelerator pedal hangs alongside and can be 'adjusted' as near as you like, its long pad making it easy to heel and toe. The front seats are comfortable without being fully wrap-around with reclining backrests and integral headrests having height adjustment via a wheel. Long-legged drivers may wish to have more tilt in the seat base, achievable by playing with the spacers under the runners. If the car has had a very sheltered life it may still have a pin across the rear of a runner limiting rearward travel; that pin can be removed without causing problems, after withdrawing its securing circlip. In this way even the Anglo Saxon ape can be accommodated in comfort.

There is no steering wheel adjustment but there are no special difficulties, with instruments straight ahead and all the lighting control stalks just behind the wheel.

To start from cold generally needs just four or so prods on the throttle pedal, a closed throttle and a turn of the key. Very occasionally a car needs use of the choke, perhaps because its float level setting is at the bottom tolerance. Starting from hot, you hold the pedal to the floor (no prods) and turn the key till she

The Bertone shape encompasses a superb range of exciting Alfas. 2000s and late model 1.3 and 1.6 Juniors looked very similar

fires. Carburation may be by twin twin choke 40mm Webers, Dell'Ortos or Solexes, all of which are sound instruments, although it is easier to find spares for the first two makes. For a given choke size there is fractionally more power from Dell'Orto but the Weber floats seem to behave a touch better in corners, under extreme duress.

Once running you are struck by the throaty thrum of induction and exhaust. There is never any doubt about there being a large four cylinder engine ahead of you, yet the instant response and the nature of the sounds, including the gentle whirr of overhead cams, tells you that it is precision machinery.

The sense of solid precision stays as you declutch (pedal fairly heavy – enough for .5g braking) and push the sturdy gearlever at first gear, not too

quickly or the gears have not stopped spinning and you'll crunch. By the way, although all five gears are synchronised, for some strange, traditional, Alfa reason the little widget that would give you synchro to change *up* into first (from neutral) has been left out. One day I'll build a 'box with one in and find out why they left it out! In the meantime those in a hurry to find bottom go via a touch at second which stops the geartrain whirling.

Bottom gear is fairly high – don't drive off in second as so many people manage to kill their clutches quickly when they will last almost for ever with proper treatment. Continuous ill-treatment will overheat the flywheel and start hairline cracking, though I've never known one break up. Driving off gently, you'll find you will soon be covering the

Alfa Romeo 2000GTV

Specification

Engine	In-line 'four'	Steering	Recirculating ball or cam and peg
Construction	Alloy block and head	Body	Monocoque, all-steel
Bearings	Five	Tyres	165 HR 14 radials
Capacity	1962cc	Length	13ft 5in
Bore/stroke	84.0mm × 88.5mm	Width	5ft 2¼in
Valves	Twin overhead camshafts (chain-driven)	Height	4ft 5¾in
		Wheelbase	7ft 8½in
Compression	9.1:1	Weight	20.6cwt
Power	131bhp (DIN) at 5500rpm		
Torque	134lb.ft (DIN) at 3000rpm	**Performance**	
Transmission	Five-speed manual	Max. speed	120mph
Top gear	22.0mph per 1000rpm	0-60mph	8.9sec
Final drive	Hypoid, 4.10:1 ratio	30-50mph in top	10.9sec
Brakes	Discs front and rear. Twin servos*	50-70mph in top	9.7sec
Suspension F.	Ind. by coils, wishbones, anti-roll bar	Standing ¼ mile	16.5sec
		Fuel	
Suspension R.	Live axle, coils, radius arms. T-bracket, anti-roll bar	consumption	21/24mpg
		* RHD only	

Typically Italian interior', complete with wood-rim wheel

All alloy Alfa 'four' has plenty of power and torque

This rather depressing illustration, left, shows the main areas of exterior 2000 GTV corrosion! The shaded portions are often the first to go and should be checked carefully; don't be too put off, though, by a sound car that has rusty exterior panels if the body is generally solid and complete. Generally speaking, GTV rust damage is cosmetic as opposed to structural and replacement panels and repair sections are readily available. Bodged body lash ups involving quantities of glass-fibre filler are to be avoided at all costs

Rear legroom is cramped but better than you might think

ground pretty rapidly using only about 4000rpm – i.e. just under 90mph in top. Lots of torque, a willing engine and the small size of the car linked to the secure knowledge via the steering wheel of what the car will do next, all provide encouragement. Both Alfa and Ferrari have this "user-friendly" feeling, maybe because both have shared that Mille Miglia test downhill on the Futa or Radicofani passes in the wet on glistening Italian tarmac.

On the standard supply 165×14 rubber, pretty pathetic when new and shall we say poor a decade later, roadholding was never a strong point. In the UK front end grip was further reduced by the need to lift the front end a touch to pass headlight height regulations. With some adjustment though, even the most menial rubber, make unmentionable, could be made to perform. What made up for it all was handling produced, not so much by balance, as by accurate control of all the contributing factors. Basically while it was balanced, in the words of one writer, like a hammer, it was a very precisely made hammer and allowed very rapid travel across country because of its progressive and consistent behaviour.

Delightful cruising ability

Another delight of the car is its cruising ability. With a red line at 5700rpm but no real risk to mechanicals, other than wear, below 7000, the car is ambling along at only 4600rpm at 100mph. For real one upmanship over lesser vehicles, try an upchange to top at around 110mph while passing!

General mechanical refinement is very good at these speeds but whereas saloons, notably Giulia Supers, have almost no wind noise, the GTV's suffer from poorer aerodynamics around the screen and sidewindow areas as well as weaker sealing of the latter. But in a fun car this matters very little.

And as a fun car, the 2000 GTV is pretty practical. For just two people there is lots of space for luggage on the rear seat and in the boot. The +2 bit is useable, provided the front seat occupants are not too tall and those in the rear are not above about 5'9" in height. They should also not be *too* heavy remembering the Giulia's stiff front spring/soft rear spring layout. Mpg is very much a matter of driver sensitivity but figures normally range from 22mpg (driven hard) to 30mpg (trickling along at legal speeds), unless in town of course.

Altogether the 2000 GTV is a car of strong character. Some may dislike its grittiness and the strong messages it provides. Others will enjoy the strong car/driver relationship that is created and the sense of security imparted.

Production history

The first of the Giulia coupé line, the beautiful Sprint GT, was built between 1963 and 1966. During that time, 21542 examples left the Arese works. Manufacture of the ultimate variant, the 2000 GTV ranged between 1971 and 1975 although the final marketing of the model did not cease until 1977. In all, 37,459 2000 GTVs were made up until the end of 1977.

Production of the 2000 GTV went hand in hand with the vastly underrated 2-litre Berlina saloon. Some Alfa connoisseurs rate this 'poor man's Quattroporte' a better-handling car than its GTV cousin though, sadly, too few of the 89,840 Berlinas made between 1970 and 1977 will be in cherished condition today.

The 2000 GTV was first shown to the Press in June 1971 but UK deliveries did not start until after October. Apart from the rather gaudy 2000 GTV SE, which was a limited-edition, special equipment version of the breed, there were no changes to the GTV's technical specification during the short five-year production run. The three-speed ZF automatic transmission offered as a Berlina option was not available on the GTV. Controversy still abounds concerning the fitment of limited slip diffs to UK market 2000 GTVs although we can confirm that lsds were standardised here from early 1972 onwards. Some minor restyling occurred with the arrival of the 2000 GTV – the grille was altered (some say for the worse!) along with the facia, seats, rear wheel arches and rear tail lights, and this theme continued onto the final GTVs, the 1.3 and 1.6 Juniors, produced from 1974 onwards. The 1.6 was available in the UK up until mid 1977 but the smaller 1.3 version was never imported, it seems.

Buyers spot check

One of the beauties about keeping any Alfa Giulia, or even Giulietta - of the 101 type - on the road is that Alfa have been producing pretty consistently much the same engines for years. Detailed specifications may change but generally there are always components around that can be fitted, sometimes after slight mods. And the models have been produced in sufficient volume to ensure good supply, both new and from breakers. Alfa are still producing 1.6 and 2-litre engines today for the Giulietta/Alfetta range and wearing components such as pistons and liners, bearings, valves and so on can be used on the older models and will be available off the shelf for many years. Chassis components are very robust but

if bushings or ball joints do need replacing supplies are ample – the Giulia Diesel was still in production until very recently.

Brakes are pretty reliable on the 2-litre, although less so on early Dunlop braked Giulias, but come in for their fair share of master cylinder and caliper faults. Twin servos on rhd cars are another complication and sometimes it is necessary to bleed the twin circuit system front and rear together, with the engine running as well, to ensure the servos are scavenged. Braking action is very powerful as the front brakes especially, are very large for the size of the vehicle, considerably larger for instance than on the Alfetta.

Many aspects of the car are in fact rather over-engineered relative to the size of vehicle, no bad fault in a car to keep. Take a look at all those alloy castings, including the massive finned sump with a cleverly arranged labyrinth of baffles to prevent surge under any circumstances. Never ever rebuild one of these engines without removing the bottom pan of the sump because you will never be able to get it completely clean otherwise.

Bodywork? Ah yes. They have been known to rust. But to be down to earth, these cars have always invited being *used* and any car run around through salt solution four months a year is going to have its problems by the time it is six years old. Caught early enough, corrosion can always be isolated to a few areas – the sills, the front and rear valances, the radiator carrier, the rear wheelarches, the rears of the front wings, one or two points on the boot floor and a couple more areas of random choice. Water that has been allowed to leak into the wrong place can do a lot of damage over a period. Badly fitted trim strips can cause their own mayhem, at the tops of the doors for instance. All these problems can be dealt with quite simply. If they are left to fester, then the problem extends within a couple of years to door frames, door posts, main box side members, floor and so on. That doesn't matter as the solutions are still there; they simply cost more and demand more work to achieve a fine result.

Maintaining an engine is simple enough from a service standpoint but as with anything costlier than the average, errors or mechanical accidents are punished. Running the engine with insufficient oil or coolant brings trouble sooner than with your average Ford. An alloy block suffers worse from freezing up with no antifreeze or corrosion if the wrong antifreeze is used. On the other hand wet liners make reboring or replacing easy to arrange for the DIY man. The high grade materials used in the twin cam layout make valve clearance adjustment difficult for Mr

The rather gaudy end-of-line 2000 GTV SE was available in the UK only

Rare and very desirable: the Touring produced Giulia GTC Cabriolet

GTVs ancient and modern grouped together at the Alfa Romeo OC's National Day

This early advertisement for the 2000 GTV underlines the car's all-round potency

DIY but then this job is scarcely ever necessary. Once set they never change. Kept on an even keel by timely sensible maintenance, engines will run to high mileages without overhaul and accept a lot of hard driving with total reliability. Take a flier and neglect them and the costs to recover the damage could be considerable.

Having said that I am constantly amazed by the way engines in hopeless condition continue to perform . . . they are pretty strong!

Dampers, particularly at the rear have a shortish life, lower front suspension ball joints wear ahead of the rest, rear radius arm bushes get blamed a lot for poor dampers or oil-destroyed T-arm bushes on the diff pivot, handbrake cables wear out or drop on the road and destroy themselves, headlamps get Carello disease, standing pedals seize on their cross shafts, second gear synchromesh deteriorates ahead of the rest, reverse gear selector forks bend allowing popping out of gear under load, centre propshaft steady bearing rubbers soften producing rumble on the tunnel, rear springs sag and rear bump stops fall off, to name but a few syndromes.

But parts are readily available both from Alfa via the dealer network and from enthusiast specialists such as EB Spares, selling direct via mail order. In fact it is only fair to say that Alfa themselves show quite a lot of enthusiasm for keeping older cars on the road. In a sense with the Giulias and especially the 2000s, we have seen for the first time in Alfas sufficient manufacturing volume for spares demand and supply to be maintainable on a reasonably economic basis.

Even now panel supply is not really any sort of problem for the coupés and as specific panels go non-available from Alfa, alternative suppliers can probably pick them up one by one.

Rivals when new

No prizes will be given to anyone who suggests that the BMW 2002 Tii was the 2000 GTV's closest rival during the time it was in production. In terms of engine sizes, specification, image and price, the two cars were (and are) remarkably similar. Performance is near identical too although some road tests show the BMW to be slightly the faster. Bavarian bravado or happy-go-lucky Italian flair? Take your pick. Both cars are stylish, compact and fast, although it's likely to be the Alfa that turns more heads in the street nowadays.

Other eligible contenders include the Fiat 124 Coupé 1800, Ginetta G21 1800 and the Lotus +2S 130 and, just conceivably, the Lancia Coupé Rally S3. The Lancia only had a 1298cc engine but it was a car definitely in the GTV mould, being fast, fun to drive, attractive-looking – and Italian.

Clubs, specialists and books

The Alfa Romeo Owners Club must be one of the UK's most active one-make organisations. An impressive range of social and competitive events occur each year, the highlight of the 1982 programme being undoubtedly National Alfa Day at Knebworth House on September 5.

While it's true that there's a strong AROC contingent participating in 750 MC and COMCC events (some of these fixtures feature Handicap Alfa-only races), the club has 11 regional secretaries and five register secretaries handling the social aspects of club life. Details of the many local pub meetings that occur each month can be found in the club's excellent magazine, which also contains plenty of Alfa-type news and reports on the AROC's varied autotests, sprints and production car trials. At the back of the

magazine, there is a series of 'For Sale/Wanted' classifieds as well as a round up of F1 news, written by the magazine joint editor, Michael Lindsay. 12 copies a year of the magazine can be yours for £12, membership details being available from Jil Maxted, Friars Way Cottage, Sheephatch Lane, Tilford, Farnham, Surrey.

By our reckoning the last 2000 GTV is now almost seven years old so some of the newer Alfa Romeo dealers might not be too keen to service these pre Alfetta coupés. Your local AROC secretary should be able to pinpoint those that will in your area but if it's official service work that you require, why not go right to the top and try Alfa Romeo London Sales at Edgware Road, London NW2 6LW (tel: 01 450 8641)? For expert body/mechanical restorations and routine servicing, Brookside Garage of 55 High Street, Wrestlingworth, Sandy, Beds (tel: 076 723 217) must figure close to the top of the list as should J & R Goodchild Engineering whose address is 2 Garrick Crescent, Parkhill Road, Croydon CR0 5PW (tel: 01 680 2120). Other recommended Alfa addresses in the London area must include Ramponi Rockwell of 47 Lancaster Mews, London W2 3QQ (tel: 01 262 2449), Bell & Colvill Ltd of Epsom Road, West Horsley, Surrey (tel: East Horsley 4671), Alfista (Special Developments Ltd) of 10/12 The Viaduct, Sherwood Road, South Harrow (tel: 01 422 4594) and Peter Hilliard & Son of 41 High Street, Penge, London SE20 7HJ. (tel: 01 778 5755).

To round off this awe-inspiring list of Alfa specialists, we must mention John Clifton, the AROC's scrutineer, whose forte is mechanical surgery (address: 'Giulia', Horsham Road, Forest Green, Dorking, Surrey; tel: 03067 0340) plus Alfacentre of Turgis Green, Basingstoke, Hants RG27 0AG (tel:

0256 882831), and EB Spares of 2 Washington Road, West Wilts Trading Estate, Westbury, Wilts (tel: 0373 823856). These last two concerns are especially useful for new and used Alfa parts. Last, but by no means least, there's Richard Banks of 7 Wenny Road, Chatteris, Cambs (tel: Chatteris 2460), whom you might like to contact should you want to buy or sell a good condition, low-mileage Giulia model.

Any review of Alfa Romeo reading matter must start with Luigi Fusi's remarkable bible, *Alfa Romeo Tutte Le Vetture Dal 1910*. This fantastic book which is a definite must for any serious Alfa buff, has been updated at least three times since its 1965 launch and is now available with an English translation at a reduced price from leading specialist bookshops such as Chater & Scott. Fusi's 870-odd page tome makes a first-rate job of identifying all the machines produced bearing the famous Alfa or Alfa Romeo name since 1910 and for that reason alone it carries an 'indispensible' rating from us. The third edition goes up until 1977 so the 2000 GTV is safely covered.

Alfissimo! (Osprey) by David Owen is a creditable review of the post-war Alfa Romeos powered by the famous four-cylinder twin overhead camshaft engine; thus the book covers in some depth the 1900 plus the myriad Giuliettas, Giulias, Alfettas and current Giuliettas as well as other Alfa topics. It's an interesting, well-illustrated book but many Alfa enthusiasts view *Alfissimo!* with mixed feelings.

The Japanese have recently produced two interesting Alfa Romeo books, the first being a soft cover catalogue of the exciting factory museum at Arese. Although there is already a large-format lavish book covering the same subject, this new work entitled simply *Museo Alfa Romeo* is well worth buying for its competitive price, delightful illustrations and English text! The other oriental offering, *The Alfa Romeo* is another book in the 'Creative Boutique Neko' series. If you can read Japanese, fine; if you can't, this book is still worthwhile for its splendid colour photos of some genuinely emotive machinery. Finally, there's *Alfa Romeo*, which is a pocket-sized, condensed history of the company up until the present day. Many of the photos have been seen before and the text (thankfully in English) is skimpy to say the least but at £2.50 one obviously can't be too critical. As a simple guide to the company's products and exploits, it is recommended reading.

On the technical front, the AROC can supply a hefty workshop manual which covers the 2000 GTV and a comprehensive Giulia 1750/2000 parts book. These two guides are official Alfa Romeo publications, incidentally. Finally, Autobooks have produced a slim workshop manual on Giulias of 1962/1978 vintage.

Prices

Over a million Giulias of all types were built by Alfa Romeo so it's no exaggeration to say that there are plenty about still. Records show that more than 37,000 2000 GTVs left Arese between 1971 and 1977 and it's now come to the point where clean, low-mileage examples are beginning to fetch fairly high prices.

Expect to pay around £1200/£1500 for a sound, comparatively rust-free example with an MOT and up to £2000/£2400 for a respectable, known-history GTV with little evidence of the dreaded body rot. Truly outstanding cars can command in excess of £3500 with concours winners topping £5000 plus, although a car in this latter category will be a rare beast indeed.

The 2000 GTV is just starting to become a sought-after motor car even though there seem to be plenty of 'average' £800/£1000 ones about. Parts are freely available either new or from decrepid Berlinas and the like but if you're thinking of buying a tired GTV to renovate, we suggest choosing one costing £600 or less. For that kind of money you can afford to deal with two out of four possible problems (engine, body, interior and the rest) and still come out on top from a financial point of view. £150 horrors can still be picked up for possible renovation and/or spares – but choose carefully.

Jon Dooley at work in his rapid 2000 GTV during the 1976 Tour of Britain. What a strange registration number for an Alfa!

The Racing Pedigree

Racegoers have strong memories of GTAs and GTAms powering their front-wheel-lifting-way around the circuits, all the way from 1965 through to 1976 when the 1300 GTAs finally bowed out of the European Touring Car Championship. I first saw the GTA at Monza in April 1965, running as a prototype in the Monza 1000kms in chunky bumperless trim. By the Snetterton 4 Hours, that August, they were Touring Cars . . . though driven up the A11 to the circuit by the Jolly Club team. And they were red.

The following year's Snetterton found Rindt, de Adamich, Bussinello and two GTAs from Team VDS taking on Lotus Cortinas for Proctor, Whitmore and one J.Y. Stewart, in pouring rain. It was sterling stuff with Rindt skating off at Riches and Stewart taking a trip behind the spectator barrier at the hairpin, leaving de Adamich to win. It was a play acted out all over Europe that year and for years to come.

By 1970, the line-up became GT Ams (Am for America for these cars relied on an extension of the US-spec injected model) and 1300 GTAs to fit the new class divisions. The GTAms had 1985cc developed inititally from the 1750 unit with 84.5mm bore obtained by using special siamesed liner sets. Both GTA and GTAm began to use a special narrow valve angle twin plug cylinder head with semidowndraft injection inlet porting for better cylinder filling and burning. The GTAms, by the way, had *steel* shells from the 1750 GTV but with some optional lightweight panels and plastic wheelarch extensions.

In spite of growing opposition from lighter cars like the Escort, these cars repeatedly took championship successes in longer events thanks to their inherent strength and reliability.

On the suspension front, they sported some Heath Robinson arrangements to drop the rear roll centre by replacing the standard locating pivot on the top of the diff by one at the bottom which slid within a vertical slot created by brackets bolted to the rear platform. At the front, the roll centre was raised by lifting the outer top ball joint relative to the upright, thus helping maintain camber on roll. The combination of the roll axis thus obtained with a very stiff front end produced the characteristic front wheel in the air pose. The sight of Nanni Galli taking down all the corner markers through Woodcote at Silverstone in a GTAm, front wheel wagging in the air is instantly recalled – he did it twice, once on the first lap of the first heat, and again on the first lap of the second heat of the '71 TT.

By the time that the 2000 GTV began to give a good account of itself in Group 1 (Production) events against much bigger cars like the 3-litre BMW, it was taken for granted that it had a lot to live up to. In this country the Roger Clark Team helped fly the Alfa flag and had many good outings in 1973, including a memorable win at the BMW Raceday at Brands Hatch!

Best result, though, was probably the Manufacturers Award in the Tour of Britain that year for the two Roger Clark cars driven by John Handley and Stan Clark.

In Europe, Autodelta appeared at Spa for the 24 Hour race and cleaned up the class with some devastatingly fast 2000 GTVs which were pulling some 145mph down the Masta straight. The lesson repeated yet again was that they were not only fast, but also very strong.

With some 12 years under its belt as a top contender in racing, and – to a lesser extent – in tarmac rallying, the 'Shape' earned the image of a classic competitor. Ownership of a GTV, in red preferably, does much to help reminiscences of a day spent on a hillside at Mugello or watching night practice at Spa.

1300 GTAs in characteristic pose at the 1972 Silverstone Tourist Trophy. GTAs, 1300 or 1600, were formidable contenders